Information Seeking Stopping Behavior in Online Scenarios

INFORMATIONSTECHNOLOGIE UND ÖKONOMIE

Herausgegeben von Christian Becker, Wolfgang Gaul,
Armin Heinzl, Alexander Mädche und Martin Schader

Band 52

Erik Hemmer

Information Seeking Stopping Behavior in Online Scenarios

The Impact of Task, Technology
and Individual Characteristics

Bibliographic Information published by the Deutsche Nationalbibliothek
The Deutsche Nationalbibliothek lists this publication in the Deutsche Nationalbibliografie; detailed bibliographic data is available in the internet at http://dnb.d-nb.de.

Zugl.: Mannheim, Univ., Diss., 2013

Library of Congress Cataloging-in-Publication Data

Hemmer, Erik, 1983-
  Information seeking stopping behavior in online scenarios : the impact of task, technology and individual characteristics / Erik Hemmer.
    pages cm. — (Informationstechnologie und Ökonomie, ISSN 1616-086X ; Band 52)
  Originally presented as the author's thesis (doctoral)—Universität Mannheim, 2013.
  Includes bibliographical references.
  ISBN 978-3-631-64352-5 — ISBN 978-3-653-03418-9 (e-book)
  1. Information behavior. 2. Electronic information resource searching. I. Title.
ZA3075.H467 2013
025.5'24—dc23
                                                                2013022664

D 180
ISSN 1616-086X
ISBN 978-3-631-64352-5 (Print)
E-ISBN 978-3-653-03418-9 (E-Book)
DOI 10.3726/978-3-653-03418-9

© Peter Lang GmbH
Internationaler Verlag der Wissenschaften
Frankfurt am Main 2013
All rights reserved.
PL Academic Research is an Imprint of Peter Lang GmbH.

Peter Lang – Frankfurt am Main · Bern · Bruxelles · New York · Oxford · Warszawa · Wien

www.peterlang.de

To my parents.

Acknowledgments

Developing and writing this dissertation was a challenging, but especially enriching endeavor. I met many people I would like to thank for their great support and their respective contributions to this work.

I want to express my deepest gratitude to my supervisor and mentor Professor Dr. Armin Heinzl, who gave me the opportunity to do both research and teaching in Information Systems at the University of Mannheim. Professor Heinzl did not only highly inspire me, but he also guided my research trajectory and gave me a substantial degree of freedom to develop initial ideas and do my research. Finally, he encouraged me to utilize every chance to present my concepts to an international audience both during conferences and in my role as a guest researcher.

Furthermore, Professor Dr. Glenn Browne invited me to a research stay at the Texas Tech University in Lubbock, where I was able to discuss and refine my research. I want to thank him for his warm welcome and this great opportunity. I am indebted to Professor Dr. Robert Kauffman, Professor Dr. Joe Valachich and Professor Dr. Shirley Gregor who served as academic advisors during the ICIS Doctoral Consortium in Shanghai. I also would like to thank Professor Dr. Georg Alpers and his team, especially Andrew White, for giving me important feedback on my work from a psychology perspective. Moreover, I thank my cousin Bettina for investing countless hours in proofreading my entire dissertation.

I am also grateful to the members of my committee, Professor Dr. Christian Becker, Professor Dr. Irene Bertschek, Professor Dr. Martin Weber and Professor Dr. Moritz Fleischmann and thank them for their commitment.

In the course of writing my dissertation, the colleagues at the chair of Business Administration and Information Systems became close friends. We did not only mutually and unconditionally support each other in our daily work, but we also had long and highly enriching, even philosophical discussions about life in general.

My thanks go to Lars Klimpke, Tommi Kramer, Thomas Kude, Tillmann Neben, Marko Nöhren, Christoph Schmidt, Alexander Scheerer, Sven Scheibmayr, Kai Spohrer, Sebastian Stuckenberg and Aliona von der Trenck. Furthermore, I want to thank my former colleagues Thomas Butter, Sina Deibert, Jens Dibbern, Tobias Hildenbrand, Miroslav Lazic, Jessica Winkler, Boris Quaing and Anja Zöller for the great atmosphere at the chair as well as our secretaries Luise Bühler and Ingrid Distelrath and the student assistants Nina Jaeger, Melanie Marnet, Olga Oster, Lea Offermann, Santana Overath and Kathrin Teupe for their administrative support. My thanks also go to all participants of my studys' experiments and the student assistants Sebastian Grünschloß, Danijel Jozic, Alexander Neff, Laura Pfannemüller, Stefan Schellhorn, Florian Spiegel and Jörn Wagener who made important contributions to my research and teaching activities and to all tutors of the lecture "Integrated Information Systems" who supported me during the last few years.

Many friends within and outside University made my life truly enjoyable. I thank you for so many enriching conversations and unforgettable activities.

My deepest gratitude goes to my family, especially to my parents Rita and Herbert as well as to my sister Kristin, my brother Florian and my aunt Cornelia for always supporting me, encouraging me and teaching me what life is about and what it's not.

Finally and above all, I thank my partner Melanie for her patience, unconditional support and valuable advice when times were rough and for enriching my life in all respects.

Mannheim, April 2013   Erik Hemmer

Contents

List of Figures

List of Tables

List of Abbreviations

ANOVA	Analysis of Variance
AR	Autoregressive
CMC	Computer-mediated Communication
EIP	Elementary Information Processes
EIS	Executive Information Systems
ECG	Electrocardiography
EEG	Electroencephalography
ELM	Elaboration Likelihood Model of Persuasion
FFM	Five Factor Model
FFT	Fast Fourier Transform
fMRI	functional Magnetic Resonance Imaging
GSR	Galvanic Skin Response
HCI	Human-Computer Interaction
HIB	Human Information Behavior
HCIB	Human Computer-based Information Behavior
HSM	Heuristic-Systematic Model of Information Processing
HTTF	Human Task Technology Fit
IS	Information Systems (Discipline)
MIS	Management Information Systems
PLS	Partial Least Squares
REI	Rational-Experiential Inventory
RSA	Respiratory Sinus Arrhythmia

SD   Standard Deviation

SE   Standard Error

SEM   Structural Equation Modeling

TAM   Technology Acceptance Model

1. Introduction

1.1. Problem Statement

For more than 150 years, numerous technological advances and disruptive innovations have been changing the way how people work, communicate and influence modern societies (Danneels, 2004; DeSanctis and Poole, 1994). Today, the entity *information* is a major production factor, hence forcing organizations to act as efficient and effective information processors in order to be able to compete in increasingly globalized markets (Capurro and Hjorland, 2003; Choudhury and Sampler, 1997; Kohli and Grover, 2008; McKinney Jr. and Yoos II, 2010; Mendelson and Pillai, 1998). On an individual level, the Internet has a strong impact on the behavior people exert when interacting with information as they now have access to a literally unlimited amount of information considering their restricted cognitive capacities (Browne et al., 2007; Simon, 1982).

From an evolutionary perspective, however, a period of about twenty years in which the Internet gained its popularity is too short for sustainably influencing behavioral patterns that were learned and shaped before today's modern information technology was developed (Kock, 2004, 2009). Therefore, it is essential for Information Systems (IS) developers, managers and users to have a clear understanding of how individuals acquire, process and make use of information they receive from technological artifacts (Wilson, 1999). Several studies have shown that by taking the specific characteristics of human computer-based information behavior into account, information needs can be fulfilled more accurately resulting in higher task performance and user satisfaction (Hong et al., 2004a; Rafaeli and Ravid, 2003; Vessey and Galletta, 1991).

In spite of the fact that human computer-based information behavior is an important early step in many organizational decision making and sense making tasks, there is still a significant lack of research (Hemmer and Heinzl, 2011). Especially the question of when and why information seekers *terminate* information seeking processes in computer-mediated contexts has been largely neglected in past research (Browne and Parsons, 2012; Browne and Pitts, 2004; Browne et al., 2005, 2007; Davern et al., 2012b). Terminating information seeking processes too early or too late, however, has detrimental effects on the information seeker's overall performance (Bearden et al., 2006, 2005; Seale and Rapoport, 1997): either the acquired information is not sufficient for answering the underlying question accurately (reduced effectiveness), or too much time and effort are invested to come to an appropriate solution (reduced efficiency).

Whereas several *normative stopping rules* have been developed in past research prescribing when a person should stop seeking for information (Busemeyer and Rapoport, 1988; Meyer, 1982; Seale and Rapoport, 1997), only a few publications decidedly investigate actual human behavior in terms of *descriptive stopping rules* (Browne et al., 2007; Nickles et al., 1995; Zach, 2005). With regard to the latter, it becomes obvious that researchers primarily follow two distinct assumptions: they *either* regard a person's decision to stop seeking for information as the endpoint of a rational information acquisition process that is guided by goal-directed reasoning *or* they interpret the stopping decision as a spontaneous reaction that is not based on rational information scrutiny (Gigerenzer and Goldstein, 1996; Stigler, 1961). To date, though, no research explains and predicts how task, technology and individual characteristics affect the two aforementioned contradictory patterns of information seeking stopping behavior.

Apart from the research gap described before, two developments in the field of web-based information provisioning underline the importance of creating advanced knowledge about human information seeking stopping behavior: On the one hand, the *quantity of information* available via online media has been growing exponentially during the last decade (Smyth and Balfe, 2006). As a consequence, the Internet is constantly replacing traditional offline media and catalyzes the development of new behavioral strategies for coping with the large amount of information provided to information seekers both in working life and private life (Andriole, 2010; Taraborelli, 2008).

However, not only the pure amount of information available via online media is rising, but, on the other hand, also the variety of channels which are used to distribute this information to its consumers – such as e-commerce websites, microblogging, social networking or company websites – is increasing continuously.

Recently, there has been an ongoing transformation from static web pages to highly interactive ones, shifting the focus to content visibly created by its users (Bawden and Robinson, 2009; Mudambi and Schuff, 2010). Consequently, issues with respect to *information quality* are another important dimension influencing online information seeking activities: information rich in social cues, i. e. information that was visibly created and rated by a heterogeneous group of people seems to be highly appreciated by today's Internet users, although it is often hard to judge the objective quality of this type of information (Bawden and Robinson, 2009; Smyth and Balfe, 2006). Social cues convey additional contextual information which go beyond "objectively correct information" (Cross et al., 2001, p. 439) and are likely to support a holistic approach for making sense of the acquired information without a thorough argument scrutiny (Petty and Cacioppo, 1986).

In summary, both from a research perspective as well as from a practitioner's viewpoint, there is a strong need for obtaining insights into the determinants of computer-mediated information seeking stopping behavior. Furthermore, it is essential not to take a purely rational view assuming that human information seekers strictly follow systematic processing rules but also to investigate factors activating spontaneous, affective reactions on part of the information seeker.

1.2. Research Objectives

Given the aforementioned research gaps in the realm of information seeking stopping behavior, this study addresses several derived questions. First, the research project analyzes two fundamentally different reasons why people terminate information seeking processes showing rational, goal-directed stopping behavior on the one hand and impulsive, spontaneous stopping behavior on the other hand. Thus, two research streams that were investigated separately in the past are combined in one theoretical model in order to answer the following research question:

(1) Why do people stop seeking for information in online scenarios?

As this study's major objective consists in the development of a holistic nomological network for explaining and predicting information seeking stopping behavior, the determinants of stopping behavior are also identified and integrated into a coherent research model. A specific focus is set on the impact of social cues on information seeking stopping behavior as information visibly created by other social actors is constantly gaining importance in the context of web-based information provisioning (Cross et al., 2001; Cyr et al., 2009; Gefen and Straub, 2004). Consequently, the following research questions are addressed:

> *(2a) Which factors influence the decision to terminate information seeking processes in online scenarios?*

> *(2b) How is information seeking stopping behavior influenced by the presence or absence of social cues?*

Answering these research questions provides various insights for several stakeholders. *First*, a central topic for the IS discipline, namely the relationship between human beings and the entity information, is addressed holistically. Therefore, existing theories from different disciplines will be combined in a multitheoretical research model. Hence, a mid-range theory of information seeking stopping behavior is developed which also informs extant theories by applying them in a new context of computer-based information processing. *Second*, by applying modern psychophysiological measures as part of a triangulation approach, new insights into cognitive processes are generated that are not amenable to traditional empirical data collection methods (Dimoka et al., 2011; Riedl et al., 2010a). *Third*, information system designers get valuable advices on how to develop information systems that adequately support their users in information-intensive task scenarios and thereby maximize their task performance. At the same time, the findings will also be helpful for the operators of e-commerce websites or online search engines because they get knowledge on how they can influence the users' information seeking stopping behavior actively and intentionally (Mudambi and Schuff, 2010).

1.3. Overview of Research Methodology

The study takes a *post-positivist epistemological perspective*, assuming that there are unilateral causal relationships which can be deduced from universal laws or principles and which can be tested empirically in order to verify or falsify them. The objective is to generate "generalized knowledge" (Orlikowski and Baroudi,

1991, p. 10) and thus, the thesis is theory-building. *The level of analysis* is the individual user of information technology although there is a continuum towards a group perspective since information seeking is usually integrated into a broader social context with several persons interacting. *Methodologically,* the study follows an experiment-based triangulation approach, combining quantitative, qualitative (Meredith et al., 1989) and innovative techniques from the field of neurosciences (Dimoka et al., 2011; Riedl et al., 2010a). The goal is to reduce method bias (Burton-Jones, 2009), balance internal and external validity of the results (Bonoma, 1985) and especially to allow for both confirming the validity of the deduced propositions and giving explanations and predictions (Gregor, 2006).

The research design comprises three sequential stages. *In the first stage,* extant research on information seeking stopping behavior will be analyzed in order to identify task-, technology- and individual-related determinants. Theories from the IS domain and adjacent disciplines will be combined to deduce theoretical explanations for the hypothesized causal relationships between independent and dependent variables. *In stage two,* these insights are summarized in a comprehensive but nevertheless parsimonious research model explaining and predicting human information seeking stopping behavior. *In the third stage,* a web-based laboratory experiment environment will be developed and used to pre-test the research model's theoretical assumptions. Furthermore, heart rate variability measurement will be employed for obtaining complementary data on human behavior in a high granularity. Post-hoc interviews with the participants of the experimental sessions will help to potentially detect additional constructs and causal relationships that were not part of the original model. Finally, the research model on human information seeking stopping behavior will be validated following a survey-based experimental approach. Figure 1.1 summarizes the research methodology.

1.4. Study Organization

The study is divided into seven chapters, reflecting the logic of the research methodology introduced in the previous section.

The major objective of *Chapter 2* consists in the development of a research model for explaining and predicting human computer-based information seeking

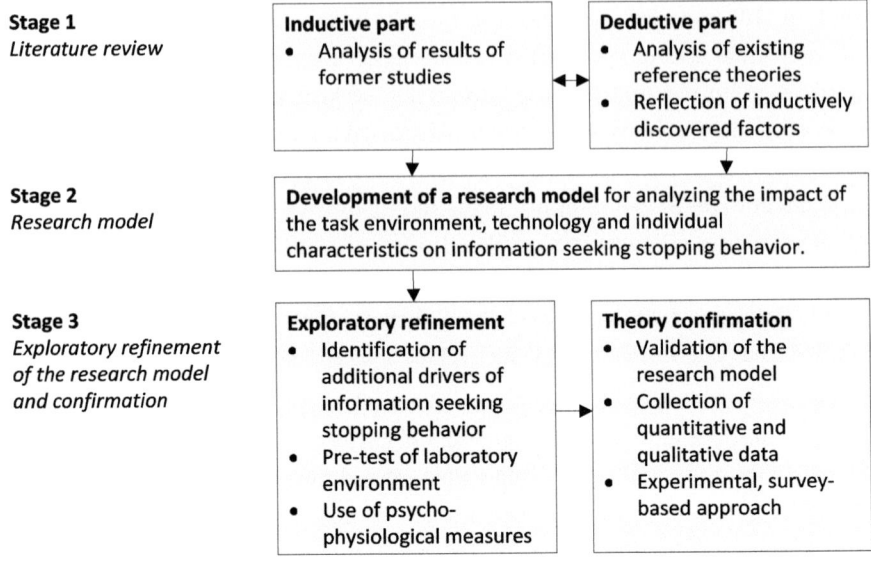

Figure 1.1.: Research Approach

stopping behavior. For this reason, the fundamental terminology concerning the entity *information*, the concept of *human computer-based information behavior* and *information seeking stopping behavior* are introduced. Based on extant literature, appropriate theoretical lenses for answering the study's research questions are identified and discussed.

In *Chapter 3*, the study's research methodology is described in detail, before major characteristics of the web-based laboratory environment are introduced which is used to collect empirical data in a triangulation approach comprising questionnaires, interviews and the use of psychophysiological methods.

Chapter 4 gives an overview of a pre-test with eleven subjects using the laboratory environment while being connected to a heart rate monitor. Furthermore, the findings of interviews that were conducted with the participants after the experimental sessions are presented and result in a slight adaptation of the research model.

In *Chapter 5*, the design and the results of the empirical main study are described. This study is conducted in order to validate the research model's hypothesized causal relationships explaining information seeking stopping behavior. Again, the laboratory environment is used for collecting data after it was improved based on the feedback by the participants of the pre-test.

In *Chapter 6*, the findings gained by the analysis of the empirical data are presented. Implications for theory and practice are discussed before the study's limitations are described and avenues for future research are stated.

The study closes with a summary in *Chapter 7*.

2. Theoretical Foundation

In this chapter, the theoretical foundation for analyzing human computer-based information seeking stopping behavior is provided. In a first step, the term *information* is introduced and its central role for the IS discipline is emphasized. Then, previous literature on human computer-based information behavior is studied setting a focus on IS literature, integrating articles from adjacent disciplines whenever appropriate. Thereafter, research on information seeking stopping behavior as an important sub-category of human information behavior is analyzed in the form of a comprehensive literature review. Based on reference theories used in past research, suitable theory candidates are selected and presented with the goal of answering this study's research questions by developing a coherent research model.

2.1. Information as the Fundamental Entity in the Information Systems Discipline

The Information Systems discipline is concerned with the development and use of technologies that support people in gathering and processing information required in various business contexts (Avison and Elliot, 2006; Heinrich et al., 2011). Hence, the question of how to provide the entity *information* to human recipients efficiently in organizational settings can be regarded as the discipline's core.

2.1.1. Definition of the term *Information*

Even though information is one of the most essential entities in IS research and many other disciplines, a precise definition of the term is not available (McKinney Jr. and Yoos II, 2010; Newman, 2001; Vreeken, 2002). McKinney Jr. and Yoos II (2010, p. 329) summarize this observation by stating that "[v]irtually all the extant IS literature fails to explicitly specify meaning for the very label that identifies it".

Several researchers define *information* in a rather generic way as "any difference that makes a difference to a conscious, human mind" (Case, 2007, p. 40, emphasis in original). Thus, "information is whatever appears significant to a human being, whether originating from an external environment or a (psychologically) internal world" (Case, 2007, p. 40). Similarly, Belkin (1980) defines information implicitly as anything that helps to reduce uncertainty in terms of a perceived discrepancy between the external world and a person's internal model of the surrounding world. In their taxonomy of views on information, McKinney Jr. and Yoos II (2010) call this perspective *Adaptation View*. These broad definitions are not specific enough in order to be used in an IS context as they are neither confined to a dedicated context of use (within organizations) nor do they make assumptions about the role of artificial technologies manipulating and providing information.

In Business Administration and Information Systems research, there is a long tradition of defining *information* in relation to *data* and *knowledge*, organizing the words in a hierarchy ranging from *knowledge* (sometimes also "action") at the top and *data* at the bottom (Davenport and Prusak, 1998; Kettinger and Li, 2010). Semiotics, the study of signs, is regularly utilized in the context of delineating the aforementioned expressions. Semiotics distinguishes between the three dimensions *syntactics*, *semantics* and *pragmatics*, suggesting that data are groups of letters and numbers that are combined following given syntactical rules. As such they symbolically represent a specific real-world issue. On a semantic level, data get a meaning as soon as they are transformed into information by adding a goal-orientation in a specific context. On a pragmatic level, knowledge is created by linking information in the recipient's mind and is thus the result of a learning process and experience (Heinrich et al., 2011; Kettinger and Li, 2010). Machlup (1983) summarizes this understanding by stating that "information is acquired by being told, whereas knowledge can be acquired by thinking" (p. 644). Thus, this definition conceptualizes information as a precursor to knowledge.

Other authors take the opposite stance, regarding information as a subset of knowledge. In this understanding, information is goal-directed knowledge supporting people to make decisions and solve problems and tasks (Wittmann, 1959). Bode (1997) adopts the basic idea of information being a subset of knowledge, but omits the goal-orientation arguing that e. g. hedonic information acquisition would not be part of Wittmann's narrow definition. An extensive overview of controversial perspectives on *data, information* and *knowledge* is given in Kettinger and Li (2010), but goes beyond the scope of this introduction.

In this study, a broad conceptualization of the term *information* is used in the sense that *information is any difference in the business environment, noticed by a person in a computer-mediated context, which causes him[1] to adapt to this difference* (McKinney Jr. and Yoos II, 2010, p. 336). This definition has several advantages compared to existing conceptualizations of the term *information*: (1) Considering the research questions of this study, a purely semiotic interpretation of information is not viable because then, the content of images would not be regarded as information but the term would be restricted to content exclusively transported by language (Newman, 2001). (2) In this study, there is an emphasis on information that is accessible for human beings via an artificial interface. Consequently, an implicit assumption is made with regard to the medium which is used to produce and transmit information as being computer-based. (3) This study's understanding of information implies goal-orientation in that it assumes that human beings especially pay attention to those differences in their environment which are important for solving a specific problem at hand. Hence, it adopts and extends the basic notion of past conceptualizations both in Business Administration and Information Systems.

2.1.2. The Importance of Information for Today's Organizations

During the last few decades, the importance of an efficient and effective use of information has increased significantly. Today, information is considered a forth production factor in addition to the traditional ones, capital, labor, and raw materials (Capurro and Hjorland, 2003). Making fast and accurate decisions has become a crucial competitive advantage in almost all industries (Eisenhardt, 1989; Miller and Ireland, 2005). Consequently, the provision and utilization of adequate information and communication technologies is essential for most companies in order to support their employees in making decisions and understanding complex phenomena (Choudhury and Sampler, 1997). Furthermore, in a "proactive"

---

1 Throughout this study, the use of the unmarked masculine form implies a reference to both genders.

mode, concepts like environmental scanning, i. e. the systematic but nevertheless exploratory surveillance of a company's market environment allow for the detection of future opportunities or the identification of potential threats (Choudhury and Sampler, 1997, p. 27).

Past research has shown that people can solve tasks most effectively and efficiently when there is a fit between the person's internal representation of a problem and the way problem information is presented to him (Vessey and Galletta, 1991). Any deviations with regard to the problem solver's information needs and the information delivered by a technological system either result in an undersupply or an over-supply of information. Whereas the former has a negative impact on decision quality, the latter leads to an information overload activating coping mechanisms which are potentially detrimental to the overall task performance (Eppler and Mengis, 2004). As people usually do not follow normative strategies when making complex decisions or solving abstract problems because of limited cognitive capacities, it is difficult for IS designers to predict how people will react when acquiring information in order to solve specific problems. Thus, many authors stress the importance of getting a better understanding of the contingencies influencing human behavior in relation to the entity information in computer-mediated contexts (Browne et al., 2007; Speier and Morris, 2003; Wilson, 1981). The major findings from past research concerning the behavior people exert when interacting with information in computer-based scenarios are presented in the next section.

2.2. Human Computer-based Information Behavior

Information seeking stopping behavior represents the last step in information acquisition activities before the information seeker proceeds to making use of the obtained information, e. g. by thinking about viable solutions to a problem or finally making a decision. As the entire process of acquiring information might have an effect on the stopping behavior, a detailed overview of existing research in the realm of computer-based information behavior in the IS domain is given.

Drawing on the notion of "Human Information Behavior" as it is used in the Information Science field, in this study's context the term "Human Computer-based Information Behavior" (HCIB) is defined as *the totality of human behavior*

Table 2.1.: Reviewed IS Top Journals and Number of Articles Selected

Title of journal	Abbreviation	Coverage	# of articles
European Journal of Information Systems	EJIS	1993 – 2010	6
Information Systems Journal	ISJ	1998 – 2010	2
Information Systems Research	ISR	1990 – 2010	17
Journal of AIS	JAIS	2003 – 2010	3
Journal of MIS	JMIS	1984 – 2010	13
MIS Quarterly	MISQ	1977 – 2010	23
		Sum	**64**

in relation to computer-mediated channels of information, including both infor-mation seeking and information use (adapted from Wilson, 2000, p. 49). The review comprises 64 articles published in the six major top-ranked IS outlets before 2011 (see Table 2.1)[2].

2.2.1. A Model of Computer-based Information Behavior

Based on Gemünden (1993) and Wilson (1999), the model in Figure 2.1 describes behavioral activities in computer-mediated, both goal-driven (active) search and interest-driven (passive) scanning scenarios (Vandenbosch and Huff, 1997).

According to the proposed model, a sequence of goal-driven information seeking activities is initiated by the awareness of a problem that requires the acquisition of information from the problem domain. Based on this ex ante information need and the emerging information seeking strategy, an adequate information chan-nel is selected, i. e. the question of where to get the information is answered. Restricted by the specific properties of the chosen information channel, the in-formation need is amended resulting in an actual, i. e. "realized" information request. After this interaction with the information system, the human infor-

---

2 A detailed list of all reviewed articles is given in Table A in the Appendix and in Hemmer and Heinzl (2011)

mation seeker has to decide (consciously or subconsciously) on how to process and evaluate the resulting information. Therefore, the seeker has to choose from various cognitive strategies and heuristics culminating in the termination of the process or a reiteration.

In passive information scanning scenarios, information is acquired independent of clearly defined problems the information seeker tries to solve. Thus, scanning is exercised when people "browse through information without a particular problem to solve or question to answer" (Vandenbosch and Huff, 1997, p. 83). Therefore, the information seeker also chooses a computer-based information channel and requests information from an information system. However, he is not necessarily guided by a clear information need and a resulting information seeking strategy (indicated by the dotted line around the "Information need" box). As a consequence, at the end of the information acquisition process, the information seeker is passively exposed to a set of information provided by a computer-based system and has to generate ideas how this information can be used, e. g. to improve organizational effectiveness by fostering creativity and supporting the formulation of new problems (Vandenbosch and Huff, 1997).

2.2.2. Phases in Information Acquisition

In this section, based on Hemmer and Heinzl (2011), the findings from past research on human computer-based information behavior are presented following the sequence of activities depicted in Figure 2.1.

2.2.2.1. Information Need

Information Need refers to a gap between the quantity and quality of information available to an individual or an organization and the quantity and quality of information required in a specific scenario, for example in a decision making process or sense making situation. Generally speaking, an "anomalous state of knowledge" (Belkin, 1980), i. e. the awareness of a lack of information triggers the formation of an information need as a means for adapting to a complex environment (Simon, 1982; Wilson, 1999). In this understanding, "information need" represents a subjective desire of a person (subjective information need;

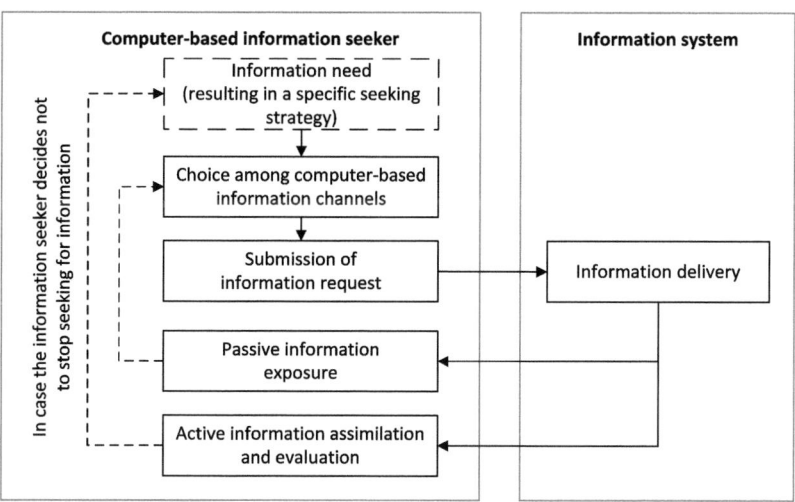

Figure 2.1.: Model of Human Computer-based Information Behavior (based on Gemünden 1993 and Wilson 1999, extended by Vandenbosch and Huff 1997)

information demand) while the term can also describe the set of information which is objectively required to solve a given organizational task (objective information need, Grunert, 1984).

A large share of articles dealing with differences in information needs is task-centered in that an organizational task is conceptualized as an independent variable influencing the seeker's perception of which information might be required (ex ante) to fulfill the given task (Melville and Ramirez, 2008; Specht, 1986; Wetherbe, 1991). Especially the importance of task complexity is stressed by several authors, though operationalized in different ways: Specht (1986) investigates task analyzability and states that tasks with a low degree of analyzability require less precise but more information than simple tasks. Heinrich et al. (2011) extend this view by regarding task variability and task structure as important characteristics of task complexity. According to Melville and Ramirez (2008), task complexity can either be reduced by increasing information processing capabilities or by decreasing information needs.

Browne et al. (2007) argue in a similar way but exclusively use the dimension of "task structure" as an indicator for task complexity and hypothesize a positive impact of task complexity on the amount of information required to solve the task and the strategy employed to find the relevant information. Sviokla (1989) additionally investigates the reciprocities between task complexity and information needs by concluding that sophisticated information technology does not necessarily help to satisfy information needs. On the contrary, they state that the underlying tasks can quickly mutate in the presence of information technology (in this case, expert systems) and produce completely new information needs.

This topic is closely related to a theme addressed by Wetherbe (1991) and Mendelson and Pillai (1998), namely the accelerating pace of business, constantly increasing information needs and information processing capabilities on an organizational level. Wetherbe (1991) proposes various guidelines for determining information needs in a quickly changing world and translating them into the design of appropriate information systems, whereas Mendelson and Pillai (1998) suggest to regard this problem from the opposite perspective: they propose to reduce organizational information needs artificially, arguing that otherwise, information supply will exceed human information processing capabilities in terms of humans' bounded rationality.

Besides explaining the genesis of information needs and describing mechanisms to identify them, recent IS literature also covers exogenous factors triggering and guiding information processing. Dou et al. (2010) build on the schema theory from the field of cognitive psychology in order to show that by priming users of e-commerce web sites, the operators of such platforms can indirectly influence the way users navigate through the web site and how intensively they seek for information. Similar studies can be found in the marketing literature with respect to the effect of advertisements on the willingness of its viewers to gather more information about the advertised product or service (MacInnis and Jaworski, 1989; Meyers-Levy and Malaviya, 1999). The authors base their assumptions on dual-process theories and argue that specific characteristics of an advertisement such as information density and the size of pictures result in varying degrees of information needs and finally activate different information processing strategies such as systematic as opposed to heuristic seeking.

2.2.2.2. Choice among Computer-based Information Channels

Advances in modern information technology result in an increasing number of different ways for acquiring information in organizational contexts. Especially the Internet has evolved to a valuable source of information created and maintained by its users. The corresponding information is accessible via channels as diverse as e-commerce web sites (customer reviews), social networks (user posts) or microblogging applications (tweets), while the term "information channel" generally describes "any medium by which a message may be transmitted from a source to a receiver" (Swanson, 1987, p. 131, Shannon, 1948). These channels can be differentiated according to dimensions such as accessibility, channel restrictiveness or transmission velocity (Dennis et al., 2008; Jones et al., 1993). Consequently, some information channels are more attractive than others in information seeking scenarios depending on several criteria such as characteristics of the task which has to be fulfilled, the information seeker's personality or the information seeker's current mood.

Jones et al. (1993) concentrate on managers' choice behavior depending on the velocity of information acquisition stating that the managers prefer written information in low-velocity situations, but acquire information from other people via channels with high information richness (which provide immediate feedback) in high-velocity situations.

Other authors emphasize information channels' propensity to reduce the effort in information acquisition tasks (Schoberth and Heinzl, 2001). Wang and Benbasat (2009) extend the effort-accuracy framework of cognition (Payne, 1982), holding that information seekers minimize their effort while simultaneously getting as accurate information as possible. Wang and Benbasat show that especially the degree of restrictiveness of decision aids has an impact on the choice of these systems that can be regarded as information channels supporting information seekers in purchasing decisions. In this terminology, a decision aid is restrictive when the decision processes or strategies desired by the decision maker are not supported. Thus, an increased perceived restrictiveness of the decision aid leads to a decreasing intention to use this tool since people generally prefer information channels that are in line with their mental problem representations.

Similarly, Jones et al. (2004) find out that users show a higher tendency to stop using online community web sites when the amount of information they can acquire in such an environment exceeds specific limits. Hence, information density also has an impact on channel choice, especially on the decision to stop using specific channels in the future.

While the aforementioned articles on choice of computer-based information channels focus on various characteristics of information channels and how these characteristics influence choice, some research considers other aspects of the channel such as the difference between internal and external information (from the perspective of a person within an organization, Jones et al. 1993). Krishnan et al. (2001) even take a more technical perspective when designing an information-retrieval agent that is capable of automatically identifying appropriate information channels for solving an organizational task. Thus, they derive design implications from the observation of human problem solvers while retrieving information from heterogeneous databases.

2.2.2.3. Information Request

The phase "Information Request" is concerned with the actual act of acquiring information from a specific information system (Gemünden, 1993). Therefore, it is significantly different from the information need concept since the latter consists of ex ante assumptions about required information based on a given problem description *before* the information acquisition process has started.

Two common themes emerge with respect to this phase: one group of articles discusses the immediate interaction between the user and the information system, e. g. in form of user-centered information retrieval systems, whereas the second group deals with broader concepts such as the amount or quality of information requested in order to fulfill a certain task (Pitts and Browne, 2004; Todd and Benbasat, 1992). With regard to the first group, Gordon and Moore (1999) concentrate on the problem of document retrieval and propose a formal language for describing documents. Also in the realm of document retrieval, Stenmark (2001) conducted a case study to evaluate an agent-based retrieval prototype putting a link between information behavior research and knowledge management literature: the author shows that organizational IS users stick to established ways of searching when locating information in a knowledge management system. Another stream of research addresses semantics and linguistic methods to develop more accurate retrieval mechanisms matching the users' natural language use, for example by building so-called "collocation indexes", i. e. groups of words carrying a distinct meaning and, therefore, reducing ambiguities (Arazy and Woo, 2007; Storey et al., 2008).

Taking a broader perspective on the phenomenon of requesting information from computer-based systems, several authors try to explain why human information seekers deviate from ex ante defined information needs and solve tasks in a less effective way by not considering available, relevant information. The major reason for this behavior is rooted in the information seekers' limited mental capacities resulting in an information overload if a specific, individual limit is exceeded (Eppler and Mengis, 2004). Beyond this point, the information seeker's task performance is reported to decline significantly (Chewning and Harrell, 1990). Even though this topic has been addressed at least marginally in about ten articles – e. g. in Jones et al. (2004) and in Liang et al. (2006) – the overall amount of articles dealing with information overload is rather small. This finding is further supported by a comprehensive study on the concept of information overload in organization science, accounting, marketing, and Management Information Systems (MIS), in which the authors conclude: "Surprisingly, MIS has not been the discipline that has dealt with information overload in the most extensive manner" (Eppler and Mengis, 2004, p. 339).

2.2.2.4. IS-enabled Information Delivery

The two major topics that emerge when looking at the role of information systems in the information delivery phase comprise (1) the visualization of information, e. g. how information is presented to the user and (2) the personalization of information to the individual's specific context.

The differing impacts of various forms of information visualization on the efficiency and effectiveness of information systems use have been analyzed broadly and extensively in the past, especially with regard to decision support systems. Starting with the effect of numerical, textual, and relational representations

(Robey and Taggart, 1982), the field has matured and intensified the research beyond the classical graph versus table discussions of the past.

Vessey and Galletta (1991) formalize the concept of cognitive fit by including the human information seeker and calling for an adequate support of human information seeking and problem solving strategies. Based on the information processing theory, they assume that only a fit between problem solving task and problem representation leads to a consistent mental representation, which is the prerequisite for reducing the effort in acquiring information. Lin et al. (1999) complement these findings by measuring improvements in human recall and precision when information is visualized in self-organizing maps. Such maps cluster terms of a specific domain so that the size of a cluster correlates with its relative importance.

In more recent research, Hong et al. (2004a) examine the effect of flash animations on online users' performance in search scenarios drawing on theories from cognitive psychology, the central capacity theory, and the associative network model. Chung et al. (2005) eventually develop new web visualization methods for facilitating mental model building in exploratory information seeking processes. Dudezert and Leidner (2011) go into a similar direction by visualizing a company's knowledge assets in knowledge maps.

Starting in 2005, significantly more articles elaborate on the personalization aspect especially in web environments. They cover various topics such as trust in recommendation agents conceptualized as "social actors" with human characteristics (Wang and Benbasat, 2005), or the effect of personalization on user satisfaction and perceived information overload (Liang et al., 2006). The reduction of information load in organizational settings by presenting customized content is also mentioned (Scheepers, 2006) as well as users' perceptions of personalized information in decision making contexts (Tam and Ho, 2006).

2.2.2.5. Passive Information Exposure

The behavior people exhibit "when they browse through information without a particular problem to solve or question to answer" (Vandenbosch and Huff, 1997, p. 83) is regarded as a mode of passive information acquisition. Thus, this category describes articles dealing with information retrieved from an information system without having a clearly stated problem in mind. Examples of such behaviors are manifold and were investigated from different perspectives in past IS research. While up to the mid 1990ies, several articles were published addressing strategic scanning behavior on a manager's level, the research focus has shifted in the last ten years. The recent three publications in IS top journals are exclusively centered around private end users' behavior dependent on various design aspects of web sites.

El Sawy (1985) and Chen (1995) present attempts to adapt Executive Information Systems (EIS) in order to reduce the amount of reports, managers have to scan on a daily basis. Thus, the problem of information overload can be reduced. El Sawy's research project was motivated by the perception that a huge number of managers spends a significant amount of time scanning information and that these tasks are regularly not delegated to employees. Descriptive evidence is presented, supporting managers' preference for personal information orally transmitted to the CEO, finally leading to high-level design recommendations with regard to future EIS.

Chen's work on the other hand is primarily problem-centered in that he proposes an EIS solution that structures information along organization models and thus delivers additional contextual information that help the managers in fitting the received information into their own mental models. The authors base their assumptions on findings in cognitive sciences as well as managerial thought processes and conclude that the combination of various information sources and organization models will lead to improved organizational learning, arguing that managers browsing through the structured set of information will better understand the shared visions and processes of the company. From today's perspective, the authors' vision reminds of what is now known as "Business Intelligence" as a comprehensive and integrative approach for delivering organizational information to members of the company in a structured way. Watson (1990) has a narrow focus on IS managers and describes their scanning behavior with regard to key issues in the IS area, conceptualizing "scanning" as "the first stage of a response mechanism that leads to an organization adapting to its environment" (p. 218).

Hong et al. (2004b) investigate a question close to marketing research. They examine the effects of two different types of information presentation, namely list versus matrix in two shopping tasks and goal-directed search versus experiential browsing. The authors conclude with the observation that information seekers experience lower degrees of mental effort when being exposed to information in a list format while experientially browsing for information. A similar question is addressed by Nadkarni and Gupta (2007), however in a broader context. The authors hypothesize a correlation between a web site's complexity and the user experience on this web site and assume that this relationship is moderated by the user's task goal, i. e. if he is performing a goal-directed search or if he is browsing. In the latter scenarios, users are intrinsically motivated to process challenging information. According to the authors, this results in an inverse U-shaped curve, i. e. optimal user satisfaction can be observed when the scanning person is exposed to information nested on a web site with medium complexity.

Liang et al. (2006) also confirm this effect in a slightly different scenario: the authors draw on least effort theories in order to explain the impact of personalized web services on user satisfaction depending on scanning versus target search. They conclude that personalized content recommendation systems can reduce information overload and hence are preferred when users retrieve information experientially from general purpose web sites.

2.2.2.6. Active Information Assimilation and Evaluation

The previous section summarized literature on users passively exposed to information in browsing tasks. Subsequently, articles dealing with behavioral and mental processes taking part after the act of requesting specific information in a goal-directed way are described. In this context, literature in the IS domain is mainly concerned with (1) the integration of information into mental models and (2) the question of when users should stop seeking for information.

Vandenbosch and Higgins (1996) take a cognitive learning perspective to investigate the relationship between information acquisition and learning in the context of executive support systems. They primarily differentiate between mental model building and mental model maintenance. The former is conceptualized as a change of an existing mental model in order to integrate new information. The latter represents a confirmation mechanism in which new information fits into the prevalent mental model. The organizational impact of these differing behavioral patterns is illustrated by the assumption that executives who are scanning information challenge fundamental assumptions and therefore build new mental models. On the other hand, executives, who answer specific questions, verify assumptions and hence maintain existing mental models (Vandenbosch and Huff, 1997). Dou et al. (2010) extend this research and show – drawing on the schema theory – that information, evaluated as being incongruent with the searcher's basic assumptions about how the world works, is more memorable and, thereby, make recommendations for the design of search engine marketing campaigns.

Pitts and Browne (2004) and Browne et al. (2007) investigate human stopping behavior in information systems design and online search scenarios. They show that the application of various cognitive stopping rules determines the quantity of information actually retrieved depending on characteristics such as task complexity and former task experience. Prabha et al. (2007) provide an extensive overview of stopping rule-related literature in the Information Science domain and conclude that also in this discipline "[it has been] neglected to study how individuals decide what and how much information is enough to meet their [the information seekers'] needs or goals" (p. 75).

2.2.2.7. Summary

The literature review on human computer-based information behavior reveals that IS top journals have published several articles on various aspects of information behavior in the last decades. However, the total number of publications is rather small and the inter-textual coherence (Locke and Golden-Biddle, 1997) with regard to the authors' awareness of a research trajectory on information behavior is low. The latter aspect is visualized in Figure 2.2 by showing that there is only a small number of cross references between articles included in the review.

Furthermore, it becomes obvious that there has been a significant amount of research on HCIB in the realm of online applications during the last ten years. This development can be regarded as an indication for a plethora of research gaps arising as a consequence of information being provided via online media.

Finally, many authors mention the impact of perceived effort on information behavior in many different steps of the information acquisition process. The phenomenon of information overload is also often noted. Nevertheless, a remarkable

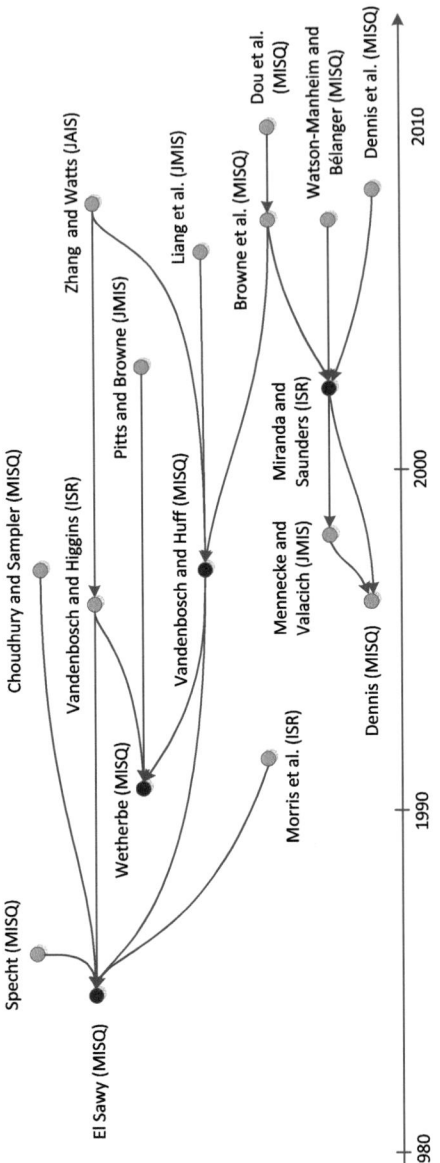

Figure 2.2.: Cross References between Publications Reviewed Above (around "Hub" Articles)

lack of research is reported on the question of when and why people stop seeking for information even though this question is related to and impacted by all preceding activities during information acquisition.

To summarize, the literature review on human computer-based information behavior emphasizes – in line with the research questions formulated in Section 1.2 – the general need for research on information seeking stopping behavior and the impact of properties of online information provisioning on information seeking behavior.

2.2.3. Research Boundaries

Research related to human computer-based information behavior has also been conducted in the field of *Information Science* and in the *Human-Computer Interaction (HCI)* community. Nevertheless, the publications presented in the previous sections are clearly distinct from articles published in the aforementioned fields where the focus has not been set on behavior concerning the access and use of information from computer-based sources.

The Information Science discipline, for example, recognizes the importance of technological artifacts for explaining information-directed human behavior, but technology itself is not a mandatory part of corresponding research models. Consequently, the Information Science discipline also examines information behavior in scenarios in which information technology is absent, e. g. information acquisition from traditional offline media.

In contrast, the Human-Computer Interaction community focuses explicitly on the interplay between humans and computers. This research is less interested in human interaction with *information* from computer-based sources, but more in the interaction between the individual and technology. In this realm, the entity information is not a conditio sine qua non of the research programs, i. e. the design of computer hardware, for example, is also of interest for the community's members (Zhang et al., 2009).

Both streams offer valuable insights into information-directed human behavior, but neither deals specifically with the information-related behaviors of organizational stakeholders as they interact with information systems. Thus, the Information Systems discipline should be the primary source of knowledge when it comes to the examination of human information seeking and processing activities since it explicitly looks at information, artificial "systems", and the users who are supported in business contexts. Consequently, this study aims at contributing to the IS discipline's knowledge base.

2.3. Information Seeking Stopping Behavior

In the previous section, an overview of literature on human computer-based information behavior was given. It became obvious that in a large variety of organizational tasks such as decision making, sense making or general problem solving, information acquisition is a crucial pre-condition for the related downstream processes. Usually, the amount of information available to the information seeker significantly exceeds the mental capabilities of this person.

As a consequence, the information seeker has to decide – either consciously or subconsciously – when to terminate the process of acquiring information. This field has only received little attention in past research (Browne et al., 2007) and will be analyzed next.

2.3.1. Conceptualization of *Stopping* in Information Search

Information seeking stopping behavior is defined as the use of "heuristics, or *stopping rules*, [...] to decide when to terminate information search [...]" (Browne and Pitts, 2004, p. 208). There is a long tradition of research regarding the question when human information seekers *should* terminate and when they *actually* terminate information acquisition in various types of organizational and non-organizational tasks. The common denominator of this research stream, which comprises several scientific disciplines, lies in the assumption of costs (e.g. mental effort) being caused by information gathering processes. Based on these costs, information seekers constantly have to make judgments about the sufficiency of information gathered while taking trade-offs between effort and accuracy into account (Payne et al., 1992, 1993; Wang and Benbasat, 2009; Zach, 2005): a fact that Simon summarized in the statement that "decision makers need to prune the full decision tree" (Katsikopoulos and Lan, 2011, p. 728).

In many situations, an optimal amount of information can be calculated by comparing the costs for acquiring additional information units with the value of this piece of information. Thus, many so-called *normative stopping rules* have been defined, especially in the field of economics, in order to carve out idealized instructions on when to stop seeking for information (Seale and Rapoport, 1997; Stigler, 1961; Zwick et al., 2003). Consequently, any deviations from the predictions of these normative stopping rules necessarily lead to a reduced task performance in terms of the problem solver's efficiency and effectiveness.

With regard to the amount of information requested by an information seeker, deviations from idealized and optimal stopping rules either result in an overacquisition or an underacquisition of information. Overacquisition leads to higher acquisition costs, whereas underacquisition is said to have consequences in terms of poor decision quality or incomplete enumeration of alternatives in terms of Simon's adaptation of systems to their surrounding complex environment (Browne and Pitts, 2004; Simon, 1996). As a reaction to the insight that decision makers rarely behave in accordance with prescriptions given by normative stopping rules, researchers proposed *descriptive stopping rules*. Descriptive stopping rules reflect the actual behavior information seekers and decision makers exercise when solving tasks, taking underlying cognitive and motivational drivers into account. However, most publications deal with problems of the choice between different alternatives both in a heuristic or purely descriptive sense, while only a few articles conceptualize the judgment of sufficiency in information search (Browne and Pitts, 2004; Browne et al., 2005, 2007; Nickles et al., 1995; Prabha et al., 2007; Zach, 2005).

A more detailed overview of existing research streams on stopping rules is given in the following section.

2.3.2. Different Perspectives on Information Seeking Stopping Behavior

2.3.2.1. Cost-Benefit-driven Stopping Behavior

A large part of literature on information seeking stopping behavior is centered around cost and benefit considerations in the realm of choice problems and decision making tasks. Many publications follow a similar pattern consisting of a normative and a descriptive, experimental part. In the normative part, a model is deduced that fulfills some optimality criteria with respect to costs and expected benefits, whereas in the descriptive part, the behavior of human beings is examined and compared to the normative model (Busemeyer and Rapoport, 1988; Kogut, 1990; Meyer, 1982; Seale and Rapoport, 1997). Very often, the research focus is set on sequential choice problems, especially the secretary problem, which requires a decision maker to choose a job applicant from a set of various applicants in a step-by-step process (Ho et al., 2011; Saad and Russo, 1996; Seale and Rapoport, 1997; Zwick et al., 2003). Usually, the decision maker has to decide after sampling the "attributes" of one applicant if he wants to proceed or go for this specific person. One reason for the remarkable popularity of this class of problems surely lies in the relative ease of developing an optimal strategy for acquiring information and terminating the search process, since a global optimum can be found and is largely independent of the rational information seeker's values and expectations.

At the same time, however, the models distinguish between maximizing and satisficing strategies. While in the former, a human being tries to maximize the benefits or accuracy of a task outcome, in the latter he aims at minimizing effort being well aware of and accepting potentially less accurate outcomes. Consequently, all models following the assumption of a maximizing strategy account for benefits or utility as a dependent variable (Brickman, 1972; Herrnstein, 1990; Prabha et al., 2007; Stigler, 1961). Satisficer models, however, do not necessarily take this variable into account but basically focus on effort as the dependent variable (Hardy, 1982; Klein and Ford, 2003; Rapoport and Tversky, 1970; Saad and Russo, 1996; Schmalhofer et al., 1986; Swensson and Thomas, 1974; Wirth et al., 2007). Most authors argue in favor of trade-off models between costs and benefits while both variables are usually operationalized as monetary values (Connolly and Gilani, 1982; Connolly and Thorn, 1987; Kogut, 1990).

Consequently, common stopping criteria combine costs and benefits in rules like "search until the perceived marginal benefit of search is equal to the perceived marginal cost" (Klein and Ford, 2003, p. 30) or "a model should be refined only as long as the cost of each additional refinement provides at least comparable improvement in information" (Spetzler and Stael Von Holstein, 1975,

p. 343). As most of these models do not take individual differences into account, the aforementioned rules are applicable without considering information seekers' individual preferences. However, Schunk (2009) shows that information seekers dynamically set reference points which they use to judge if additional pieces of information increase or decrease future pay-offs. Since people tend to be loss-averse, reference points are a means for making sure that the "current level of well-being" (p. 1723) can at least be retained and – on an organizational level – that the employees' behavior is aligned with the company's goals (strategic reference point theory, Fiegenbaum et al. 1996). Kogut (1990) shows that information seekers calculate an overall profit while seeking for information and, thus, contradict assumptions of the prospect theory suggesting that people calculate the expected utility of alternatives as the sum of weighted gains and losses.

Interestingly, Brickman (1972) hypothesizes in line with Kogut (1990) that costs of information acquisition might be largely ignored by information seekers because they are regarded as sunk costs and thus even intensify the seekers' commitment to continue also in situations in which additional benefits cannot be expected (sequential choice with descending benefit distributions). However, based on empirical data, Kogut (1990) finds that seeking costs result in a premature stopping as they are not considered as sunk costs by the participants of the experiment, but as costs that reduce the overall profit in the search tasks.

An increasing number of publications sets a focus on stopping behavior in the context of web applications. Klein and Ford (2003), Kuruzovich et al. (2008), Sundar (2007) and Taraborelli (2008) report that the Internet reduces the overall effort for acquiring information by offering access to a large variety of sources and delivering information instantaneously to the receivers. However, this high degree of source accessibility forces the information seeker to judge constantly which source might contain the most valuable information for solving a given problem. In order to explain the resulting browsing behavior, Pirolli (2005) and Taraborelli (2008) draw on information foraging theory, which holds that information seekers follow those "external information scent cues" (e. g. web links, Pirolli, 2005, p. 352) that are expected to have the maximum utility in a given context.

In summary, the cost and benefit-oriented models take a rather narrow and partly "technical" view on how information seeking processes should be terminated. On the one hand, many models are based on fairly artificial assumptions such as that the costs and benefits of alternatives in choice problems can and will be considered rationally by information seekers and therefore, have limited explanatory power when it comes to actual human behavior guided by limited information processing capabilities. On the other hand, past research shows that perceived effort and expected benefits are important and contrary drivers of human information seeking stopping behavior.

2.3.2.2. Cost-Benefit-independent Stopping Behavior

The aforementioned models and theories of information seeking stopping behavior are regularly based on the assumption that information seekers process information by actively comparing costs and benefits of acquiring additional pieces of information. Deviations from "optimal" predictive models (Berryman, 2008) are primarily explained by dynamic, non-rational adaptations of the information seekers' cost and benefit evaluations. Another stream of research tries to explain actual stopping behavior by focusing on heuristic information processing that largely ignores cost and benefit considerations. Authors such as Gigerenzer and Goldstein (1999), Simon (1955) and Kahneman et al. (1982) argue that human beings do not possess the mental capabilities which would be required to judge the value of every piece of information they acquire and to compare this value with all the information they have obtained before. Thus, the cognitive and motivational processes guiding information seeking in the absence of cost-benefit considerations are analyzed below.

Choice Problems

There is a huge body of knowledge in the realm of heuristic decision making in choice problems. Research in this field addresses cognitive strategies which are used by human beings to simplify complex tasks by not processing the complete set of information available to the person but by focusing on a specific subset, thus ignoring a large portion of information. Kahneman et al. (1982) claim in their "Heuristics and Biases" program that the use of the aforementioned simplification strategies (heuristics) does not necessarily result in a higher task performance, but might also lead to poor (biased) judgments (Gilovich et al., 2002; Kahneman, 2011; Tversky and Kahneman, 1971). Proponents of the predominantly positive effects of heuristic information processing report about findings indicating that "fast and frugal" information processing approaches often outperform complex cognition (Gigerenzer and Brighton, 2009; Gigerenzer and Goldstein, 1996; Marewski et al., 2010).

Gigerenzer et al. (1999) give a profound overview of heuristics that describe human information behavior in choice tasks. Gigerenzer and Goldstein (1999), for example, differentiate between three stopping rules, calling them "The Minimalist", "Take the last" and "Take the best". The minimalist approach is relying on another popular heuristic termed "recognition heuristic" which holds that decision makers often come to correct conclusions about which one of two alternatives to select by simply going for the alternative they recognize[3]. If the recognition heuristic is not applicable, the subject following a minimalist approach randomly searches for information cues describing the two alternatives and repeats this process until he finds one cue to be superior of the other. "Take the last" is driven by prior experience and lets a decision maker seek for those information cues which terminated a similar seeking process conducted in the past. In the "Take the best" scenario, the information seeker has additional information on the validity of information cues and processes them in the order of highest to lowest validity and apart from that follows the minimalist approach. All heuristics mentioned above process information sequentially. The decision to stop seeking for additional information is made based on just one specific cue (one-reason decision making). Similar heuristics restricted to binary choices between two alternatives have been proposed by Aschenbrenner et al. (1984) and Schmalhofer et al. (1986).

A theme often emerging in research on heuristics is the importance of information validity and credibility. Hausmann and Lage (2008) propose a threshold model stating that information seekers stop seeking for information as soon as they reach a "desired level of confidence", which is interpreted as an individual aspiration level of the corresponding subject. Beach and Strom (1989) take the

---

3 Experiments on the recognition heuristic often contain questions like "Which city has the larger population: Milan or Modena?" (Gigerenzer and Goldstein, 2011, p. 106). Here, the recognition heuristic in the form "If one of two objects is recognized and the other is not, then infer that the recognized object has the higher value with respect to the criterion" (Gigerenzer and Goldstein, 2011, p. 101) is shown to result in a significant amount of correct answers even though no additional information is requested by the subject from external sources.

opposite perspective and analyze rejections of alternatives in choice problems. The authors show that subjects terminate the acquisition of information on a specific alternative as soon as a given threshold of acceptable violations of desired goal criteria is exceeded. In another study, Metzger et al. (2010) investigate credibility assessments made by web site visitors based on dual-process theories. They find that the subjects rarely use systematic approaches to make credibility judgments but often rely on simple heuristics such as counting positive comments about a specific topic made by other users. Negative credibility judgments though are reported to be triggers for terminating sub-processes in information seeking activities, i. e. subjects quickly leave web sites they do not trust and switch to alternative information channels.

Sufficiency of Information

Since most studies on information seeking stopping behavior are related to decision making tasks and choice problems, only a few research projects focus on the identification of stopping rules that are used in information search tasks, in which the sufficiency of acquired information is the major trigger for terminating the search (Browne et al., 2007).

Browne and Pitts (2004) and Browne et al. (2007) introduce two scenarios in which the aforementioned sufficiency of information is the central aspect. In the former study, they differentiate between an early design and a late choice phase in decision problems and argue that the major objective of the design phase consists in the identification of alternatives in terms of divergent thinking. The goal of the choice phase lies in the selection of one specific alternative (convergence). They summarize that in design problems, considerations of information sufficiency guide the decision when the search for alternatives should be terminated. Similar decisions have to be made in online search tasks, which are addressed in the latter research. Also in this scenario, the goal of seeking for information is not necessarily to condense the information in order to make a decision for a specific alternative, but to obtain a sufficient amount of information.

In their research, Browne et al. primarily use four cognitive stopping rules which had been defined by Nickles et al. (1995) and which were extended by a fifth rule in Browne et al. (2005) and Browne et al. (2007). Cognitive stopping rules describe actual human behavior in information seeking scenarios, not being

Table 2.2.: Cognitive Stopping Rules (Browne et al., 2007, p. 92)

Rule	Description
Mental List	Person has a mental list of items that must be satisfied before he stops collecting information.
Representational Stability	Person searches for information until his mental model, or representation, stops shifting and stabilizes. The focus is on the stability of the representation.
Difference Threshold	Person sets an *a priori* difference level to gauge when he is not learning anything new. When he stops learning new information, he stops his information search.
Magnitude Threshold	Person has a cumulative amount of information that he needs before he will stop searching. The focus is on having "enough" information.
Single Criterion	Person decides to search for information related to a single criterion and stops when he has enough information about that criterion.

restricted to choice tasks. As such, they make assumptions about conscious cognitive processes guiding the information seeking process. The use of a specific stopping rule is said to be dependent on properties of the task environment such as task complexity or task structuredness and individual characteristics such as former experience (Browne and Pitts, 2004; Browne et al., 2007). Browne et al. find that task structuredness is a strong predictor of the *mental list* and *single criterion* stopping rule. Both stopping rules assume that the information seeker has a clear understanding of which specific information cues he needs before terminating the search. Low task structuredness is shown to cause the use of *magnitude threshold* and *representational stability* stopping rules. These rules do not focus on specific information entities but assume that the subject is seeking until an a priori defined amount of information has been acquired ("enough" information) or until the mental representation of the problem space shifts only gradually by acquiring additional information. An overview of all cognitive stopping rules identified by Browne et al. is given in Table 2.2.

Explaining information seeking behavior is traditionally one of the core research objectives in the Information Science discipline. Consequently, also Information

Scientists report findings on information seeking stopping behavior, but strictly limit their research to specific groups of people (e. g. arts directors or academic library users). Zach (2005) only gives rather vague insights into the stopping behavior of senior arts directors by indicating that they quit seeking when reaching an "arbitrary level of comfort with the input they had acquired" (p. 30). However she mentions that this decision to stop was either made consciously or subconsciously and thus, moves away from the classical assumption of purely rational behavior.

Kraft and Lee (1979) primarily distinguish between a *satiation rule* and a *disgust rule*, assuming that people either stop seeking because they have found all documents they were looking for in an information retrieval system (satiation) or because they received too many irrelevant documents (disgust). Prabha et al. (2007) exploratively analyze differing patterns of stopping behavior based on the role theory stating that the role of a person (in this case undergraduate and graduate students versus faculty members) strongly predicts information needs, motivations and perceptions. As a result, they present several quantitative and qualitative stopping rules in the context of document search in libraries which offer limited opportunities for generalizations.

Motivational Factors Influencing Stopping Behavior

The termination of information seeking activities is not solely the result of active cognitive processes or intuitive judgments but can also be triggered and influenced by external factors, emotional states and individual predispositions.

Time-pressure is described as one of the most prominent and intuitively reasonable external factors triggering the early termination of information seeking processes (Browne et al., 2007; Hausmann and Lage, 2008; Nickles et al., 1995; Zach, 2005). But also the current mood of the information seeker, which can be influenced – among other factors – by a lack of time, is said to have significant consequences on the subsequent stopping behavior. Martin et al. (1993) find that people in positive mood process more information when they enjoy the task, but less if they follow a strict information sufficiency heuristic (in comparison to people in negative mood). Furthermore, negative mood is a predictor of systematic information processing with the goal of reducing the bad mood condition, whereas positive mood activates heuristic information processing (Bless et al., 1990).

Various individual characteristics of the information seekers have been identified as predictors of differing processing styles and stopping behaviors. For instance, individuals with high need for cognition or such individuals showing general maximizing tendencies usually search for information more systematically and also consider a higher amount of information before terminating the seeking process. In this context, "need for cognition" is usually defined as "an individual's tendency to engage in and enjoy effortful cognitive endeavors" (Cacioppo et al., 1996, p. 197), whereas maximizing tendencies are thought to be an individual predisposition indicating if a person generally strives for global maxima or optimal solutions when making decisions (Schwartz et al., 2002). Another individual characteristic, the need for cognitive closure defined as an "individual's desire for a firm answer to a question and an aversion toward ambiguity" (Kruglanski and Webster, 1996, p. 264), predicts lower resistance to persuasive messages if no prior knowledge is available (Webster and Kruglanski, 1994). This means that people high in need for cognitive closure terminate information acquisition earlier if they receive convincing information about a topic they do not have knowledge about (compared to individuals with low need for cognitive closure). David et al. (2007) analyze the impact of the individual level of motivation to solve a specific task on the depth of information seeking and report an increased level of exploration with positive effects on overall task performance.

2.3.2.3. Summary

The discussion above indicates that past research on information seeking stopping behavior set a strong focus on normative, later also descriptive stopping behavior in choice tasks. However, there is a significantly smaller amount of articles dealing with stopping behavior in situations in which the sufficiency of information is the major reason for terminating the search. Furthermore, there is a large share of publications assuming that information seekers terminate the information acquisition process based on primarily rational considerations of the information they received so far, thus ignoring spontaneous, experiential stopping behavior. Additionally, only a few articles decidedly address the topic from an

Information Systems perspective, taking characteristics of the technology used to acquire information, an organizational task and individual characteristics of the information seeker into account.

Consequently, this study aims at closing the gaps shown above by building and testing a holistic theory of IS-mediated information seeking stopping behavior. For this reason, the next section presents existing work from adjacent disciplines serving as reference theories in the context of this study.

2.3.3. Theoretical Lenses for Analyzing Information Seeking Stopping Behavior

Considering the limited amount of IS literature on human information behavior and information seeking stopping behavior, it becomes obvious that for filling the research gaps identified in this work, theories from adjacent disciplines have to be integrated. In the next section, the most suitable theories are selected and discussed subsequently, before a final evaluation is conducted.

2.3.3.1. Selection of Theoretical Lenses

Following the approach of Dibbern et al. (2001), theory selection requires that *first*, a specific research problem is available guiding the selection process. In this study, the research problem was characterized in Chapter 1 and insights into existing literature were given in the previous sections. *Second*, several theories with similar explanatory claims regarding information seeking stopping behavior have to be available. Based on the literature review in the previous sections, Table 2.3 summarizes those theories that were mentioned frequently in existing literature on human information behavior and information seeking stopping behavior as well as theories that appear promising in the context of this work. The applicability of these theories in the context of the present study is discussed next.

Even though both in Economics and in Psychology impressive efforts have been made to gain a better understanding of information seeking strategies in decision making and choice tasks, these findings cannot be transferred to questions of stopping behavior in search tasks without taking the special characteristics of

Table 2.3.: Selected Theories Used in Extant Literature on Information Seeking and Stopping Behavior

Theory	Selected articles using the theory	Theory's core assumptions
Information processing		
Dual-process theory	Metzger et al. (2010); Wirth et al. (2007)	Human beings follow two different ways of processing information: either effortless, heuristic or effortful, systematic.
Information foraging theory	Pirolli (2005); Taraborelli (2008)	Information seekers consume those pieces of information they assume to get the highest benefit from.
Effort-accuracy framework of cognition	Rapoport and Tversky (1970); Todd and Benbasat (1992)	When solving problems, human beings invest as little effort as possible to gain as accurate results as possible (cf. bounded rationality, satisficing).
Social influence		
Social presence theory	Hemmer and Heinzl (2012); Kumar and Benbasat (2006, 2004)	Artificial communication media and information technologies can convey the feeling of another person being present while a user is interacting with these systems, thus influencing information behavior.
Role theory	Prabha et al. (2007)	The social position a person holds influences the amount and quality of information he is looking for.
Choice between alternatives		
Rational choice theory	Herrnstein (1990); Prabha et al. (2007)	In choice situations, problem solvers know all alternatives, acquire information about these and choose the alternative which promises to have the highest benefit.
Prospect theory	Kogut (1990)	When making choices that involve risk, problem solvers calculate the expected utility of alternatives as the sum of weighted gains and losses and try to reduce losses.

this task into account. As pointed out earlier, sufficiency of information is the main criterion for terminating information search activities whereas convergence of information is the dominant trigger for making decisions about alternatives in choice tasks (Browne and Pitts, 2004). Consequently, *rational choice theory* and *prospect theory* are not considered core theories in the domain of information seeking stopping behavior because they decidedly focus on decision making and choice problems. *Role theory* is also excluded because it is the goal of this work to build a mid-range theory of information seeking stopping behavior which explains human behavior independent of a specific role the information seeker holds.

The literature review in the previous section reveals that there is an obvious conflict between two fundamentally different perspectives on human behavior: *on the one hand*, especially economists develop prescriptive stopping rules based on trade-offs between costs and benefits of information cues. Thus, they assume that both people are capable of judging the value of information constantly and that they actually perform these calculations regularly when acquiring information. *On the other hand*, it is generally accepted now that people often deviate from these prescriptions and usually consume less information than reasonable (see Section 2.3.2.1 and Bearden et al., 2006, 2005; Sonnemans, 1998). *Dual-process theories* have been used to account for this effect and explain the deviations by reflecting both individual predispositions (Epstein et al., 1996) and situation-specific activators (Novak and Hoffman, 2009). This class of theories originates from research in Psychology and supposes that human beings process information in two fundamentally different ways, namely either rationally or heuristically (Evans and Chi, 2008; Kahneman, 2011). It appears promising to utilize this well-established and validated set of theories in order to explain systematically which determinants affect the activation of rational, thoughtful versus experiential, impulsive stopping behavior (Browne et al., 2007; Cacioppo et al., 1996).

Derivatives of dual-process theories such as the Elaboration Likelihood Model of Persuasion (ELM) have been used in various IS and non-IS contexts to analyze the persuasive impact of information cues that were visibly created by other social actors (Chaiken, 1980). Surprisingly however, there is only a small number of publications explicitly integrating these observations into research projects on stopping behavior even though there is evidence for a strong link between the presence of persuasive cues and premature stopping (Petty and Cacioppo, 1986; Sundar, 2007). Hence, a close investigation of derivatives of classical dual-process theories also appears to be a rich source for gaining insights into mechanisms underlying information seeking stopping behavior.

Since this work focuses on computer-mediated information acquisition, it is important to assure that the results of existing research on dual-process theories are amendable to "computerized" contexts. For this reason, (para-)social presence theory is analyzed subsequently in order to show that artificial information systems can also be perceived as actual social actors under specific circumstances (Kumar and Benbasat, 2006, 2002).

One major theme emerging from the literature review on stopping behavior in choice tasks consists in the observation that human beings consistently deviate from optimality because they want to reduce effort. Consequently, it can be assumed that effort – in the case of information acquisition basically *cognitive effort* – also plays an important role in information search tasks. Thus, effort-accuracy theories fit into the context of this study since they suppose that people accept less accurate solutions as long as they can reduce their perceived effort for reaching it – a finding which is also reported in several research projects on dual-process strategies of information acquisition (Chaiken, 1980; Kahneman, 2003; Smith and DeCoster, 2000).

As mentioned in this section's introductory part, the selected theories must make similar explanatory claims and should be commensurable (Chalmers, 1999). Both criteria are fulfilled:

- *Individual* as level of analysis;

- *Positivism* as epistemological stance;

- *Information* as a major entity, especially the concept of message persuasiveness;

- *Information processing effort* identified as important determinant of information behavior;

- *Bounded rationality* as guiding principle;

- Theories that both predict *and* explain the observed phenomena.

Table 2.4.: Variety of Terms Attached to Dual-Processes (based on Evans, 2008, p. 257)

References	System 1	System 2
Epstein (1994); Epstein et al. (1996)	Experiential	Rational
Chaiken (1980)	Heuristic	Systematic
Sloman (1996)	Associative	Rule based
Stanovich and West (2000)	System 1	System 2
Lieberman (2003); Lieberman et al. (2004)	Reflexive / X-System	Reflective / C-System
Strack and Deutsch (2004)	Impulsive	Reflective

The following sections give a detailed overview of dual-process theories and its derivatives before the concept of para-social presence is introduced. Finally, the idea of effort-accuracy models is presented briefly.

2.3.3.2. Dual-Process Theories and Derivatives

On a cognitive level, human beings seek and process information in two distinct ways, which were given many different labels in past research. The most neutral and widely-used terms are "System 1" and "System 2" (Evans and Chi, 2008; Kahneman, 2003, 2011; Lieberman, 2003; Stanovich and West, 2000) to distinguish between automatic, effortless and heuristic information acquisition and evaluation on the one hand (System 1) and deliberate, effortful, conscious and systematic information acquisition and evaluation on the other hand (System 2, see Table 2.4). This duality has been shown to have a significant impact on the way people make judgments and decisions and it was also possible to identify brain regions which are activated when System 1 or System 2 thinking take place.

Lieberman (2003) detects neural correlates of System 1 and System 2 activation and finds "amygdala, basal ganglia and lateral temporal cortex" (p. 48) to be associated with the reflexive system while "anterior cingulate cortex, lateral prefrontal cortex, and the medial temporal lobe" (p. 50) is associated with the reflective system. According to Lieberman, reflexive, i. e. automatic processing is invoked when social meaning is linked to information cues whereas reflective thinking takes place when System 1 processing cannot handle the given situation. The latter effect, however, can only be observed when cognitive load does not exceed a specific threshold as cognitive load seems to suppress systematic information processing. Consequently, the neural correlates of System 1 and System 2 do not act in terms of isolated entities but highly depend on each other.

Strack and Deutsch (2004) take the opposite stance and claim that "judgments and decisions are made in the reflective system" (p. 241). Hence, they limit the important role, other dual-process theories attach to System 1 processes. In their understanding, heuristic information processing, i. e. the use of "shortcuts to circumvent effortful and time-consuming systematic processing" (p. 240), takes place in the reflective system by consciously applying cognitive simplification rules. This perspective, however, is not validated by extensive empirical evaluations. As a consequence, the majority view among cognitive psychologists still consists in the assumption that heuristic information processing and reasoning mainly takes place outside the reflective system and, therefore, also outside the full consciousness of the corresponding person (Evans, 2008).

Many authors emphasize the importance of long-term and short-term memory (Evans, 2003; Lieberman et al., 2004; Schneider and Shiffrin, 1977; Smith and DeCoster, 2000). As System 1 thinking is said to be based on associations made by the information seeker in response to given stimuli, it highly depends on former knowledge and experience which have been built up over a long period of time and, therefore, can be requested from long-term memory. System 2 thinking systematically follows cognitive rules and thus poses higher requirements towards short-term (working) memory in order to keep record of the information cues acquired before and put them into a coherent context (Smith and DeCoster, 2000).

With regard to the variables that activate reflective and reflexive information processing, researchers distinguish between individual predispositions and situation-specific triggers. Epstein (1994) developed the cognitive-experiential self-theory supposing the existence of an analytical-rational and an intuitive-experiential mode of information processing, setting a focus on the information processor's individual characteristics that are rather time-invariant. They identify need for cognition (cf. Section 2.3.2.1) as a stable personal predisposition

directly affecting a person's overall tendency to seek more information and re-
member more information (recall) if need for cognition is high. Individuals low
in need for cognition are more prone to accepting persuasive messages and using
cognitive heuristics in order to evade effortful thinking (Cacioppo et al., 1996).
Additionally, gender is reported to affect the processing mode, even though contradicting results were found. Whereas Epstein et al. (1996) claim that male
persons show a tendency towards rational thinking, Darley and Smith (1995) for
example state that women usually process all available information in a systematic way before making judgments. Major situation-specific triggers consist of the
information seeker's current mood, motivation to solve a given task and characteristics of the information which are discussed in more detail in the context of the
elaboration likelihood model of persuasion and the heuristic-systematic model.

In summary, even though the above introduction of two fundamentally different modes of information processing suggests a certain superiority of System 2
in terms of the accuracy of downstream decisions, several authors agree on the
fact that heuristic information processing can also result in highly accurate and
efficient solutions. Thus, they argue that System 1 processing can be the more
appropriate way of accessing information when the information processor has a
sufficient amount of prior experience in solving similar tasks, a fact that was
observed in medical treatment for example (Kahneman, 2003; Novak and Hoffman, 2009). Both the positive and negative effects of the two different thinking
and information processing styles were also investigated in IS research, albeit the
number of corresponding publications is considerably low (Majchrzak and Jarvenpaa, 2010; Sussman and Siegal, 2003; Tam and Ho, 2005, 2006). The two
major dual-process models used in IS research primarily deal with persuasiveness of information in computer-mediated contexts. Since they have a significant
potential for explaining the impact of this type of information on information
seeking stopping behavior, they are presented below.

**Heuristic-Systematic Model of Information Processing and Elabora-
tion Likelihood Model of Persuasion**

Both the heuristic-systematic model of information processing (HSM, Chaiken,
1980) and the elaboration likelihood model of persuasion (ELM, Petty and Cacioppo, 1986) represent dual-process theories in the context of message persua-

siveness. The models suggest the existence of two different ways in which people decide to accept or reject messages they receive from other persons either in real-life or in computer-mediated communication scenarios. The corresponding authors argue that messages influence the attitudes of their receivers either via a "central (cognitive) route" following a systematic processing or via a "peripheral route" relying on heuristic cues.

It is important to consider the models in the realm of terminating information seeking activities because during web-based information seeking, information seekers access increasing amounts of information which is difficult to evaluate with regard to its objective validity (e. g. costumer reviews). HSM and ELM help to explain the process of the aforementioned belief formation and also give explanations for differences in depth of information processing as an antecedent of stopping behavior (Petty and Cacioppo, 1986). In line with the dual-process theories of reasoning and judgment presented before, HSM and ELM follow the idea of least effort stating that heuristic processing is used to cope with limitations of human cognition and systematic processing is only exerted when more detailed evaluations are necessary. Therefore, the models share the widely accepted notion of information sufficiency underlying stopping decisions in information search that are also reflected by many theories presented in Section 2.3 in the context of stopping behavior research. The models differ in the labels they attach to the types of information processing and in the assumption that heuristic and systematic validity assessments can take place at the same time (HSM) versus an isolated, exclusive activation of central or peripheral route in ELM (Zhang and Watts, 2008).

Both models assume that elaboration likelihood as the sum of the receiver's motivation and ability (e. g. prior experience in the given domain) affect the way in which the message validity is assessed. Under conditions of high elaboration likelihood, subjects primarily rely on the objective quality of arguments in a given message, i. e. "recipients carefully consider the issues presented by the message" (Sussman and Siegal, 2003, p. 50). However, if recipients are not willing or not able to scrutinize information quality, they switch to heuristic processing in the peripheral route, relying on "peripheral cues", i. e. information indicators that go beyond the content itself (Sussman and Siegal, 2003). Examples for such peripheral cues are source credibility evoked by the statement that the information sender is a field expert, or group validity signals indicating that a specific number of persons think that a given information is valid (Areni et al., 2000; Chaiken, 1980; Zhang and Watts, 2008).

Apart from the fact that high elaboration likelihood increases the probability of central route validity assessments, it was also shown in past research that opinions formed after processing a message via the central route are more stable. Furthermore, information processors show lower degrees of regret in the long run (e. g. after having made a decision based on the information they acquired), which might be a signal for higher accuracy of central processing (Bhattacherjee and Sanford, 2006). This finding is especially important in combination with effort-accuracy principles which are part of many research projects on stopping behavior stating that information seekers regularly sacrifice accuracy for information processing effort (Payne et al., 1992).

The practical applicability of HSM and ELM for describing and explaining phenomena in the realm of IS research has been proven in various projects. Bhattacherjee and Sanford (2006) and Angst and Agarwal (2009) use ELM in combination with the Technology Acceptance Model (Davis, 1989) to investigate the effect of central versus peripheral route processing on the acceptance of new information technology. Angst and Agarwal (2009) introduce the "privacy concern" construct as a barrier to the adoption of electronic health records. They report that people with low task involvement strongly rely on peripheral cues, in this case credible messages about electronic health records. This finding is in line with the claim of ELM that low elaboration likelihood activates the peripheral route.

In e-commerce research, Kim et al. (2009) find that the price shown for a specific product positively affects the systematic scrutiny of information indicating that for high involvement products argument content is the main driver for information acquisition. Tam and Ho (2005) and Yu et al. (2011) show that personalized product recommendations on e-commerce web sites are perceived as peripheral cues that activate the heuristic, peripheral route of assessing message validity following simple rules like "This is a personalized product for me, so it should be good" (Tam and Ho, 2005, p. 275).

In addition to the examples given above, several researchers investigate persuasive effects of messages dynamically created by other web users (user-generated
content) stating that there is a significant research gap with regard to the impacts of user-generated content on validity assessments (Metzger et al., 2010).
Modern interactive web sites allow users to share opinions about specific topics
in a collective sense which results in consensus information, e. g. overall star
ratings of products in e-commerce applications. These "consensus cues" (p. 50)
or additional background information about the person who created a message
may serve as triggers for activating peripheral routes resulting in less complete
information acquisition and processing (Sussman and Siegal, 2003). A similar example is given by Zhang and Watts (2008) in the context of information adoption
in online communities. Here, the authors find that text can also convey social
cues – i. e. contextual information that evokes the impression of a social interaction – in the form of collective popularity ratings in online forums activating the
same mechanisms as reported by Sussman and Siegal (2003).

The high density of research on social cues acting as triggers for peripheral route
processing in computer-mediated persuasion contexts (Yu et al., 2011) published
in the last few years suggests that user-generated content increasingly changes
the way information is searched and processed in online settings. The general
propensity of artificial information technologies to convey social cues to its users
was examined in research programs on social presence. As social presence influences the way information is processed and, therefore, also the way information
seeking processes are terminated, the major findings from past research are presented subsequently.

2.3.3.3. Social Presence Theory

Social presence theory postulates that there are differences in communication
medias' propensity to convey "rich" information in terms of non-verbal social
cues such as facial expressions and body gestures to evoke the impression of
other persons' physical presence in a communication process (Short et al., 1976).
Consequently, the terms "social presence" and "social richness" have been used
interchangeably in past research (Kumar and Benbasat, 2002; Venkatesh and
Johnson, 2002). The theory claims that face-to-face interactions between two

individuals evoke the highest degree of perceived social presence because many of the aforementioned non-verbal cues can be transmitted to and received by the communication partner. According to the theory, computer-mediated communication is necessarily characterized by lower degrees of social presence because media like e-mail or online chats can only transport a small fraction of additional non-verbal cues compared to face-to-face communication. As a consequence, the highest performance in conducting a communication task can be achieved by creating a fit between the required level of social presence in a given situation and the degree of social presence that can be provided by a specific medium (Short et al., 1976; Straub and Karahanna, 1998). In line with media richness theory, the social presence theory assumes that ambiguous and equivocal tasks can be handled more efficiently by using socially rich media whereas quick transmission of facts is more compatible with socially lean media (Dennis et al., 2008; Yoo and Alavi, 2001).

With regard to the perception of social presence by the users of computer-mediated communication (CMC) media, those media having a high degree of social presence are "judged as being warm, personal, sensitive and sociable" (Short et al., 1976, p. 66). Furthermore, the degree of social presence is reported to have an effect on the depth of information seeking, even though no insights are given into the underlying causality (Kumar and Benbasat, 2002).

In spite of the theory's extensive use in many research projects, it has also been criticized by various authors. For example, Walther (1992) challenges the basic assumption of social richness being exclusively influenced by characteristics of the technology used (e. g. e-mail versus video conferencing). He develops a theory of social information processing stating that the construction of meaning based on a given message is a subjective cognitive process. Thus, he suggests that the degree of social presence depends on the personal interpretation of the CMC user and not only on the properties of the CMC technology itself. Kock (2004) develops the media naturalness theory (also called *psychobiological model*) in order to question the social presence theory's presumption of face-to-face communication allowing for the highest degree of social presence. He argues that modern information technology has spread so quickly that the human brain has not had a chance to adapt to these developments. Naturalness of a CMC is defined as the similarity of a medium with a face-to-face conversation, while in his view, a modern CMC can be even richer than a face-to-face conversation. Hence, he assumes that all deviations from a face-to-face conversation's degree of social presence – either positive or negative – will result in an increase in mental effort to process the transferred information because of deviations from evolutionary-shaped communication patterns (Kock, 2004, 2005, 2009). Thus, Kock indirectly argues in favor of unconscious, heuristic information processing for individuals using CMCs with high social presence.

The social presence theory was originally developed to describe differences between CMCs. In more recent research, however, it is used in a broader sense: an increasing amount of authors shifts the focus from computer-mediated communication between two human beings to the more abstract communication process between a person and a computer (Benbasat, 2010). This stream of research is of particular interest from an information seeking perspective, because information seeking can also be understood as a communication process in which a person requests information from an artificial system, thus communicates with that system.

Hemmer and Heinzl (2012) show that subjects prefer information channels high in social presence when seeking for information in the context of complex organizational tasks. Gefen and Straub (2004) even find that "the lack of an interpersonal interaction is a key defining characteristics of e-Commerce!" (p. 410). However, they report that although e-commerce web sites usually do not allow immediate interactions with other persons, appropriate design of such web sites can create the feeling of social presence, which finally results in higher perceived trust in the contents of that site. Kumar and Benbasat (2002) introduce the concept of "Para-Social Presence" to the IS community, defining it as "the extent to which a medium facilitates a sense of understanding, connection, involvement and interaction among participating social entities" (p. 7). Thus, they treat a web site as a social actor showing similar characteristics as those which can be observed in social interactions between human beings. Later, Kumar and Benbasat (2006) extend and evaluate this framework in a laboratory experiment and show that recommendation engines and the provision of consumer reviews on e-commerce web sites can improve the level of social presence perceived by the subjects. Cyr et al. (2009) also address online shopping scenarios by substantiating that human images in web sites evoke a feeling of social presence and thereby increase trust in the specific web site.

The fact that artificial web sites can induce an impression of social presence and, thus, increase credibility and persuasiveness of arguments conveyed to the visitor of the web site, has motivated researchers to explore the specific design elements that are responsible for the emergence of perceived social presence. Besides fitting the users' information needs with the information delivered to them via product recommendation engines (Kumar and Benbasat, 2006), social presence is strongly invoked by pictures of other people (Fogg, 2003; Gefen and Straub, 2004) on which facial features are perceptible (Cyr et al., 2009). Furthermore, language itself is identified as providing mechanisms for transporting social cues. Here, especially the role of a personal welcoming of a web site user by his name is emphasized by Fogg (2003) and Gefen and Straub (2004).

2.3.3.4. Effort-Accuracy Framework of Cognition

The effort-accuracy framework of cognition, proposed by Payne (1982), holds that when making decisions, human beings can follow various strategies, trading off between decision accuracy and cognitive effort the decision maker has to invest. With regard to *accuracy*, a decision maker usually makes assumptions about the likelihood that employing a specific decision strategy will result in the selection of the best alternative in a set of different options. *Cognitive effort* can be measured by counting the number of so-called *elementary information processes (EIP)*, for example (Payne et al., 1993; Shugan, 1980). An EIP represents one singular cognitive operation such as reading some words or performing a comparison between two alternatives.

As a consequence, decision makers are said to employ basically one of the following two options to trade off between effort and accuracy: they either choose the decision strategy with the more accurate outcome (when two strategies are expected to yield an equivalent level of cognitive effort) or they prefer the decision strategy that requires less cognitive effort (when two strategies yield the same outcome, Payne, 1982; Payne et al., 1992; Todd and Benbasat, 1992). Interestingly, several research projects have shown that people regularly strive for reducing effort at the price of reduced accuracy (Todd and Benbasat, 1992, 2000; Wang and

Benbasat, 2009). This observation is justified by the argument that people "will seek ways to reduce their problem solving effort, since they are limited information processors" (Vessey and Galletta, 1991, p. 65), hence referring indirectly to Simon's assumptions of bounded rationality inherent to human problem solvers (Simon, 1955). Wang and Benbasat (2009) report that decision makers "focused more on effort reduction than advice quality" (p. 308) in experiments with interactive decision aids. Todd and Benbasat (1992) find that using a computer-based decision aid does not result in an increased accuracy of decisions but makes the participants of the experiments use less information; i. e. by using decision aids, the subjects improve their efficiency instead of their effectiveness.

In IS research, the effort-accuracy framework of cognition was utilized to prove that both in information seeking and in decision making, information technology can reduce cognitive effort and increase outcome accuracy if there is a fit between the mental model a person has about the problem to solve and the format in which information is presented or pre-filtered by decision aids (Vessey and Galletta, 1991; Wang and Benbasat, 2009). Relating the concept of cognitive fit to dual-process theories suggests that information technology can activate heuristic information processing without sacrificing accuracy: a view that is especially hold by proponents of heuristic processing in non-IS contexts (Kahneman, 2003; Novak and Hoffman, 2009).

As decision making is the result of processing information about alternatives, seeking for information is an important first step in decision making tasks. Consequently, the phenomena and theoretical assumptions about effort-accuracy trade-offs reported above in the context of decision making can be transferred to information seeking in general, as shown by Kuo et al. (2004) for example. Thus, the effort-accuracy framework of cognition helps to explain why human beings usually refrain from cognitively demanding strategies when solving complex tasks that necessitate a high information seeking intensity.

2.3.3.5. Summary

A comprehensive theory of computer-mediated information seeking stopping behavior does not exist yet. Therefore, it is necessary to combine such reference theories that share similar fundamental assumptions (e. g. same level of analysis, same epistemological stance, similar explanatory claims) and provide explanations about the central constructs as well as about the relationships between those constructs in the context of this study's research topic. In the previous sections, dual-process theories, the social presence theory, and the effort-accuracy framework of cognition were presented after they were shown to fulfill the aforementioned criteria.

Dual-process theories and their derivatives, the heuristic-systematic model of information processing and the elaboration likelihood model of persuasion differentiate between two fundamentally different ways of processing information on a cognitive level. According to these theories, people seek and process information either in an effortless, automatic way (System 1) or they access information following an effortful, deliberate thinking process (System 2). From the perspective of terminating information seeking activities, this class of theories is promising for three reasons: (1) After former research has regularly chosen a one-dimensional view, concentrating on rational *or* intuitive information seeking and stopping behavior, dual-process theories integrate both dimensions in one nomological network. (2) Dual-process theories predict both the effect of individual characteristics and the specificity of tasks on the way information is processed. Furthermore, they offer explanations for these phenomena on the level of neural correlates. (3) The theories take properties of the entity *information* into account, showing that framing effects can have an influence on the persuasiveness of the information delivered to the recipient.

As dual-process theories were developed in the field of cognitive and social psychology, they do not necessarily consider the impact information technology can have on information behavior. Therefore, the *social presence theory* was analyzed as a means for complementing the predictions of dual-process theories. The social presence theory has often been applied in the realm of media choice research, but was used in recent research projects to explain technology-induced trust and information source credibility phenomena. Consequently, the theory extends the HSM and the ELM by suggesting that (artificial) information technology can be perceived as a concrete social actor and thus influences the depth of information processing.

Finally, the *effort-accuracy framework of cognition* states that people tend to minimize mental effort when solving tasks even if they have to expect a lower accuracy of the task outcome as a result of the reduced effort invested. This framework emphasizes the fit between an organizational task and the supporting technological artifacts. Thus, it can be regarded as a more general boundary spanner between the two classes of theories mentioned before, as those take mental effort into account, but pay less attention to the interplay between task and technology constructs.

2.4. Development of the Research Model

In the following, hypotheses are developed and integrated into a research model explaining information seeking stopping behavior from an IS perspective. IS research intends to investigate the interplay between individuals, tasks and information technology (Burton-Jones and Straub, 2006; Heinrich et al., 2011). This scientific objective is reflected in Figure 2.3, which serves as a preliminary framework for guiding the process of developing the aforementioned research model.

The research framework addresses the absence of a consensus on the question if information seekers decide for a specific information seeking and stopping strategy as soon as they start solving a task or if the stopping decision is a consequence of the information seeking process itself (Browne et al., 2007). The former assumption about the direction of causality implies that an information seeker actively thinks about and rationally follows a specific strategy. It neglects the possibility of the information seeker being influenced by the quantity and quality of information he receives *while* seeking for information, potentially resulting in deviations from logical, rule-based seeking and stopping behavior. Since this study aims at building a holistic theory of information seeking stopping behavior accounting for both rational and experiential stopping behavior, it is assumed that the information processing behavior – operationalized in terms of dual-process theories – mediates the impact of the aforementioned independent variables on information seeking stopping behavior. The constructs and causal relationships shown in Figure 2.3 will be extended and refined next. An operationalization and validation will take place in the course of this study.

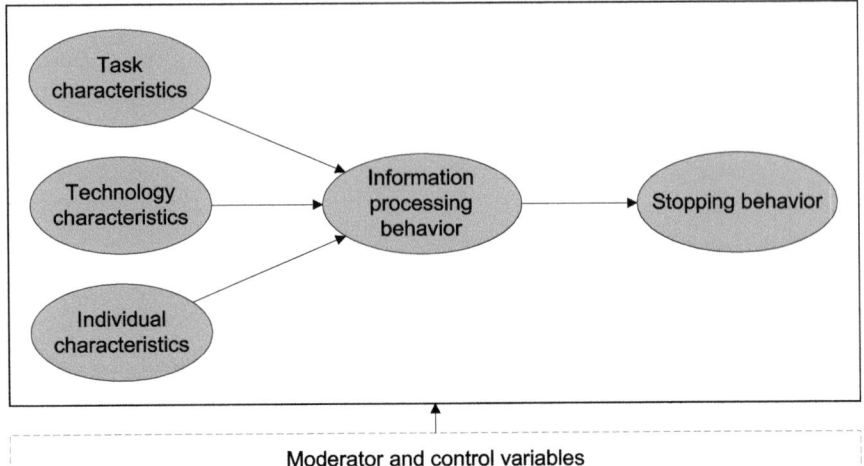

Figure 2.3.: Overview of Construct Categories and Fundamental Causal Relationships (without Propositions)

2.4.1. Development of Hypotheses

Building on the theories introduced in the previous section, a more detailed analysis of their applicability in the realm of information seeking stopping behavior is presented below. An overview of all relevant constructs and their definitions is given at the end of this section in Table 2.5 (p. 65).

2.4.1.1. Dependent Variable: Information Seeking Stopping Behavior

Research on information seeking stopping behavior suggests – primarily implicitly – that there are two fundamentally different ways how people come to the conclusion to terminate information acquisition processes. On the one hand, there is a large research stream assuming that information seekers intensively scrutinize the information they get and stop these activities following a process of logical, content-wise reasoning. To recall the discussion in Section 2.3.2, fact-based, rational stopping can either be the consequence of acquisition costs exceeding the value of retrieving additional information cues (which requires an active assessment of costs and benefits on the part of the information seeker) or the result of an active dissemination of a given task into a sequence of isolated information seeking sub-tasks and the fulfillment of all derived information needs (e. g. mental list stopping rule, Browne et al., 2007).

On the other hand, there is evidence for the fact that information seekers often make implicit judgments on the sufficiency of information based on intuition and affect (Gigerenzer and Goldstein, 1996, 2011; Gigerenzer et al., 1999). In this case, information is not assessed in a purely rational way, but spontaneously without the information seeker being fully aware of specific issue-relevant pieces of information that made him stop in a given situation. Consequently, following the terminology proposed by Epstein (1994) and Epstein et al. (1996), the broad concept of *stopping behavior* is operationalized dually, differentiating between *rational*, i. e. reasoning- and fact-based stopping behavior and *experiential*, i. e. spontaneous and intuitive stopping behavior (Miller and Ireland, 2005).

The termination of information seeking processes can be regarded as the last step in a sequence of information acquisition activities. Hence, the way in which people seek for information and think about it, appears to be a good predictor of downstream stopping behavior. As shown in Section 2.3.3.2, dual-process theories of cognition represent a well-established set of theories delivering insights into thinking processes and the persuasiveness of messages received by an information seeker by differentiating between System 1 and System 2 information processing.

Even though most dual-process theories do not distinguish between information seeking on the one hand and stopping behavior on the other hand, they implicitly acknowledge two fundamental underlying causalities: (1) In the System 1 information processing mode, judgments are regularly made "without argument scrutiny" (Petty and Cacioppo, 1986, p. 132) or based on "non-content cues" (Chaiken, 1980, p. 752), whereas (2) in the System 2 information processing mode, the aforementioned effect is attenuated, resulting in judgments that are logically justified by the information seeker (Chaiken and Maheswaran, 1994). Since System 1 and System 2 information processing are not activated in a dichotomous sense, but can occur concurrently, information seekers primarily operating in a System 2 information processing mode should be able to give a rational reasoning why they stopped seeking for information (as opposed to individuals using System 1 information processing). Summarizing the above argumentation, the following hypotheses are put forth:

Hypothesis 1: The higher the degree of System 1 information process-
ing, the higher the propensity to use experiential stopping rules.

Hypothesis 2: The higher the degree of System 2 information process-
ing, the higher the propensity to use rational stopping rules.

The fact that System 1 and System 2 information processing can take place
at the same time, has been emphasized by many authors (Angst and Agarwal,
2009; Evans, 2003; Lieberman, 2003; Novak and Hoffman, 2009; Zhang and Watts,
2008). It is generally accepted that the neural correlates of System 1 are evolutionary older and that System 2 emerged as a control mechanism handling
situations which cannot be solved by exclusively relying on past experiences and
intuition. Thus, a strong activation of System 2 information processing attenuates or even neutralizes insights delivered by System 1 (Chaiken and Maheswaran,
1994; Evans, 2003). This is put forth in the following hypothesis:

Hypothesis 3: The higher the degree of System 2 information process-
ing, the lower the degree of System 1 information processing.

2.4.1.2. Impact of Technology Characteristics

Persons retrieving information from online sources are increasingly confronted
with information that was created by other (private) Internet users, thus conveying the impression of another person's physical presence (Kumar and Benbasat,
2006, 2002; Short et al., 1976). This effect can be further intensified by showing
pictures of the person who provided a given set of information (Cyr et al., 2009;
Gefen and Straub, 2004) or a personal salutation to the information seeker (Fogg,
2003). These mechanisms for inducing social presence into artificial web sites are
often used in e-commerce scenarios to evoke positive feelings and to make web
sites more trustworthy (Gefen and Straub, 2004). The well-documented positive
effect of social presence on the affective state of a person also has an impact on
information processing styles in terms of positive affection leading to heuristic
information processing. This is due to the fact that people in positive-mood
states regard their environment as not threatening and thus are less motivated to
systematically process information, as the latter is a means for overcoming prob-
lematic situations (e. g. situations in which contradicting information is received,
Bagozzi et al., 1999; Schwarz, 2000).

Furthermore, the availability of peripheral cues, i. e. information that goes beyond issue-relevant facts, is a necessary precondition for System 1 information processing. As System 1 information processing requires less cognitive effort, information seekers can be assumed to assimilate easily accessible contextual cues provided by channels high in *social richness*. However, it is important to note that this effect can be attenuated by a strong motivation to process information systematically, as stated in hypothesis 3 (Chaiken and Maheswaran, 1994). Nevertheless, from an evolutionary perspective, social richness activates behavioral patterns that have been learned over a long period of time and that help to reduce effort while still being able to maintain a high task performance (Kock, 2004, 2005, 2009). Consequently, processing information from other social actors helps to reduce uncertainty by receiving confidence or assurance entailed in the information, hence acting as a simple means for increasing a message's persuasiveness (Cross et al., 2001). Thus, the following hypothesis is proposed:

> *Hypothesis 4a: The higher an information channel's social richness, the higher the degree of System 1 information processing.*

2.4.1.3. Impact of Individual Characteristics

Individual differences between information seekers have rarely been taken into consideration in IS research on human computer-based information behavior (see Section 2.2). One reason for the absence of interest in this class of variables might be an article by Huber which reports contradicting findings with regard to the impact of decision makers' cognitive style on their information behavior. The article recommends not to invest too much effort into investigating similar phenomena in future IS research (Huber, 1983). A related perspective is taken by Simon who states that the task environment in which an artifact operates, influences the artifact's design, underlining the importance of task characteristics in the realm of human problem solving and decision making (Simon, 1996).

In recent IS research, individual differences are considered more intensively (Devaraj et al., 2008; Junglas et al., 2008; McElroy et al., 2007). For this reason and since it was shown in Section 2.3.3.2 that individual differences strongly affect information processing behavior, a mediated cause-effect relationship on information seeking stopping behavior is proposed. The constructs *perceived task experience, perceived task motivation* and *need for cognition* are analyzed subsequently in more detail since they represent – following the literature review in preceding sections – some of the most important determinants in the realm of dual-process theories.

A person's individual knowledge on how to solve a specific task has commonly been built over a long period of time and can be seen as the result of a slow and implicit learning process (Lieberman, 2000; Vakkari, 1999). This set of *past experiences* was found to be easily accessible by human problem solvers in an associative fashion, i. e. observations about the task environment made in the past often influence the person's behavior when he finds himself in a similar, future situation again. Interestingly, problem solvers possessing a high degree of task experience often do not process information systematically but try to match the received information with information they got in a task that resembles the task they currently have to solve (Smith and DeCoster, 2000). The matching procedure itself is executed cognitively without the experienced problem solver being aware of all the single steps necessary to come to a conclusion. Similar findings are reported by Lieberman et al. (2004) concerning autobiographical memory using functional magnetic resonance imaging (fMRI). The results indicate that when persons read words being part of a domain they are experienced in, those regions of the brain are activated which are responsible for processing information automatically and subconsciously. Traditional research on the impact of task experience on information processing and recent neuroscience results lead to the following hypothesis:

> *Hypothesis 5: The higher the degree of perceived task experience, the higher the degree of System 1 information processing.*

Apart from task experience, the problem solver's involvement in a task, i. e. his *motivation to perform well*, represents an intensively-analyzed and important determinant of the effort the person is willing to invest in the course of task fulfillment (Petty and Cacioppo, 1986; Sussman and Siegal, 2003). Basically, higher involvement levels result in increased task effectiveness as problem solvers try to increase the chance of receiving rewards and reduce the risk of being punished when monetary incentives are offered in the context of positive task outcomes (Engelmann et al., 2009). In addition to an external, utilitarian activation, a problem solver's motivation to perform well in a task can also be the result of intrinsic, affective forces such as enjoyment in executing a specific task (c. f. open source software development projects, Bitzer et al. 2007; Hertel et al. 2003, and the components of the Technology Acceptance Model (TAM), Bhattacherjee and Sanford 2006; Davis et al. 1989). Consequently, task motivation does not describe a time-invariant personal predisposition, but is highly situation-specific.

Besides the abstract cause-effect relationship between motivation and task performance, from a cognitive perspective, motivation is an influential antecedent of systematic, effortful information processing. The elaboration likelihood model of persuasion conceptualizes task motivation as the main determinant of central route, i. e. System 2 information processing, arguing that problem solvers – generally acting as effort minimizers – will elaborate a message's content quality only if they are personally affected by task outcomes (Bhattacherjee and Sanford, 2006; Tam and Ho, 2005). Otherwise, economic considerations are dominant and result in the less demanding reliance on peripheral cues which can be assessed easily and still promise to lead to sufficient task performance (Chaiken, 1980).

Furthermore, motivation increases a person's willingness to achieve an improved accuracy of task outcomes. As reliance on heuristic information processing constantly bears the risk of inducing biases into problem solving activities, motivation is considered an important prerequisite for supervising and correcting potentially wrong conclusions evoked by peripheral cues (Smith and DeCoster, 2000). This effect again is due to the higher levels of effort necessary for scrutinizing messages systematically, which will be done especially in situations of high personal involvement into a topic. In addition to the reasoning given above, many authors simply confirm the described effects without giving explanations for the observed phenomena (Metzger et al., 2010; Petty and Cacioppo, 1986). In summary, the following hypothesis is put forth:

Hypothesis 6: The higher the perceived task motivation, the higher the degree of System 2 information processing.

Individual differences with respect to task experience and task motivation are situation-specific. Hence, a person showing high values on a corresponding score in one scenario might report low values on the same score in another treatment condition. This class of situation-specific variables is complemented by stable

individual characteristics that have an impact on human behavior independent
of time and environmental factors.

From a dual-process perspective underlying the development of this study's research model, individual differences concerning the degree of enjoyment a person
experiences when engaging in cognitive activities are reported to have a significant
impact on actual information processing (Cacioppo et al., 1996; Petty and Cacioppo, 1986; Thompson et al., 1993). The aforementioned behavioral tendency
was termed *Need for Cognition* (Cohen et al., 1955) and acts as a predictor of the
use of systematic information processing strategies. Need for cognition can be
understood as an intrinsic motivation triggering information seekers to effortfully
scrutinize information about a problem in order to receive hedonic satisfaction.
Individuals with high scores in need for cognition have a basic desire for getting
involved in cognitively demanding tasks (Thompson et al., 1993).

However, the presence of high degrees of need for cognition does not imply
that a person completely ignores peripheral information cues and acts perfectly
rationally. In fact, high need for cognition also results in a more thorough evaluation of the problem solver's *own* thoughts so that impressions that are generated
based on the use of heuristics and intuitions are questioned and revised critically
while seeking for information. This phenomenon is called *metacognition* or *self-
validation* (Petty et al., 2009, p. 321). Thus, high need for cognition does not
necessarily suppress System 1 information processing but indirectly attenuates
its impact on the overall task outcome. Consequently, the following hypothesis
is proposed:

> *Hypothesis 7: The higher a person's need for cognition, the higher the
> degree of System 2 information processing.*

2.4.1.4. Impact of Task Characteristics

As indicated earlier, the task environment in which an artifact is used, strongly
determines the artifact's design features and behavior (Simon, 1996). Thus, a
third category of variables that have to be considered in the realm of technology-
supported information behavior comprises characteristics of the task to be solved.
Task-related constructs identified in the literature review in Sections 2.2 and 2.3
range from *task complexity* over *task importance* to *task type*. Concerning the

latter, a significant amount of articles deals with choice problems and decision making tasks, whereas a noticeable lack of research was reported with regard to tasks in which the sufficiency of information has to be judged in online settings (Section 2.3.2.3). As a consequence, *task type* is not manipulated in this study but restricted to those tasks, in which information sufficiency considerations are in the center of attention.

The role of task complexity has been analyzed in the context of all three theories that serve as reference theories for this study's research model (Maynard and Hakel, 1997; Straub and Karahanna, 1998; Todd and Benbasat, 1992; Yu et al., 2011). The construct itself is usually conceptualized as a combination of task structure, i. e. the degree to which task inputs, operations on task inputs and outputs are obvious to the problem solver and task variability, i. e. the predictability of task outcomes (Campbell, 1988; Haerem and Rau, 2007; Wood, 1986). Based on this definition, it becomes clear that the degree of a task's complexity perceived by the problem solver highly depends on the person's interpretation of the task and the format in which problem-relevant information is transmitted to this person.

Independent of the subjective interpretation of problem-relevant information, increasing task complexity poses higher demands towards the problem solver's cognitive processing as both *more* information and *more contradicting* pieces of information have to be evaluated in complex scenarios (Speier and Morris, 2003; Todd and Benbasat, 1992). As a consequence, the problem solver's cognitive effort increases in order to retain the acquired information in the short-term memory (Speier and Morris, 2003). In line with human beings' basic tendency to reduce mental effort, a common coping strategy consists in ignoring large portions of the information available by using heuristic information processing (Lai, 2010). Hence, in highly complex tasks, aspects that are not related to the problem itself – such as the source of information – have a dominant impact on information processing as they help to easily evaluate the validity and persuasiveness of information (Chaiken, 1980). At the same time, a complex task's immanent low degree of structure makes it difficult for the information seeker to seek for information in a goal-directed manner following System 2 information processing. To summarize the above discussion, relying on heuristics and non-content cues usually results in less demanding information processing to cope with cognitive effort, which motivates the following hypothesis:

> *Hypothesis 8: The higher the perceived task complexity, the higher the degree of System 1 information processing.*

Using effort-reduction strategies often results in a reduced problem solving effectiveness. However, in organizational settings both effectiveness *and* efficiency have to be kept at a high level when fulfilling tasks. Consequently, problem solvers are faced with a trade-off between minimizing their cognitive effort and maximizing the accuracy of the task outcome. The latter can be activated by exercising pressure by making the problem solvers aware of the *task's importance* for their personal and the organization's well-being. This external pressure "to offer accurate judgments on the task in question" (Baron et al., 1996, p. 915) is reported to have a positive impact on systematic information processing because the person is willing or even forced to invest time and effort to optimize task outcomes and to give a clear reasoning for his problem solving strategy (Chaiken and Maheswaran, 1994). Hence, it can be argued that in organizational settings, task importance is related to reward and punishment mechanisms and thus influences the problem solver's involvement in the task, i. e. his motivation to perform well (Sussman and Siegal, 2003). The aforementioned mechanism is proposed in the next hypothesis.

> *Hypothesis 9: The higher the task importance, the higher the perceived task motivation.*

2.4.1.5. Moderating Variable

The information channel's social richness is not only assumed to influence System 1 information processing directly but also to interact with the complexity of the underlying task. In an evolutionary sense, face-to-face interactions used to be the common means of communication between human beings. Hence, face-to-face communication is perceived to be "natural" in that it does not consume noteworthy resources on the part of the participants since they are familiar with this type of communication (Kock, 2004, 2005). Especially in ambiguous situations as they typically result from high task complexity, problem solvers prefer to receive relevant information directly from other people because they are used to getting and evaluating information cues that go beyond "objectively correct information" (Cross et al., 2001, p. 439), i. e. they quickly assess the trustworthiness of the information source or follow consensus information resulting from recommendations made by a group of people, e. g. in e-commerce settings (Gefen and Straub, 2004; Sussman and Siegal, 2003).

As the availability of peripheral information cues is a necessary precondition for the application of heuristic information processing strategies, information channels conveying the impression of an interaction with another social entity will enforce the use of heuristic processing. As proposed above and in hypothesis H8, this is especially the case when the problem solver suffers from high cognitive load because then the person is looking for options that help to reduce the mental workload. The above reasoning is summarized in hypothesis 4b.

Hypothesis 4b: The higher an information channel's social richness, the stronger the impact of perceived task complexity on the degree of System 1 information processing.

2.4.2. Development of Control Hypotheses

The research model developed in the previous section explains the impact of technology-, individual-, and task-related determinants on information processing and stopping behavior. The underlying constructs were deduced from conceptual and empirical studies in the realm of dual-process theories, social presence theory and effort-accuracy frameworks and represent the most influential antecedents of the phenomena investigated in this study. In order to retain the model's parsimony, several constructs that might have a weak effect on mediating and dependent variables were not included into the main model. These variables originate from research projects that were analyzed in Section 2.3, but only received limited attention in the context of information seeking and stopping behavior, still possibly having measurable and significant effects on selected variables of the main model.

As pointed out in Section 2.3.2.1, normative stopping rules assume that there is a global optimum with respect to an adequate amount of information that should be gathered before the seeking process is terminated. Due to limited cognitive

resources, human beings regularly deviate from such optimal strategies by simpli-
fying the problem space. Nevertheless, the attempt to achieve optimal solutions
to given problems by analyzing all available problem-relevant information can be
regarded as a personality trait that remains stable over a long period of time
(Lai, 2010; Schwartz et al., 2002).

Following Simon's terminology, a person's intention to find the best instead of a
"good enough" option in a choice problem is called *maximizing tendency* (Simon,
1996). Individuals showing this tendency process information systematically in
order to be sure to make the best decision in a given situation. Furthermore, high
scores with regard to a person's maximizing tendency are positively correlated
with scores in need for cognition (Lai, 2010). This link implies that modeling
a direct relationship between maximizing tendency and System 2 information
processing in the main model would not increase the latter's level of explained
variance significantly. Furthermore, the impact of need for cognition on information processing behavior has been investigated more rigorously in the past and is
not necessarily bound to choice problems and decision making tasks as it is the
case for a person's maximizing tendency. Though, in order to ensure that a person's maximizing tendency does not act as a confounder, the following hypothesis
is put forth:

> *Hypothesis 10: The higher a person's maximizing tendency, the higher
> the degree of System 2 information processing.*

Instruments for measuring maximizing tendencies and need for cognition were
developed explicitly for explaining information processing behavior and decision
making activities. The five factor model (FFM), however, was introduced as part
of a descriptive trait theory of personality to gain insights into the impact of
dispositional character traits on human behavior in general. The FFM catego-
rizes character traits along the dimensions *Neuroticism, Extraversion, Openness
to Experience, Agreeableness* and *Conscientiousness* (Alexander et al., 2011). The
model was used in the IS discipline to investigate the impact of personality variables on technology acceptance (Devaraj et al., 2008), privacy concerns (Junglas
et al., 2008), and Internet use (McElroy et al., 2007).

Hemmer and Heinzl (2012) report that a person's extraversion score is a weak
but significant predictor of the use of computer-based information channels that

convey the feeling of other persons' social presence. This might be due to the fact that extraverts generally embrace close interpersonal relationships (Watson and Clark, 1997) and are characterized by a need for social relationships (Junglas et al., 2008). When using information channels that transmit social context information, extraverts might find an environment which resembles their traditional patterns of interacting with other people because they are used to dealing with these socially created contextual cues. This might result in paying close attention to peripheral social cues in general as these are an important component of extraverts' information processing habits, which is expressed in the following hypothesis:

Hypothesis 11: The higher a person's extraversion score, the higher the degree of System 1 information processing.

Gender differences have been analyzed with respect to many questions in the realm of Information Systems research, ranging from trust in web sites over buying behavior on the web to attitudes towards computers. A comprehensive overview is given in Riedl et al. (2010b). In the context of information processing and stopping behavior, empirical findings on the impact of gender differences are contradictory. Epstein et al. (1996) assume that male subjects commonly think in a logical, rational way, thus arguing for higher shares of System 2 information processing among male populations. However, Darley and Smith (1995) find that women generally show maximizer tendencies, processing all available information before making judgments – a mechanism which might help female persons to reduce uncertainty as they are believed to be less trusting in other people (Riedl et al., 2010b). Thus, gender differences obviously have some impact on message credibility evaluations and information processing in general. However, a clear causality cannot be deduced from literature. Therefore, two control hypotheses are introduced in order to make sure that gender differences do not have a significant influence on information processing activities:

Hypothesis 12a: Gender differences do not have an effect on the degree of System 1 information processing.

Hypothesis 12b: Gender differences do not have an effect on the degree of System 2 information processing.

Table 2.5.: Definition of Model Constructs

Construct	Conceptualization
Variables related to Technology, Task and Individual	
Information channel's degree of social richness	An online medium's propensity for conveying the impression of other persons' physical presence in an information seeking process, thus transmitting additional contextual cues (Gefen and Straub, 2004; Kumar and Benbasat, 2006, 2002).
Perceived task complexity	Combination of task structure (degree to which task inputs, operations on task inputs and outputs are obvious to the problem solver) and task variability (predictability of task outcomes, Campbell, 1988; Haerem and Rau, 2007; Wood, 1986).
Task importance	Degree of pressure exerted on an information seeker "to offer accurate judgments on the task in question" (Baron et al., 1996, p. 915).
Perceived task experience	Extent of the information seeker's prior knowledge with respect to a given task (Vakkari, 1999).
Perceived task motivation	Level of the information seeker's involvement in a task as a function of the task's relevance and importance for the recipient (Petty and Cacioppo, 1986; Sussman and Siegal, 2003).
Need for Cognition	Individual predisposition with regard to an "individual's tendency to engage in and enjoy effortful cognitive endeavors" (Cacioppo et al., 1996, p. 197).
Gender	Subject's gender being male or female.

Construct	Conceptualization
Extraversion	Degree of the information seeker's sociability and need for social relationships: Dispositional character trait (Borkenau and Ostendorf, 2008; Watson and Clark, 1997).
Maximizer	Individual predisposition with regard to a person's tendency to solve tasks in a (globally) optimal way by considering all information available in a specific context (Schwartz et al., 2002).

Variables related to information processing

System 1 information processing (heuristic)	Degree to which information is processed in an effortless, associative way, taking past experiences into account and following simple information cues (Kahneman, 2003; Lieberman, 2003; Novak and Hoffman, 2009).
System 2 information processing (systematic)	Degree to which information is processed in an effortful, logical way, sequentially following specific rules of reasoning (Kahneman, 2003; Lieberman, 2003; Novak and Hoffman, 2009).

Dependent variables

Propensity to use experiential stopping rules	Tendency to rely on affect and intuition when making the decision to terminate the information seeking process in a spontaneous and impulsive way (Browne et al., 2007; Cross et al., 2001).
Propensity to use rational stopping rules	Tendency to decide consciously to stop seeking for information based on a content-wise analysis of issue-relevant information (Browne et al., 2007; Cross et al., 2001).

2.4.3. Summary of Hypotheses

All hypotheses that were developed in the previous section in order to explain computer-based information seeking and stopping behavior are summarized in Table 2.6. Figure 2.4 visualizes the main hypotheses in the form of a research model.

2.5. Summary

In the first part of this chapter, IS literature on human information behavior has been analyzed. It was found that human behavior in relation to the entity *information* was the subject matter of many influential publications in the field, informing software developers and managers about the design of more user-centric information systems. However, research was rather eclectic in terms of the absence of a coherent research trajectory consistently dealing with human information behavior. Additionally, it became obvious that the last phase of information seeking activities, namely the decision of human beings when to stop seeking for information in computer-mediated contexts, was largely ignored. Browne and Pitts (2004) and Browne et al. (2007) set out that extensive knowledge about this topic is crucial from an IS perspective since the amount of information available via online applications is increasing constantly and thus exceeding limited mental capacities of its users.

At the same time, the impact of user-generated content on different aspects of information behavior was explored in past research. A detailed literature review of publications in the realm of information seeking stopping behavior revealed that there is no research project to date studying the combined effect of information quantity and quality aspects, i. e. the role of information visibly created by other actors on stopping behavior in online scenarios. Furthermore, there are no studies investigating differences with respect to rational versus experiential stopping behavior either – aspects which were treated in two separate research streams in the past.

To address the aforementioned research gaps, appropriate theoretical lenses have been identified. Dual-process theories, the social presence theory and the effort-accuracy framework of cognition were selected and described. Since there is not one specific theory that can be used to close the research gap, a multi-theory approach is followed in this study. For this reason, the selected theories were evaluated with respect to commensurability and the existence of both similar and complementary explanatory claims. Dual-process theories account for the coexistence of two different ways in which information is processed by human beings and state that social cues can have a persuasive impact on its recipients. This view is extended by social presence theory and the effort-accuracy framework of cognition in that human information processors were shown to act as effort-minimizers strongly responding to the impression of social interactions conveyed by artificial information systems.

Finally, based on the aforementioned theoretical lenses, hypotheses were developed explaining the impact of major technology-, task- and individual characteristics on information processing and stopping behavior. The resulting research model will be refined later, before it is validated in a computer-based experiment setting by triangulating data from different sources such as interaction data, questionnaires and qualitative data. For this reason, the underlying research design is introduced in the next chapter.

Table 2.6.: Summary of Hypotheses

No.	Hypothesis
H1 (+)	The higher the *degree of System 1 information processing*, the higher the propensity to use experiential stopping rules.
H2 (+)	The higher the *degree of System 2 information processing*, the higher the propensity to use rational stopping rules.
H3 (−)	The higher the *degree of System 2 information processing*, the lower the degree of System 1 information processing.
H4a (+)	The higher an *information channel's social richness*, the higher the degree of System 1 information processing.
H4b (+)	The higher an *information channel's social richness*, the stronger the impact of perceived task complexity on the degree of System 1 information processing.
H5 (+)	The higher the *degree of perceived task experience*, the higher the degree of System 1 information processing.
H6 (+)	The higher the *perceived task motivation*, the higher the degree of System 2 information processing.
H7 (+)	The higher a person's *need for cognition*, the higher the degree of System 2 information processing.
H8 (+)	The higher the *perceived task complexity*, the higher the degree of System 1 information processing.
H9 (+)	The higher the *task importance*, the higher the perceived task motivation.
H10 (+)	The higher a person's *maximizing tendency*, the higher the degree of System 2 information processing.
H11 (+)	The higher a person's *extraversion score*, the higher the degree of System 1 information processing.
H12a	*Gender differences* do not have an effect on the degree of System 1 information processing.
H12b	*Gender differences* do not have an effect on the degree of System 2 information processing.

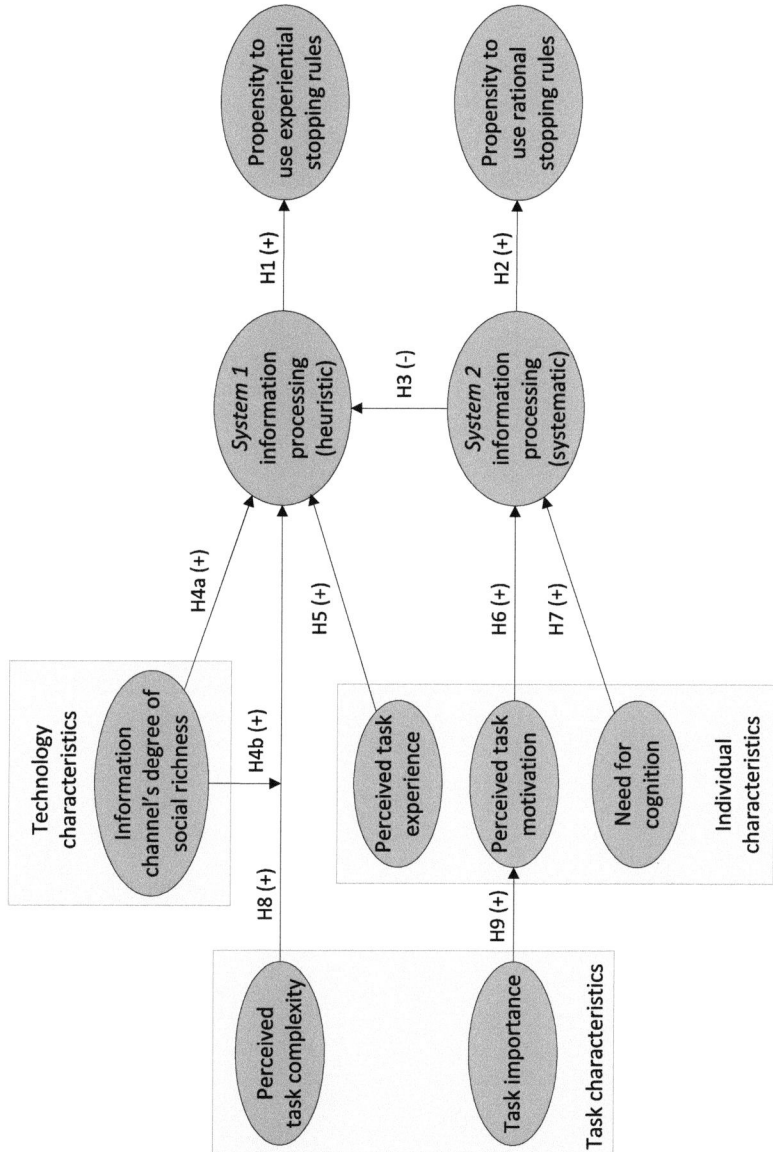

Figure 2.4.: Explanatory Research Model of Information Seeking Stopping Behavior

3. Research Design

The objective of this study consists in the explanation and prediction of human information seeking and stopping behavior in online settings (Gregor, 2006; Weber, 2012). To address the underlying research questions, appropriate reference theories have been selected and combined in a multi-theoretical model. Consequently, two of three major and interdependent building blocks of academic research, namely *aims* and *theories* have been described (Dibbern et al., 2004; Laudan, 1984). As the third component of "The Triad Network of Justification" (Laudan, 1984, p. 63), the *methods* that will be used to validate the hypothesized relationships between the research model's variables are introduced in this chapter. For this reason, epistemological and ontological assumptions guiding the use of various research strategies are outlined before a suitable research methodology is selected. Thereafter, instruments for collecting and analyzing data are developed and the data collection process itself is specified (Bhattacherjee, 2012). Due to the fact that the theories underlying the model of information seeking and stopping behavior have been used and validated in many different contexts before, it appears instrumental to follow a confirmatory approach. However, in order to make sure that the theory amalgamation conducted in Section 2.4.1 covers all aspects relevant for addressing the research questions, an exploratory pre-study is conducted first, which helps to refine and corroborate the research model and to validate the research design.

3.1. Epistemological and Ontological Grounding

From a philosophical point of view, every researcher either implicitly or explicitly makes assumptions about how new knowledge is generated (*epistemology*) and if the world surrounding the researcher is objective and exists without human intervention (*ontology*, Orlikowski and Baroudi 1991). The researcher's epistemological and ontological beliefs have a strong influence on the question which research methods are used in a given research endeavor.

In the past, there were intense debates between proponents of *rationalism* on the one hand and *empiricism* on the other hand. The former is characterized by logical deductions from existing axioms leading to new scientific insights. The latter sets a focus on observations made via human senses based on systematic measurement of phenomena of interest (Bhattacherjee, 2012; Dibbern et al., 2004). In recent decades, more sophisticated and more specific epistemological stances emerged, such as *positivism, constructivism, pragmatism, interpretivism* or *critical rationalism* (Creswell, 2009; Klein and Myers, 1999; Lee, 1991; Orlikowski and Baroudi, 1991; Trochim and Donnelly, 2008). From an IS perspective, the most dominant positions are *positivism, interpretivism* and, to a less prominent degree, *critical research* (Dibbern et al., 2004; Lee, 1991; Orlikowski and Baroudi, 1991; Weber, 2004; Wynn and Williams, 2012).

Ontologically, *positivism* assumes that the world exists independent of human intervention and thus can be investigated systematically by mapping real-world phenomena into simplified, artificial models of the world. Consequently, a positivist researcher postulates a direct link between the constructs and relationships stated in his model and the actual physical or social world. Hence, *epistemologically,* the researcher's main task consists in developing techniques for reliably and consistently measuring the phenomena and hypotheses expressed in the model and observable in the objective world (Orlikowski and Baroudi, 1991). This implies a rejection of metaphysics and a strict reliance on a priori defined cause-effect relationships that can either be confirmed by observation or are proven wrong in terms of falsificationism (Chalmers, 1999; Straub et al., 2004). Post-positivism acknowledges that human observation is always biased by the researcher's former experience or the immanent characteristics of the techniques being used for observation. For that reason, post-positivists recommend the use of triangulation approaches to get a less-biased picture of the world. In summary, post-positivism moves away from the assumption of deterministic, law-like interactions between objects of the real world towards a probabilistic conceptualization of conducting research (Trochim and Donnelly, 2008).

In contrast, the *interpretive philosophy* is built on a different ontological base: Reality as perceived by a human observer emerges from the person's subjective meaning attached to physical and social phenomena. As a consequence, a person following the interpretive philosophy is necessarily involved into a process of social construction, interpretation and the attempt of understanding what he receives via his senses against the background of past experiences. Thus, interpretive researchers create new knowledge by iteratively interpreting the potentially ambiguous meanings expressed by "language and tacit norms shared by humans working towards some shared goal" (Orlikowski and Baroudi, 1991, p. 14; Kaplan and Duchon, 1988).

Differences with respect to epistemological and ontological assumptions underlying positivist and interpretive research result in diverging methods being employed (Kaplan and Duchon, 1988). Positivists generally prefer – but do not exclusively use – *quantitative and structured methods* such as surveys and laboratory experiments in order to validate hypotheses derived from theories about physical and social phenomena (Lee, 1991; Weber, 2004). Interpretivists, however, show a tendency of relying on *qualitative approaches* such as action research or hermeneutics to understand the surrounding world holistically, setting a focus on theory building (Eisenhardt, 1989; Meredith et al., 1989; Weber, 2004). Nevertheless, in the recent past, an increasing amount of publications combines quantitative and qualitative research methods in mixed-method triangulation approaches in order to benefit from the advantages of both epistemological and ontological stances (Lee, 1991; Trochim and Donnelly, 2008).

This study follows a post-positivist research philosophy assuming that human information seeking and stopping behavior is causally determined by various technology-, task- and individual-related factors that can be derived logically from existing knowledge. Furthermore, these determinants and the resulting behavioral outcomes are thought to be quantifiable either directly or indirectly as latent variables in a highly reliable way. Nevertheless, the existence of potential measurement biases is acknowledged and attenuated by the use of both quantitative and qualitative research methods and modern approaches for examining latent variables using psychophysiological devices. The focus is set on the individual user of an information system as the study's level of analysis.

3.2. Selection of a Research Methodology

A research methodology, also called *research strategy*, represents a set of activities that have to be conducted in order to gain results that answer a pre-specified research question (Heinrich et al., 2011; Mingers, 2001; Yin, 2009). While there is a large variety of research methodologies available to academics such as laboratory experiments, case study research or survey research, extant literature agrees on the fact that there is not *one* methodology that is superior to all others (McGrath, 1981). In fact, trade-offs have to be made along several dimensions in order to identify a methodology that is suitable in a specific research scenario.

One set of dimensions for differentiating research methodologies considers the methodologies' degree of internal and external validity. *Internal validity* describes a research methodology's general power to yield precise results in terms of low measurement biases and errors (Bonoma, 1985; Scandura and Williams, 2000). *External validity* characterizes a research method's power to produce findings that are generalizable and transferable to other units of analysis, related research questions or time (Bonoma, 1985). According to Bonoma (1985), laboratory experiments are characterized by high degrees of internal but rather low degrees of external validity whereas case research is located at the opposite end of this continuum. Yin (2009) indirectly mentions "the *extent of control* an investigator has over actual behavioral events" (emphasis added, p. 8) as a major determinant of a research methodology's internal and external validity, arguing that laboratory experiments are best suited for projects in which the researcher has to manipulate independent variables. Meredith et al. (1989) highlight the *role of the epistemological and ontological assumptions* underlying the research project as a third dimension influencing the selection of an appropriate research methodology.

Considering the dimensions identified above, it seems reasonable to conduct experimental research in order to explain and predict human information seeking and stopping behavior. The most important arguments guiding this decision are listed below:

1. This research endeavor's major goal consists in theory confirmation and follows a clearly positivist approach of deducing and formulating causal relationships about variables that can be measured reliably. Experimental research is considered "the gold standard" (Trochim and Donnelly, 2008,

p. 186), if internal validity is of primary concern (Bonoma, 1985; Meredith et al., 1989)

2. In natural settings, information seekers have access to a literally infinite amount of information sources. These information sources and the quality of information they contain, show huge discrepancies: While some information sources are easily accessible but contain outdated information, others might be more difficult to access but contain up-to-date information, for example. Characteristics like accessibility, information quality or synchronicity might significantly affect the user's information behavior. Since this study is interested in the effects of specific task, technology and individual characteristics, it is essential to make sure that only those variables are affected and manipulated that are related to the aforementioned characteristics. At the same time, sufficient degrees of external validity are ensured by designing the experimental environment in a way that is similar to state-of-the-art website designs, using content taken from actual web applications.

3. Experimental research approaches have been used in many research projects dealing with information seeking and stopping behavior. In the realm of human computer-based information behavior, laboratory experiments even represent the most dominant research methodology (c. f. Table A.1 in the Appendix) allowing to analyze specific stimulus-response patterns that would remain undetected or overlaid with noise induced by confounding variables in more natural research designs.

4. Experimental research allows for high degrees of freedom in terms of data collection methods used while the experiment is conducted. Since the researcher usually owns control over the experiment environment, the user's interaction behavior with a computer-based system can be measured automatically and with high degrees of precision. Consequently, a more complete picture of the research domain can be created going beyond the pure validation of theories.

After experimental research has been selected as the most appropriate research methodology in the realm of this research project, the research strategy will be

specified in more detail next, including an introduction of relevant data collection
methods and techniques.

3.3. Specification of the Research Methodology

When conducting experimental research, many important design decisions have
to be made before data can be collected.

First of all, it is crucial to choose between two classes of experiment designs,
namely *field experiments* and *laboratory experiments* (Meredith et al., 1989). The
former take place in a rather natural setting, e. g. in the subjects' workplace,
whereas the latter are conducted in settings which guarantee the full control of all
variables that might have an effect on the dependent variable. Laboratory experiments were selected to investigate information seeking and stopping behavior for
two major reasons: (1) Compared to field experiments, laboratory experiments
allow to control for variables like time and space. That is, it can be assured that
all subjects taking part in the experiment solve the tasks at a similar time of
day and that all participants work under comparable environmental conditions
without external interruptions. This appears to be fundamental for the design of
this study, as in organizational, natural settings, information seeking processes
might be terminated as a reaction to external stimuli such as a colleague entering the room or a phone ringing close to the subject. However, the goal of
this research endeavor consists in the analysis of cognitive processes resulting in
information seeking stopping behavior, not in the exploration of environmental
stimuli. (2) The theories underlying the research model in Figure 2.4 have been
validated intensively in the IS domain and adjacent scientific domains. Nevertheless, the research model itself offers a multi-theoretical perspective on information
seeking and stopping behavior that has not been tested before. Consequently,
a laboratory experiment helps to reduce the impact of potential biases and to
provide first evidence concerning its validity. Commonly, field experiments are
conducted subsequently in order to test some well-defined sub-dimensions of the
original model.

Second, experiments can be clustered into *true experimental* and *quasi-experimental* designs (Bhattacherjee, 2012). In true-experimental designs, subjects are

assigned randomly to treatment and control groups whereas in quasi-experimental settings, this requirement does not hold. In both designs, however, the researcher assumes to have probabilistically equivalent groups, i. e. the members of each group do not differ statistically with regard to attributes that are investigated within the experiment (Trochim and Donnelly, 2008). In this study, a quasi-experimental approach is selected, as experiments are conducted in University classes of about 20-30 students. Since the students are assigned to the classes in a largely randomized way and every experimental task is presented to at least two different groups, probabilistic equivalence between groups can be assured.

Following common guidelines on experimental research, a *pre-test* (c. f. Chapter 4) is conducted before the main data collection phase starts (Trochim and Donnelly, 2008). During the pre-test, the design of the laboratory environment (c. f. Section 3.4) is evaluated and the fundamental validity of the research model is tested exploratively. In the main phase, a factorial design is used to manipulate three binary variables being part of the research model. The remaining variables are measured, but not manipulated, because for these variables the laboratory experiment simply serves as a frame for presenting traditional questionnaires in a controlled environment. Furthermore, a combined *between- and within-subject design* is chosen in which every subject has to solve several tasks. Thus, differences in information behavior can be attributed to intra- and interpersonal characteristics.

In order to reduce method bias, data collection and analysis follow a *multi-method approach*, i. e. independent and dependent variables are measured differently and complimentary data is used whenever possible to corroborate the findings by increasing convergent validity and to get a more complete picture of human information seeking and stopping behavior (Burton-Jones, 2009; Dimoka et al., 2011; Léger et al., 2010). Among other parameters, psychophysiological reactions are captured based on the subjects' heart rate variability during the pre-test phase. The use of psychophysiological approaches is especially reasonable in situations in which it is difficult for the subjects to verbalize feelings or impressions in real-time, e. g. the perception of information overload while solving a demanding task (Dimoka et al., 2012). Furthermore, from a philosophy of science perspective, such innovative methods for observing reality help to get more robust findings or even new insights into complex phenomena that could not be obtained with traditional instruments (Chalmers, 1999). In the main experiment phase, questionnaires with both quantitative and qualitative questions are employed and analyzed via *Structural Equation Modeling* (SEM) as a well-established means for validating complex nomological networks. Using questionnaires in experimental settings to get insights into behavioral phenomena is a common method for obtaining data on constructs that are not directly manipulated in the experiment (Haines and Mann, 2011; Qiu and Benbasat, 2009; Zhang et al., 2011). The following sections will introduce the aforementioned methods.

3.3.1. Introduction to Heart Rate Variability

Heart rate variability (HRV) measurement allows for the collection of complimentary real-time data on problem solvers' cognitive activities by analyzing small variations in the duration between a subject's heart beats. As many studies have shown a link between heart rate variability and mental workload metrics, the method appears to be suitable for getting additional evidence for a person's System 1 or System 2 information processing (Cinaz et al., 2011; Henelius et al., 2009; Murata and Iwase, 1998).

Contractions of the human heart are controlled by the *cardiac sinoatrial node* which is influenced by both *parasympathetic and sympathetic autonomous nervous system activity* (Berntson et al., 1997). Thus, it is difficult to manipulate the rhythm consciously, as the autonomous nervous system operates largely beyond a person's active control. *The sympathetic nervous system* shows increasing levels of activation if a person is in a condition of high arousal, e. g. induced by a complex task to be solved. As a reaction, the person's stress level rises and results in shorter intervals between heart beats. *Parasympathetic activity* is characterized by an increase in the time between heart beats and can usually be observed when a person is in a more relaxed state (Cinaz et al., 2011). Even though a person's heart rate is manipulated dually via sympathetic and parasympathetic systems, e. g. in response to external stimuli, there are still significant between-subject differences with respect to heart rate variability. Consequently, in between-subject designs, a baseline measurement of HRV is recommendable in order to make the person-specific measurements comparable to each other (Henelius et al., 2009).

The most dominant approaches for measuring a person's heart beat rhythm consist in the use of electrocardiography (ECG) or heart rate monitor watches. Both methods are non-invasive and record the heart's action potentials. Therefore, in order to get a time series containing a person's inter-beat intervals, the so-called QRS complex is detected, representing the heart's ventricular depolarization (Malik, 1996). Software products such as Kubios HRV[1] or Kardia[2] take these time series as input in order to calculate several metrics of parasympathetic and sympathetic nervous activation. Berntson et al. (1997) cluster these metrics into *descriptive statistics* (including time-domain measures) and *spectral analyses*, noting that the former "have limited application in basic psychophysiological research, however, where a more precise parsing of the frequency components of heart rate variability is desired" (p. 629). Consequently, only the latter approach is described below.

Using *spectral analysis*, the variation of heart beat intervals in a time series is decomposed into its underlying frequency bands, usually in the form of a spectral density function (Berntson et al., 1997). Today, Fast Fourier Transform (FFT) algorithms and autoregressive (AR) modeling are commonly used to compute the density function after artifacts were eliminated from the data series (Berntson et al., 1990). FFT approaches work deterministically by taking all available data into account, whereas parametric AR techniques focus on "significant peaks" in the data series to exclude noise and thus regard data "as a composite of deterministic and stochastic components" (Berntson et al., 1997, p. 629). Figure 3.1 shows an example of an FFT spectral analysis.

In HRV analyses, frequency bands are commonly segmented into *Very Low Frequency (VLF)*, *Low Frequency (LF)* and *High Frequency (HF)*. LF and HF are correlated with primarily sympathetic and parasympathetic activity, respectively, while the effect is less pronounced for LF than for HF components (Berntson et al., 1997; Malik, 1996). HF power is partly influenced by *Respiratory Sinus Arrhythmia (RSA)*, i. e. a changing heart rate depending on a person's inspiration and expiration periods (Berntson et al., 1993). However, RSA is believed to originate "largely or exclusively from fluctuations in vagal control" (Berntson et al., 1993, p. 186) and hence predicts parasympathetic activation. As it is

---

1 http://kubios.uku.fi/ (20012/10/26)
2 http://sourceforge.net/projects/mykardia/ (20012/10/26)

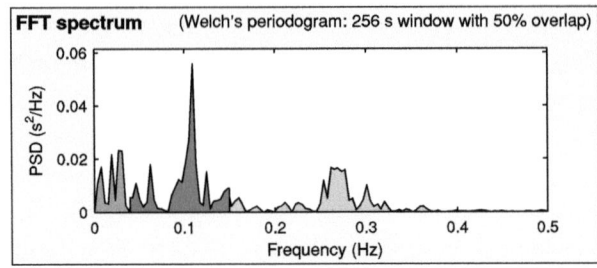

Figure 3.1.: Example of an FFT Spectral Analysis Created with Kubios HRV,
Version 2.0

Table 3.1.: Heart Rate Variability Metrics Based on Frequency Domain Methods

Frequency component	Frequency interval	Autonomous nervous system
High Frequency (HF, RSA)	0.15 – 0.5 Hz	Parasympathetic origin
Low Frequency (LF)	0.04 – 0.15 Hz	Both sympathetic and parasympathetic origin
Very Low Frequency (VLF)	0.003 – 0.05 Hz	Possibly represents thermoregulatory effects
LF / HF ratio	0.04 – 0.5 Hz	Increases in the ratio represent an activation of the sympathetic and a concurrent inhibition of parasympathetic nervous system

difficult to obtain valid VLF results from short-term HRV recordings and because
contradicting effects of VLF components on behavioral outcomes were reported
in the past (Malik, 1996), HF and LF power is often normalized by subtracting
the VLF power from the total power of the spectral analysis. The aforementioned
frequency components are summarized in Table 3.1.

In order to get valid FFT results, extant literature recommends to capture data
series of at least one minute if HF bands are analyzed and at least two minutes in
case of LF bands in order to make sure that the recording has at least the length
of ten times the lower bound of the frequency band that is analyzed (Berntson

et al., 1997, p. 634). For AR-based analyses, the requirements are less strict, but not specified in detail (Malik, 1996; Tarvainen and Niskanen, 2008).

As stated earlier, HRV measures have been used in many studies before to get objective information about subjects' mental workload while solving various tasks. The inhibition of the parasympathetic nervous system and the reciprocal activation of the sympathetic nervous system or the isolated decrease of parasympathetic nervous system activation represent a pattern that predicts the presence of a high mental workload or cognitive stress, respectively (Backs, 1998; Hjortskov et al., 2004; Murata and Iwase, 1998). Correspondingly, HF power increases, i. e. the parasympathetic inhibition is reduced, when the mental workload decreases. Following this logic, HRV can be used to get complimentary evidence for a person processing information in a System 1 mode that is characterized as imposing lower cognitive demand on the problem solver compared to System 2 information processing.

3.3.2. Introduction to Structural Equation Modeling

Structural equation modeling is widely used in the IS and adjacent disciplines to validate causal relationships in both simple and complex nomological networks (Gefen et al., 2000; Reinartz et al., 2009). Compared to traditional linear regression approaches, SEM as a "second-generation multivariate technique" (Chin, 1998b, p. 296) allows to get insights into the strength of "hypothesized causal paths" (Gefen et al., 2011, p. iv) between constructs and the quality of the constructs' measurement simultaneously (Gefen et al., 2000). Thus, it combines an *econometric perspective* emphasizing the empirical prediction with a *psychometric perspective*, setting a focus on the measurement of *latent variables* (or *constructs*). A latent variable is "a conceptual term used to describe a phenomenon of theoretical interest" (Edwards and Bagozzi, 2000, p. 157) that cannot be measured directly such as personality traits or attitudes (Chin, 1998a, p. vii).

Gefen et al. (2011, p. iv) even regard SEM as the *method of choice* when the path diagram contains latent variables as SEM acknowledges for unavoidable measurement errors that originate from multi-item operationalizations of these variables (Homburg and Baumgartner, 1998). In addition to the aforementioned advantages of SEM over linear regression, Chin (1998a) stresses the technique's applicability in the realm of confirmatory analyses in which a priori defined causal relationships are validated based on empirical data.

As indicated above, SEM consists of two major components: (1) a *structural model / outer model* and (2) a *measurement model / inner model* (Chin, 1998b). The former contains the hypothesized causal relationships between latent variables, while these variables are categorized as either *exogenous / independent variables* when they are not influenced by other variables in the model or *endogenous / dependent variables* if they are affected by other constructs in the model. The measurement model encompasses all items that are used to measure a specific latent variable. Consequently, a separate measurement model has to be defined for every latent variable in the model (Homburg and Baumgartner, 1998). In this context, the term *item*, also known as *measure* or *indicator* represents "a quantified record, or datum, taken as an empirical analog to a construct" (Edwards and Bagozzi, 2000, p. 156). Item values can be "obtained through self-report, interview, observation, or other empirical means" (Petter et al., 2007, p. 625) and thus are indirect measures of the latent variable.

The measurement model can either be operationalized *formatively* or *reflectively* (Chin, 1998b; Götz et al., 2010). In the *formative mode*, the observed values of a construct's items are supposed to cause the level of the latent variable (Bollen and Lennox, 1991; Chin, 1998a). Hence, when operationalizing formatively measured variables, the researcher has to make sure that all items together explain the essential dimensions of the underlying latent variable (Fornell and Cha, 1994; Petter et al., 2007). This implies that items cannot be deleted or substituted easily as this would have an effect on the latent variable's characteristic. In the *reflective mode*, the items are caused redundantly by the underlying latent variable, i. e. items should be positively correlated (multicollinearity) and, consequently, can be replaced by similar items that fulfill this criterion (Bollen and Lennox, 1991; Petter et al., 2007). A change of one item in a given direction should also be reflected by all other item values shifting in the same direction and with similar intensity (Chin, 1998b).

An example of a path model and its above-mentioned sub-models as well as a differentiation between reflectively and formatively measured constructs is given in Figure 3.2.

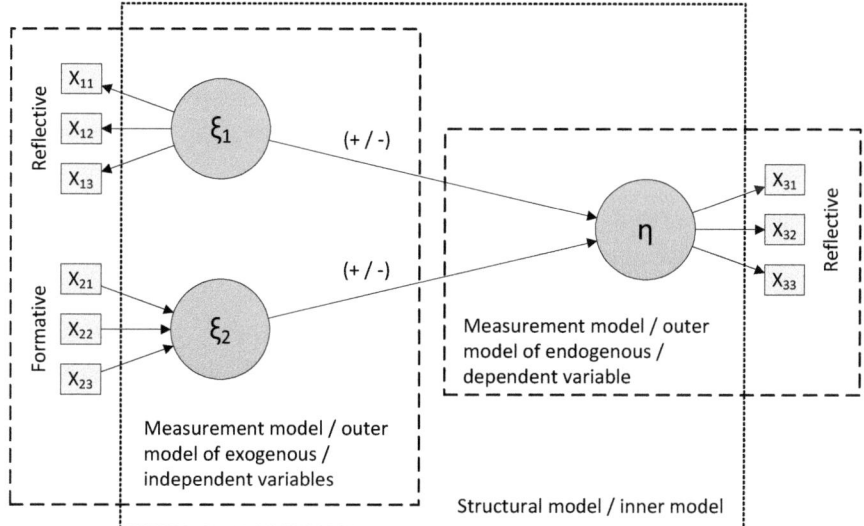

Figure 3.2.: Example of a Path Model (based on Chin 1998b)

3.3.2.1. Model Estimation Approaches

In order to be able to make conclusions about the strength of causal relationships in the structural model and the quality of the measurement model, several model parameters such as *path coefficients* between constructs and *factor loadings* (for reflectively measured constructs) or *factor weights* (for formatively measured constructs) have to be estimated based on the empirical data collected by the researcher (Götz et al., 2010). For this purpose, two approaches are available: (1) *Covariance-based techniques* and (2) *variance-based / component-based / Partial Least Squares (PLS) techniques*. As both approaches differ in terms of assumptions regarding the empirical data and in the way the model parameters are calculated, one best approach does not exist.

Using the empirical sample data set, the *covariance-based* SEM algorithm calculates a matrix of covariances between all items of a given model. Thereafter, model parameters are estimated iteratively with the aim of finding such parameters that optimize the fit between the empirical covariance matrix and the estimated one. As a result, "the covariance-based procedure provides optimal estimations of the model parameters" (Chin, 1998b, p. 301) as long as the empirical data follows a normal distribution and the sample size is sufficiently large (Chin, 1998b; Homburg and Baumgartner, 1998). Popular software packages in the realm of covariance-based SEM comprise the products AMOS[3], LISREL[4] or Mplus[5].

The *component-based* SEM algorithm aims at minimizing the residual variance of the model's depending variables, relying on the iterative application of ordinary least square regressions (Gefen et al., 2000). Therefore, an approximating component score is calculated for every latent variable based on the weighted sum of its indicators, called *outside approximation* (Chin, 1998b, p. 301). Afterwards, path coefficients between latent variables are calculated using regression analysis to obtain *inner approximations* (Chin, 1998b; Reinartz et al., 2009). These regression results are then used to specify the indicator weights more precisely in another round of outside approximation. The sequence of iterative outside and inside approximations is terminated after a specific limit (e. g. only a small improvement compared to the previous round) is reached (Chin, 1998b). Since the latent variable scores are calculated as weighted sums of the observed variables, the results are biased (because every reflectively measured item is influenced by a specific measurement error). As a consequence, in component-based SEM, factor loadings are overestimated whereas path coefficients are underestimated (Gefen et al., 2011). This effect can be reduced by increasing the sample size and the number of indicator variables at the same time ("consistency at large", Wold 1982, p. 25). Since these requirements regarding an unlimited amount of indicator variables and sample size cannot be met in practice, the aforementioned inconsistency is a necessary characteristic of PLS results. SmartPLS[6] and PLS-Graph[7] represent common tools for evaluating models relying on the component-based approach.

As the covariance-based and the component-based approaches differ significantly in the way model parameters are estimated, the measures for assessing the model quality are also different. Gefen et al. (2011) and Götz et al. (2010) give

---

3 http://www-01.ibm.com/software/analytics/spss/products/statistics/amos/ (2012/10/26)
4 http://www.ssicentral.com/lisrel/ (2012/10/26)
5 http://www.statmodel.com (2012/10/26)
6 http://www.smartpls.de (2012/10/26)
7 http://www.plsgraph.com (2012/10/26)

a profound overview of various quality metrics that should be reported in SEM research. These guidelines will be followed in Section 5.2.2 when this study's research model is analyzed.

3.3.2.2. Selection of an Appropriate Model Estimation Approach

Among many other authors, Reinartz et al. (2009) and Chin (2010) intensively discuss various criteria that should be considered before either covariance-based or component-based SEM is used. Some of these criteria, which appear especially important in the context of this study, will be discussed below:

1. Focus on theory confirmation

2. Path model's complexity

3. Sample size requirements

4. Normal distribution requirement of sample data

In extant literature, there is a general consensus on the fact that covariance-based SEM is better suited for *confirming theories* relying on well-established measurement models that have evolved over a substantial period of time. Component-based SEM is especially applicable in studies with an exploratory character, theories in an early stage or measurement item specifications that have not been tested in detail yet (Gefen et al., 2011).

With regard to a *path model's complexity* in terms of a high number of items involved in measuring the underlying constructs, component-based SEM is the method of choice. In situations of high model complexity, covariance-based approaches tend to show low model fits. Therefore, especially in research projects which set a focus on the completeness of the theoretical model they investigate and if many factors related to "attitudes, opinions, and behavior over time" (Chin, 2010, p. 661) are analyzed, the use of the former method is recommendable.

For several decades, the use of PLS was motivated in various research projects by arguing that covariance-based SEM does not provide trustworthy results if the *sample size* does not meet a specific limit which was regularly set to 200 data sets (Reinartz et al., 2009). PLS, however, was already reported to provide meaningful results in cases of only 20 empirical observations (Chin and Newsted,

1999). Goodhue et al. (2012a) and Goodhue et al. (2012b) challenge the aforementioned recommendation and claim that it is worth investigating if there are
differences with respect to the applicability of component-based SEM as opposed
to covariance-based SEM in small samples. In a Monte Carlo simulation, the
authors find that PLS – like component-based approaches – produces increased
standard deviations and reduced statistical power when used to analyze small
samples (Goodhue et al., 2012b).

In addition to sample size requirements, the presence of *non-normally distributed sample data* was often employed as an argument for not using covariance-
based SEM in past research (Chin, 1998a; Reinartz et al., 2009). This criterion
is now obsolete as modern covariance-based techniques easily tolerate moderate
deviations from normal distribution (Gefen et al., 2011; Goodhue et al., 2012b).

As pointed out above, sample size and distribution requirements are of secondary importance for choosing an appropriate SEM algorithm. This study aims
at explaining human information seeking and stopping behavior. The research
model is based on theories from the field of psychology and the IS domain that
have been tested intensively in past studies. Nevertheless, their combination in
one research model is novel, thus representing an early stage of theory building.
Furthermore, many of the measures underlying the research model's latent variables have not been tested thoroughly in the context of IS research. For that
reason and because of the research model's complexity with regard to the number of constructs, relationships between constructs and measurement items, it
appears reasonable to use the component-based PLS approach.

3.4. Web-Based Laboratory Experiment Environment

In order to validate the research model on human information seeking and stopping behavior, a web-based laboratory experiment environment was developed.
The degree of external validity is increased by designing tasks that are regularly
solved in organizational settings and by providing problem-relevant information
that is directly taken from existing web sites and that was pre-validated by actual
web users. Both the design of the laboratory environment and the tasks are described in this section before the manipulations on several independent variables
are explained.

3.4.1. Design of the Laboratory Experiment Environment

The laboratory environment was implemented as a web-based application in order to be able to imitate the look and feel of traditional web applications as well as possible. All information that can be accessed by the subjects in text format is displayed on the screen upon user request, i. e. participants have to request information actively by clicking on specific links (Vandenbosch and Huff, 1997). This mechanism has been used in many so-called "mouselab" studies in past decision making experiments because it allows the researcher to track which pieces of information were actually accessed and read by the information seeker throughout the experiment (Payne et al., 1993; Reisen et al., 2008; Riedl et al., 2008). Any interactions between the subject and the laboratory experiment environment are recorded in combination with a time stamp so that all processing steps can be synchronized with the heart rate variability data, which are acquired with a separate device. Additionally, the recording of user interactions allows a detailed analysis of the information seeking stopping behavior in terms of duration and amount of information requested by the subjects (Reisen et al., 2008).

All questionnaires that have to be answered by the subjects during the experiments are fully integrated into the experiment software so that the risk of distractions is reduced. Furthermore, a detailed workflow can be defined by the researcher so that no interventions are necessary during the experiments. Instead, participants get all instructions and tasks they have to solve in a standardized, unambiguous pattern, which increases the comparability of the results. Finally, this approach allows to define training tasks that have to be processed before the main experiment starts.

3.4.2. Task Design

As this study focuses on the investigation of information seeking and stopping behavior in *organizational settings*, simulated task scenarios are chosen as stimuli. For this reason, following common task designs in several studies on information seeking and decision making (Beach and Strom, 1989; Connolly and Thorn, 1987; Zwick et al., 2003), the subjects are given context information about a hypothetical organizational task they have to solve. In order to be able to answer this study's research questions, the key features of these scenarios are:

- Subjects have to solve an *original information seeking task*, i. e. they do not have to make choices between alternatives. Specifically, the participants are told that they have to gather information about one specific product (e. g. a printer) and based on this information, they have to give a recommendation about the product's suitability for the given company. Hence, a focus is set on judgments regarding the *sufficiency* of information gathered by the subjects (Browne et al., 2007).

- Based on the information provided during the experiment, recommendations regarding *two different classes of products*, namely printers and monitors, have to be given by the subjects. This choice was made because it can be expected that experience with these product categories is characterized by significantly large degrees of variance among the subjects. Furthermore, these categories were also used in past research (Browne et al., 2007; Liang and Doong, 1999).

- In order to put an emphasis on information acquisition in organizational contexts, subjects are told that they are in a *specific position within an organization* (e. g. CEO – depending on manipulations of the *task importance* variable).

- Attributes such as task complexity, task importance and social richness can be manipulated easily so that all relationships between the research model's constructs can be validated.

- All textual information that is accessible for the participants is *taken from original websites* to increase external validity.

During the experiment, every subject has to solve several information seeking tasks (c. f. Section C.1 in the Appendix). After every task, subjects are asked to fill out a questionnaire with items capturing the major latent variables of the research model. A questionnaire addressing time-invariant personality differences and general personal preferences and attitudes is shown at the end of the experiment after all tasks have been completed.

3.4.3. Experimental Manipulations

Laboratory experimental research settings allow for systematic manipulations of independent variables (Trochim and Donnelly, 2008; Yin, 2009). In addition to the advantage of being able to control for various confounding factors, the afore-mentioned aspect is one major reason for the use of laboratory experiments in this study. As many constructs of the research model are measured but not ma-nipulated, only the constructs *task complexity*, *task importance* and the informa-tion channel's *degree of social richness* are manipulated actively in corresponding treatment conditions. The manipulations are summarized in Table 3.2.

Task complexity is manipulated by inducing differences with regard to the construct's main components *task structure* and *task variability* (Campbell, 1988; Haerem and Rau, 2007; Wood, 1986). Even though four combinations of the aforementioned dimensions exist, only such tasks are created for the experiment which show both high degrees of task structure *and* task variability or both low degrees of task structure *and* task variability. Thus, the extreme values on the task complexity scale are addressed, presumably resulting in significant differences in the construct's variance.

In the low task complexity condition, the information seekers are informed about all product attributes that are relevant in the given scenario (e. g. the monitors should not consume a lot of energy and they should provide high video quality). Furthermore, the participants are told that the product they seek in-formation about is the only one available at the moment. Hence, task variability is low because the number of possible task outcomes is restricted explicitly.

In the high task complexity condition, however, neither information on specific product attributes is given, nor the number of possible task outcomes is restricted. Here, the subjects simply get a task description such as "You are responsible for the IT Systems of a large enterprise. In the future, all employees are supposed to get their own inkjet printer. Based on the information on the next screen page, evaluate if the printer 'Printer A', mentioned there, is appropriate for that purpose". In this case, the subjects have to develop their subjective idea of which criteria are relevant in the given scenario, i. e. a decomposition strategy is not suggested in the task description (Browne et al., 2007).

Table 3.2.: List of Experimental Manipulations

Independent variable	Manipulation
Perceived task complexity	*High:* Subjects get a vague task description. *Low:* Decomposition of task in task description: Subjects are informed about the aspects they have to concentrate on while seeking for information.
Task importance	*High:* Subjects are told that they are part of a small sample of persons that was selected for the experiment. In the simulated task, their performance affects all employees of the organization described in the task. Additionally, a researcher is physically present during the experiment (without interacting with the subjects). *Low:* Subjects are told that they are part of a large sample of persons that was selected for the experiment. In the simulated task, their performance affects one or two persons of the organization described in the task. The researcher is not physically present during the experiment.
Information channel's degree of social richness	*High:* Subjects get textual, problem-relevant information and, additionally, see a picture of the person who wrote the text, see consensus cues and are welcomed by their first name. Furthermore, the text is written in a first person perspective. *Low:* Subjects get only textual, problem-relevant information. The text is written in a third person perspective.

In Section 2.4.1, the construct *task importance* was defined as the degree of pressure exerted on an information seeker "to offer accurate judgments on the task in question" (Baron et al., 1996, p. 915). In an experiment on attitude judgments, Chaiken and Maheswaran (1994) created this pressure artificially by telling the subjects in the high task importance group that they belong to a small sample of people that is surveyed in the specific experiment. Members of the low task importance group, however, were told that they belong to a large sample and that their individual performance is not important because the results of the entire group will be averaged. In this study on information seeking and stopping behavior, a similar approach is chosen and two manipulations of task importance are induced: (1) At the beginning of the experiment, participants of the low task importance condition are informed about the large sample they belong to and learn that their questionnaire results will finally be averaged. Furthermore, the researcher leaves the room during the experiment. (2) Before every task the subjects have to solve, they receive context information. In the low task importance condition they learn that they work in a small company and their performance in the task will only affect one or two persons in the company. In the high task importance group, the subjects are told that they work in a large enterprise and task outcomes will have an effect on all employees.

Information channels high in *social richness* convey the impression of other persons' physical presence in an information seeking process (Gefen and Straub, 2004; Kumar and Benbasat, 2006, 2002). According to extant literature, a website's degree of perceived social richness can be increased e. g. by

- including consensus cues into the website. These cues represent the opinion of several persons in a format that is easily interpretable, e. g. a star rating (Sussman and Siegal, 2003);

- welcoming website users by their name (Fogg, 2003; Gefen and Straub, 2004);

- including pictures of other people into websites (Cyr et al., 2009; Fogg, 2003; Gefen and Straub, 2004).

Consequently, in the high social richness condition, the participants of this study's experiment receive textual product descriptions written in a first person perspective combined with a picture of the person who evidently wrote the text. Furthermore, consensus cues are shown in the form of star ratings and an indication of how many persons consider the information helpful. Additionally, the person is addressed by his first name which has to be entered at the beginning of the experiment. The low social richness group simply receives the textual process description in a third person perspective, i. e. without any contextual information that is believed to increase the degree of perceived social richness.

An overview of the specific experimental manipulations among the treatment groups is given in Appendix C. Furthermore, screenshots of the laboratory environment are part of the aforementioned Appendix.

3.5. Operationalization of Constructs

In this section, the latent variables of the research model are operationalized, i. e. measurement items are developed that capture the essence of the latent variables. Whenever possible, measurement instruments are used that have already been validated in past research. In some cases, new items are developed if valid operationalizations do not exist in extant literature. The items' wording is amended to make the items fit into the context of information seeking and stopping behavior research. Most variables are measured on a seven point Likert scale ranging from "strongly disagree (-3)" over "neutral (0)" as a mid-point value to "strongly agree (3)". In addition to using Likert scales, the constructs capturing the subjects' actual stopping behavior are measured qualitatively and coded manually. As most of the subjects are native German speakers, all items in the final questionnaire are in German (see Section D in the Appendix for an overview of the German questionnaire items).

3.5.1. Independent Variables and Moderator Variables

Perceived Task Complexity. Even though task complexity was manipulated in the experiment, its analysis is based on the degree of task complexity *perceived* by the subjects, i. e. its level is measured during the experiment (subjective instead of objective task complexity). Thus, the manipulation of objective task complexity serves as a mechanism for indirectly inducing variance in the perceived task complexity construct. In Section 2.4.1, task complexity was defined as a combination of task structure and task variability resulting in high task complexity when task structure is low and task variability is high (Campbell, 1988; Heinrich et al., 2011; Wood, 1986). As many studies concentrate on objective task complexity, a consensus on how to measure subjective task complexity has not been found yet. Consequently, in this study, the construct is measured by combining two items taken from Maynard and Hakel (1997) with two items developed by Haerem and Rau (2007). The former concentrates on measuring task complexity indirectly by asking for mental effort induced by the task, whereas the latter differentiates between task analyzability (structure of the task) and task variability (see Table 3.3).

Table 3.3.: Operationalization of the Construct *Perceived task complexity*

ID	Indicator	Source
Perceived task complexity refers to the combined influence of task structure and task variability on the difficulty a person feels while solving a task.		
TC1	This task was mentally demanding.	Adopted from Maynard and Hakel (1997)
TC2	This task required a lot of thought and problem solving.	Adopted from Maynard and Hakel (1997)
TC3	This task was well-structured.*	Based on Haerem and Rau (2007)
TC4	While solving this task, I came across problems which made me feel unsure.	Based on Haerem and Rau (2007)

*Inversely coded item

Perceived Task Experience. In Section 2.4.1, based on Vakkari (1999), *perceived task experience* was defined as "the extent of the information seeker's prior knowledge with respect to a given task". As the subjects are confronted with tasks in which they have to evaluate the suitability of different physical products in a given organizational context, it appears instrumental to develop a new measurement instrument that reflects the aforementioned requirements. The degree of experience with regard to the products relevant for the information seeking tasks is measured by asking for general knowledge about attributes of the products and by asking if and how often the subject bought a similar product in the past. The resulting three items are summarized in Table 3.4 containing placeholders for the product categories "printer" and "monitor" (separate instances of the questionnaire for the two categories are shown during the experiment).

Perceived Task Motivation. In Section 2.4.1, based on Petty and Cacioppo (1986) and Sussman and Siegal (2003), *perceived task motivation* was defined as the "level of the information seeker's involvement in a task as a function of the task's relevance and importance for the recipient". Unfortunately, both aforementioned studies which were used to develop a definition of the construct do not contain measurement instruments. In order to make the construct accessible in a questionnaire design, three reflective indicators are adopted from the study of Maynard and Hakel (1997). This set of indicators is especially suitable in the

Table 3.4.: Operationalization of the Construct *Perceived task experience*

ID	Indicator	Source
Perceived task experience refs...	*Perceived task experience* refers to the extent of the information seeker's prior knowledge with respect to a given task (buying and using *monitors, p*=1 and *printers, p*=2).	
TE1_1, TE2_1	I am experienced with regard to buying and using <product category>.	Developed for this study
TE1_2, TE2_2	I bought <product> several times in the past.	Developed for this study
TE1_3, TE2_3	I only have a very limited knowledge of <product category>.*	Developed for this study

*Inversely coded item

context of this study, as it conceptualizes task motivation as a "motivation to perform" (Maynard and Hakel, 1997, p. 313). Thus, it regards task motivation as a person's desire to invest effort into solving a task at hand in order to come to a solution of high quality – an operationalization which reveals strong parallels to effort-accuracy frameworks which are an important component of the research model. Table 3.5 shows a summary of all indicators.

Individual Characteristics: Need for Cognition, Extraversion and Maximizer Tendencies. Measurement instruments for operationalizing need for cognition, degree of extraversion and maximizer tendencies have been discussed intensively in the field of psychology. Since the constructs are measured reflectively by 12 to 16 indicators which were adopted from research articles without making changes to the wordings, summaries of the specific indicators are shown in the Tables D.4, D.5 and D.6 in the Appendix and are not included in this section.

Need for cognition refers to an individual predisposition with regard to an "individual's tendency to engage in and enjoy effortful cognitive endeavors" (Cacioppo et al., 1996, p. 197). Cacioppo and Petty (1982) developed an instrument for measuring need for cognition comprising 45 items. In order to reduce fatigue effects resulting from surveys overwhelming participants with too many questions, Cacioppo et al. (1984) refined the instrument by reducing it to a set of 18 indicators. A similar approach – however in German language – was followed

Table 3.5.: Operationalization of the Construct *Perceived task motivation*

ID	Indicator	Source
Perceived task motivation refers to the level of the information seeker's involvement in a task as a function of the task's relevance and importance for the recipient.		
TM1	I was motivated to perform well on this task.	Adopted from Maynard and Hakel (1997)
TM2	This task was interesting to me.	Adopted from Maynard and Hakel (1997)
TM3	I put a lot of effort into coming up with the best possible solution.	Adopted from Maynard and Hakel (1997)

by Bless et al. (1994). The authors translated the original questionnaire into German and eliminated all items showing a factor loading of $<.42$ in a study with 226 persons. As a result, they provide a validated measurement instrument comprising 16 items, which is used in the study at hand.

Extraversion represents a dispositional character trait referring to the degree of an information seeker's sociability and need for social relationships (Borkenau and Ostendorf, 2008; Watson and Clark, 1997). Extraversion is one of the dimensions of the *five factor model* as a widely respected and commonly used framework for measuring personality traits (Devaraj et al., 2008; Junglas et al., 2008; McElroy et al., 2007). Borkenau and Ostendorf (2008) give an extensive overview of existing approaches for measuring the degree of extraversion by using English items. Furthermore, they create a German questionnaire consisting of 12 indicators and conduct several tests on the validity of these items, which are summarized in Table D.5 in the Appendix. Again, the aforementioned German version of the measurement instrument is employed with the goal of increasing construct validity by using pre-validated indicator variables.

Maximizer tendencies refers to a person's attempt to solve tasks in an optimal way by considering all information available in a specific context (Schwartz et al., 2002). The authors propose and validate a list of 13 items for measuring a person's predisposition for showing maximizer tendencies. The instrument was developed in the realm of choice problems arguing that – opposed to the assumptions of rational choice theory – having more options does not necessarily result in the choice problem appearing more attractive to decision makers. One explanation for this observation, which makes the instrument especially appropriate for studying information seeking and stopping behavior, is the fact that more options lead to increased information needs, affecting information seeking behavior (Schwartz et al., 2002). The corresponding items are listed in Table D.6 in the Appendix.

3.5.2. Variables Referring to Information Processing

Based on an extensive literature review, in Section 2.4.1 two complementary information processing styles were identified, namely System 1 (effortless, automatic, experiential) and System 2 (effortful, systematic) information processing. It was emphasized that current research assumes the possibility of a simultaneous activation of both systems (Angst and Agarwal, 2009; Chaiken and Maheswaran, 1994; Evans, 2003; Zhang and Watts, 2008). Several measurement instruments have been proposed in various dual-process theory contexts: Epstein et al. (1996) developed the Rational-Experiential Inventory (REI) consisting of 31 items for measuring a person's predisposition with regard to cognitive versus intuitive information processing. The instrument was refined by Pacini and Epstein (1999) to eliminate both content-related and reliability weaknesses. In the context of this study, however, task-induced differences in information processing styles are of primary concern. Consequently, the aforementioned predisposition-oriented measurement instruments are less suitable.

Instead, Shiv and Fedorikhin (1999) come up with indicators for analyzing the task-induced interplay of cognition and affect in consumer decision making on a bipolar scale. The bipolarity, however, is in contrast with this study's assumption of the non-exclusive activation of System 1 versus System 2 information processing. Novak and Hoffman (2009) propose a measurement instrument which fulfills all of the criteria mentioned above: It was designed for measuring task-induced information processing styles following the idea of common dual-process theories and uses two independent blocks of indicators (rational versus experiential processing). The words "While solving the task" were put in front of five items in order to underline that the questions are related to the task that had to be solved in the experiment. The resulting indicators are summarized in Table 3.6.

Table 3.6.: Operationalization of the Constructs *System 1 information processing* and *System 2 information processing*

ID	Indicator	Source
System 1 information processing refers to the degree to which information is processed in an effortless, associative way, taking past experiences into account and following simple information cues.		
Sys1_1	While solving the task, I used my gut feelings.	Based on Novak and Hoffman (2009)
Sys1_2	While solving the task, I relied on my sense of intuition.	Based on Novak and Hoffman (2009)
Sys1_3	While solving the task, I used my instincts.	Based on Novak and Hoffman (2009)
System 2 information processing refers to the degree to which information is processed in an effortful, logical way, sequentially following specific rules of reasoning.		
Sys2_1	While solving the task, I reasoned things out carefully.	Based on Novak and Hoffman (2009)
Sys2_2	I tackled this task systematically.	Adopted from Novak and Hoffman (2009)
Sys2_3	While solving the task, I figured things out logically.	Based on Novak and Hoffman (2009)

3.5.3. Variables Referring to Stopping Behavior

Following the standard procedure for measuring information seeking stopping behavior in the IS discipline, the constructs *Propensity to use experiential stopping rules* and *Propensity to use rational stopping rules* are not analyzed based on Likert scales as the latent variables above, but qualitatively (Browne et al., 2007). Therefore, two open questions are asked after every task completed by the subjects (see Table 3.7).

This approach has three advantages:

- *Reduction of common-method bias*: Independent and dependent variables are not measured using the same method, but independent variables are analyzed quantitatively, whereas dependent variables are investigated following a qualitative approach (Burton-Jones, 2009).

- *Reduction of demand effects* (Dimoka et al., 2012): Since every subject solves at least two information seeking tasks, questions regarding the stopping behavior based on a Likert scale would bias the results of the questionnaire shown after the first and all subsequent tasks. This is due to the fact that, when filling in the questionnaire after the first task, the subject would learn about possible rules that are applicable for terminating information seeking activities and would possibly adapt his behavior in subsequent tasks. This adverse effect is reduced by not disclosing possible stopping rules to the participants of the experiment.

- *Identification of "new" stopping rules*: Research on information seeking and stopping behavior is eclectic in that researchers from many fields provide knowledge on many different aspects of the phenomenon. Research addressing the sufficiency of information, however, does not specifically differentiate between experiential and rational stopping rules. Hence, based on a qualitative approach, it is not only possible to confirm this study's research model but also to identify reasons for terminating seeking activities that have not been reported in past research.

Table 3.7.: Operationalization of the Constructs *Propensity to use experiential / rational stopping rules*

ID	Indicator	Source
Propensity to use experiential stopping rules refers to the tendency to rely on affect and intuition when making the decision to terminate the information seeking process, whereas *Propensity to use rational stopping rules* refers to the tendency to decide consciously to stop seeking for information based on a content-wise analysis of issue-relevant information.		
Stop1	Why did you stop searching for information when you did?	Adopted from Browne et al. (2007)
Stop2	How did you decide to stop searching for information?	Adopted from Browne et al. (2007)

3.6. Data Collection

After instruments for measuring the research model's latent variables were developed in the previous section, the selection of participants taking part in the experiments is discussed next. Thereafter, the design of the questionnaires used during the experiments is explained.

3.6.1. Sample Selection

Laboratory experiments offer the possibility to minimize the effect of confounding variables that are not part of the underlying research model. In order to further reduce potentially biasing implications induced by age and education differences, a homogeneous group of people has to be selected for this study. All participants are required to have a Business Administration and Information Technology background without having entered the job market yet. Thus, it can be guaranteed that the information seeking and stopping behavior the subjects show during the experiments, has not been shaped by cultural influences of a specific company, but is innate to the participants. Furthermore, relying on student subjects narrows down the focus on such people that will soon enter the job market and are a highly interesting target group from the perspective of both IT and E-Commerce responsibles.

Another argument for acquiring student subjects lies in the fact that these persons belong to the group of *digital natives* (Prensky, 2001), i. e. they have entirely grown up using computers and information technology. Hence, it is important to test if existing, well-established theories on information seeking, stopping behavior and derivatives also hold for the above-mentioned group of people, even though the theories were developed when computers only slowly gained importance both in organizational settings and private life.

Consequently, for this study, a course of business administration students was chosen to recruit participants for the experiments. The course deals with the use of Enterprise Resource Planning Systems in organizational settings and thus especially fulfills the criterion of establishing a basic knowledge of information technology on part of the participants. Additionally, all subjects are in a similar age with comparable degrees of experience with regard to the use of computers and have attended similar education programs. Hence, potentially confounding effects of a series of variables that are not in the research model's core can be minimized.

3.6.2. Questionnaire Design and Pre-Test of Experiment

According to the guidelines proposed by Dillman (2007), a questionnaire should be designed in a "respondent-friendly" way (p. 81) to improve response rates and to reduce the risk of measurement errors. Specifically, Dillman recommends to define *navigational paths* that guide the respondent through the questionnaire. To accomplish this goal, in the study at hand, the participants have to fill in several questionnaires. The first questionnaire contains questions regarding nationality, age and education of the subjects. Thereafter, the participants have to deal with two to six information seeking tasks. After every task, another questionnaire is shown that addresses specific aspects of the behavior the subjects exerted while solving the task. Finally, at the end of the experiment, the subjects have to answer questions related to time-invariant personality dimensions.

Accordingly, all questions are grouped contentwise and a clear navigational structure is visible to the subjects. Furthermore, mechanisms are implemented into the laboratory environment that make sure that the subjects fill in all questionnaires completely, i. e. it is not possible to accidentally skip a question. Thus, the risk of subject-induced measurement errors is minimized.

The validation of the measurement instruments and the questionnaire itself are of high importance for the research endeavor's overall quality and reliability. Dillman (2007) suggests a four-stage approach for validating questionnaires. In *stage 1*, the questionnaire is supposed to be "reviewed by knowledgeable colleagues and analysts" (p. 140), before it is evaluated in interviews (*stage 2*). These interviews can either be conducted as *cognitive* or as *retrospective interviews*. In cognitive interviews, the respondents are asked to comment on the survey contents and layout while the researcher is present. In retrospective interviews the respondents are not interrupted while filling in the questionnaire but report their impressions afterwards (Dillman, 2007, p. 142). In *stage 3*, a small pilot study should be conducted to evaluate the questionnaire under conditions that are comparable to the main study. Finally, in *stage 4*, a final check should be exerted with a person who was not involved in one of the previous steps (p. 147).

The questionnaires embedded into the laboratory environment software were validated based on the above-mentioned guidelines. Therefore, the initial version of the survey was discussed in detail with a professor working in the field of information seeking and stopping behavior at a University in North America. Additional researchers knowledgeable in the information seeking and stopping behavior domain were contacted and provided feedback both on the survey and on the experiment itself. As a consequence, some questions were slightly reworded and the order of questions was amended (stage 1).

In the second stage, researchers working at the Psychology Department of the University of Mannheim were asked to make detailed comments on the questionnaires and the laboratory environment. In two sessions of about one hour each, the researchers sat in front of a computer screen and solved all experimental tasks. The questionnaires shown between tasks were discussed following the cognitive interview approach, i. e. the researchers commented on the understandability and suitability of every question. Finally, the measurement instrument for the variable *Need for Cognition* was replaced by a shorter but still highly reliable version in order to reduce the risk of fatigue effects.

In a pilot study with 11 students, it was checked if the subjects can answer all questions in a reasonable period of time. Apart from that, the subjects took part in retrospective interviews and gave some important advice with respect to wording issues and two spelling mistakes (stage 3). All these aspects were addressed before the final version of the laboratory environment software with the most recent version of the questionnaires was evaluated by two persons. Therefore, these persons who had not been part of a previous evaluation cycle were asked to work with the laboratory environment software to find potential mistakes that had not been detected before. No further comments were made by these subjects.

3.7. Summary

At the beginning of this chapter, a laboratory experiment was selected as the most appropriate research methodology for analyzing human information seeking and stopping behavior.

An introduction to heart rate variability measurement and structural equation modeling was given as these methods are used within the laboratory experiment environment to collect and analyze both psychophysiological and questionnaire data.

In the experiments, three different independent variables will be manipulated by the researcher, whereas all other variables shown in the research model will be measured but not manipulated. Consequently, a comprehensive but parsimonious nomological network will be validated with the help of well-established measurement instruments.

The questionnaire design used in the laboratory experiment environment was pre-tested comprehensively and improved iteratively.

In the next chapter, the results from a first round of experiments are discussed. The aim of that chapter consists in the refinement and preliminary confirmation of the research model before it is validated in more detail in the main study in Chapter 5.

4. Pre-Test and Theory Refinement

In Chapter 3, this study's research design has been described and a laboratory experiment has been chosen as a suitable means for evaluating the research model proposed in Section 2.4.1. In this chapter, a pre-test of the laboratory experiment environment and the experimental tasks is conducted. The objective of this pre-test is threefold: it aims at (1) evaluating and adapting the laboratory experiment software, (2) evaluating and adapting the tasks that are shown during the experiment and (3) making sure that the research model captures all relevant aspects of the real world it reflects. To accomplish these goals, the pre-test is designed in a way that is very close to the main study which is conducted later to validate the research model.

In the experiments of the pre-test phase, 11 subjects solved a series of six information seeking tasks in the laboratory experiment environment. Additionally, heart rate variability data were captured and the subjects were interviewed after the experiment. The results are discussed subsequently and changes being made to the experiment software are described. Furthermore, it is explained how the triangulation of data collected via different quantitative and qualitative methods informed the refinement of the study's research model.

4.1. Experimental Design

The experimental design basically consists of three phases (Figure 4.1). In the *initial phase*, the subjects are welcomed and asked to fill in some questionnaires concerning demographic aspects. Furthermore, the subjects read an experiment description with varying content depending if they belong to the low or high task importance group (c. f. Section C.1 in the Appendix for the exact wording of the description). During the *main phase*, the subjects have to solve six tasks sequentially. In all tasks, the subjects are asked to seek information about different IT-related products and proceed in the workflow by clicking on a "Next"

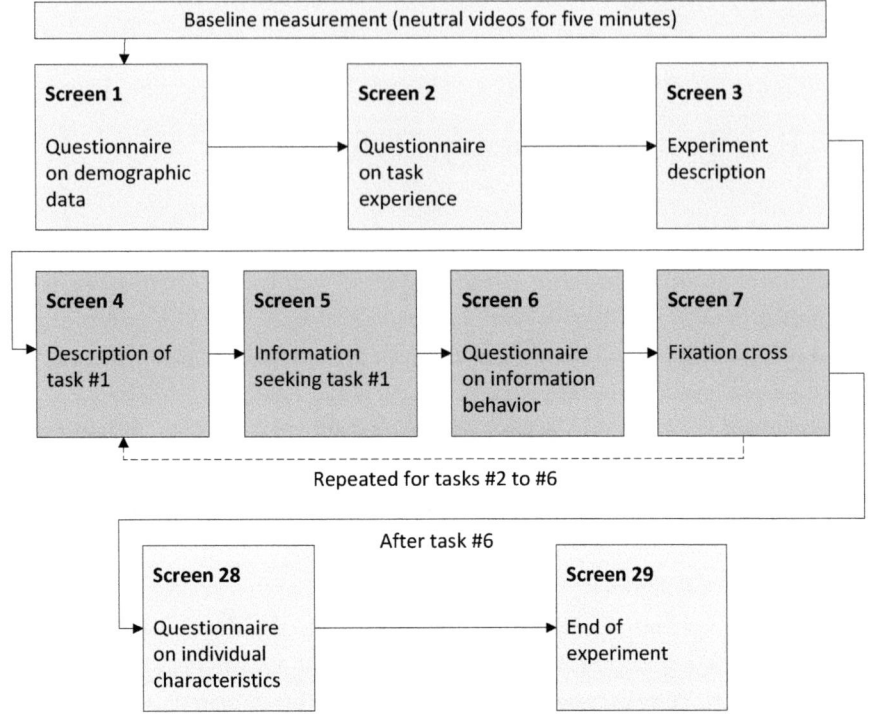

Figure 4.1.: Experimental Design in Pre-test Phase

button as soon as they are confident of having acquired a sufficient amount of information (c. f. Section 3.4.2). Every task starts with a short description before problem-relevant information is shown on the screen reflecting the experimental manipulations introduced in Section 3.4.3. Thereafter, the subjects have to fill in a questionnaire on constructs related to information seeking and stopping behavior. Finally, a fixation cross is displayed to neutralize the impressions the subjects received while solving the tasks (Riedl et al., 2010b). Then, the next task description is shown. In the *final phase* of the experiment, a questionnaire tapping into several individual characteristics mentioned in the research model is shown before the experiment is finished.

Before the experiment starts, every subject attaches a heart rate measurement device on his chest (above the sternum), which transmits heart beat data wirelessly to a heart rate monitor watch positioned about two meters away from the subject. The heart rate monitor watch records data with a sampling rate of 1,000 Hz, which is at the upper end of the recommended 500 – 1,000 Hz (Berntson et al., 1997). Thereafter, the subject watches neutral videos for five minutes while baseline data are recorded. The basal heart rate has to be determined to make the results comparable between subjects as every subject has a different heart rate in a resting condition (Jennings et al., 1992). While the subjects watch the videos and solve the experimental tasks, they are alone in the laboratory without any distractors being present.

In order to create a highly standardized environment, all experiments are conducted in a narrow time frame during the afternoon of several consecutive weekdays. Furthermore, a protocol formatted as a checklist is used to make sure that the experiment environment and the video player as well as the heart rate monitor watch are configured consistently whenever a new subject starts the experiment. The entire protocol is listed in Table C.1 in the Appendix.

The 11 participants of the pre-test are healthy, right-handed members of business-related degree programs and are instructed not to consume coffee or alcohol on the day of the experiment as these substances might bias the psychophysiological measurements.

4.2. Data Analysis and Findings

4.2.1. Descriptive Statistics and Overall Evaluation of the Laboratory Experiment Environment

The subjects have an average *age* of 24.6 years ($SD = 2.1$ years); thus they belong to a rather consistent age group which minimizes undesired age-related effects. The sample consists of three female (27%) and eight male (73%) subjects taking part in the experiment voluntarily. The women's average age ($M = 25.7$, $SD = 2.5$) is slightly higher than the men's age ($M = 24.3$, $SD = 2.0$)[1].

On average, the subjects needed about 31 minutes to complete the experiment. Additionally, it took about 15 minutes to attach the heart rate monitor sensor to

---

1 All statistical analyses in this study were computed with IBM SPSS Statistics, Version 20 and Microsoft Excel 2007 if not stated differently.

Table 4.1.: Subject Age and Processing Times

	M	SD	Min.	Max.
Subject age (female subjects) [years]	25.7	2.5	23.0	28.0
Subject age (male subjects) [years]	24.3	2.0	22.0	27.0
Duration of experiment [min.]	31:12	06:00	24:36	42:24
Duration of initial phase [min.]	01:23	00:24	00:51	01:57
Duration per task [min.]	04:00	01:08	02:11	06:38
Duration of final phase [min.]	06:06	01:19	04:36	08:34

the subjects, to instruct them and to let them watch the neutral videos for recording baseline data. While it was easy for the subjects to follow the instructions at the beginning of the experiment ($M = 01:23$ minutes, $SD = 00:24$ minutes), it took significantly longer ($M = 04:00$ minutes $SD = 01:08$ minutes) to complete one of the six tasks and fill in the corresponding questionnaire. Especially the final questionnaire asking for the subjects' individual characteristics demanded considerable effort and concentration ($M = 06:06$ minutes, $SD = 09:19$ minutes). Consequently, immediately after the experiment, many subjects mentioned that the overall processing time of about 45:00 minutes was challenging, but nevertheless, they were confident of having solved all tasks properly. Both subject age and processing times are summarized in Table 4.1.

Apart from fatigue effects, the subjects reported some *minor spelling mistakes* in the laboratory environment, which were corrected immediately. The first subject was confronted with a *non-critical error message* issued by the web browser right at the beginning of the experiment, which could be solved easily by clicking on the message's "OK" button (the subject did not have to interrupt the experiment). The error message could not be reproduced afterwards and did not appear in any of the remaining experiments. As the issue could be resolved easily by the subject himself, it can be assumed that it did not have noteworthy negative effects on the experiment session.

No other technical problems were reported by the subjects and a validation of the data captured during the experiment (questionnaire responses, time stamps

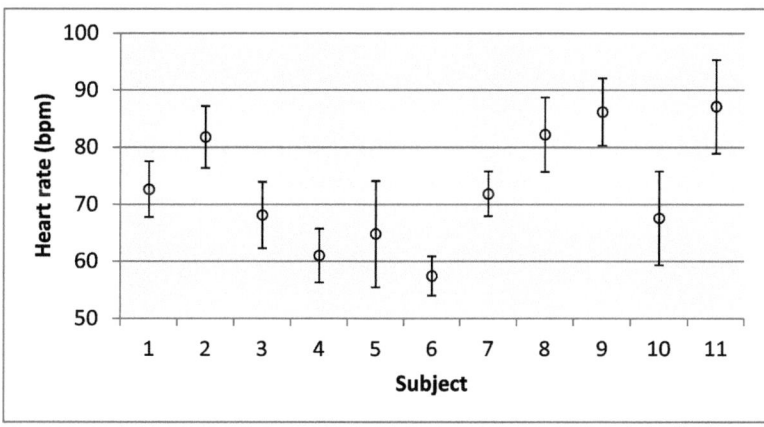

Figure 4.2.: Subjects' Average Heart Rate (and SD) during Baseline Measurement

for calculating the duration of sub-tasks) confirmed the laboratory experiment software's proper functionality and overall reliability under real-life conditions.

As predicted by Jennings et al. (1992), the eleven subjects showed substantial differences with respect to their average *heart rate* measured before the start of the experiment. An overview is provided in Figure 4.2 and underlines the necessity of comparing heart rate metrics in between-subject designs by focusing on deviations from individual-specific baseline conditions. Consequently, all calculations on heart rate data will be performed based on deviations from basal heart rate characteristics.

4.2.2. Evaluation and Adaptation of Experimental Tasks

In order to obtain sufficient degrees of variance between the experimental tasks' perceived complexity, two tasks have to be selected for the main study that are significantly different with respect to their complexity. The subjects reported the highest task complexity scores for task 6 ($M = 3.93$, $SE = 0.33$) calculated as the average value of the four task complexity items used in the questionnaire. Task 3 ($M = 3.25$, $SE = 0.42$) and task 4 ($M = 3.14$, $SE = 0.42$) showed the lowest scores. A paired t-test was conducted to test if the mean of task 6 is significantly higher than the mean of task 3 and task 4, respectively. Both alternative hypotheses

Table 4.2.: Paired *t*-Test of High Frequency Component for Task 3 versus Task 6 and Task 4 versus Task 6 Including Test for Normal Distribution (Sample Data: Deviation From Baseline in %)

	Normal dist. (Kolmogorov-Smirnov)			Paired *t*-test with task 6 (complex task)				
	df	Statistic	p	M	SE	df	Statistic	p
Task 3	11	0.131	> .2	18.18	4.45	10	3.641	< .01
Task 4	11	0.200	> .2	-0.78	5.31	10	0.129	> .2
Task 6	/	/	/	-1.77	3.84	/	/	/

can be confirmed, i. e. task 6 is perceived to be significantly more complex than task 3 and task 4 ($t(10) = 2.488$, $p < .05$ for task 3 and $t(10) = 2.692$, $p < .05$ for task 4). As the differences between the task complexity scores are normally distributed (Kolmogorov-Smirnov test: $D(11) = 0.182$, $p > .20$ for task 3 and 6 $D(11) = 0.219$, $p > .1$ for task 4 and 6; visual inspection of Q-Q plots), the paired *t*-test's assumptions are fulfilled (Field, 2009). Furthermore, both p values are below .025 (.05 / 2) as required when conducting two pairwise comparisons.

Since the complexity scores for the low complexity task candidates are on a similar level, it is necessary to make an informed decision about which of the tasks will be used in the main study. For this reason, HRV data was analyzed following the assumption that higher task complexity and the thereby induced increased information processing requirements will inhibit the activation of the parasympathetic nervous system. This effect would be reflected by a decrease in the relative HF component density calculated in the spectral analysis (c. f. Section 3.3.1). To test this assumption, the first 40 seconds of the HRV data series of task 3 and task 4 were compared with the first 40 seconds of task 6. Due to the small sample size, the autoregressive approach was used to calculate the power densities (Tarvainen and Niskanen, 2008) as relative HF deviations from baseline. Table 4.2 contains the results of the analysis indicating that task 3 induced significantly lower cognitive demands than task 4 compared to the complex task 6 (significantly higher HF component for task 3 compared to task 6). Thus, task 3 will be used in the main study to represent a task with low complexity.

Furthermore, the heart rate variability data confirmed a prediction concerning human behavior when solving complex tasks made by Payne et al. (1993). The authors assumed that – following effort-accuracy trade-offs – decision makers often choose decision strategies that result in low cognitive effort when they have to deal with complex problems. To test this assumption, the first 40 and the last 40 seconds of the problem solving process were analyzed with regard to changes in heart rate variability for every subject solving the complex task 6. For this reason, the deviation of the relative HF component from the baseline measurement was computed (autoregressive approach).

The deviation during the first 40 seconds was significantly lower than in the last 40 seconds with $M = -1.8$, $SE = 3.8$ at the beginning and $M = 14.68$, $SE = 4.66$ at the end of task 6 ($t(10) = -2.79$, $p < .05$). Again, the test for normal distribution of the difference scores between the two aforementioned groups following a Kolmogorov-Smirnov test ($D(11) = .19$, $p > .2$) and the visual inspection of Q-Q plots were positive. This finding suggests that in complex tasks, subjects invest high mental effort when they start solving the task and then switch to a heuristic problem solving approach towards the end, which is reflected by a reduced inhibition of the parasympathetic nervous system in the last 40 seconds. This result can be regarded as a preliminary validation of Hypothesis H8 of this study's research model suggesting that higher task complexity results in higher levels of System 1 information processing. Furthermore, the HRV data analysis is in line with the subjects' self-reported values on perceived task complexity. Hence, also from a psychophysiological perspective, task 6 represents an appropriate task for an experimental high task complexity scenario.

4.3. Refinement of Research Model

After every experiment session, retrospective interviews were conducted with the subjects in which they were asked to describe which information seeking strategies they used and how they decided to terminate the seeking process. The interviews were recorded and transcribed, resulting in 35 pages of interview transcripts comprising about 11.000 words. An analysis of the interviews did not reveal any significant deviations of the subjects' seeking behavior from that predicted by the research model developed in Section 2.4.1, with one exception:

many subjects mentioned variables such as *source credibility* and *trust* and argued that their levels varied with the information channel's degree of social richness. In order to better understand the underlying mechanisms, the transcripts were coded with the software tool NVivo[2] focusing on such statements that are related to the information channel's degree of social richness, source credibility and information processing mode. The results of this analysis are presented below.

Several subjects explained that the differing degrees of social richness during the experiment did not have any effect on their behavior, partly because they completely ignored such cues. For example, subject 6 reported:

> *"I did not pay attention to pictures [of the persons who produced the acquired information] at all."*

Subject 5 commented on the impact of the presence or absence of contextual social cues in a similar way:

> *"I did not classify the information differently."*

However, most subjects described either explicitly or implicitly that social richness affected their perception of the information source's credibility. For example, subject 1 reported:

> *"Especially the additional contextual information resulted in a positive impression."*

Surprisingly though, several subjects mentioned that the presence of contextual social cues resulted in reduced credibility assessments of the acquired information because they had the impression to receive highly subjective information that solely represents the opinion of one specific person. Subject 3 and 7 stated:

> *"When I saw contextual information, I immediately doubted the credibility, because the information had a highly subjective touch." (Subject 3)*

> *"Information containing personal recommendations seemed to represent subjective opinions. In such cases I need additional information in order to be able to compare." (Subject 7)*

---

2 http://www.qsrinternational.com (2012/10/26)

Hence, a clear pattern does not emerge with respect to the impact of the degree of an information channel's social richness on the source's credibility. Nevertheless, since many subjects *did* recognize a connection between the aforementioned variables, a closer examination of the source credibility construct and its impact on information seeking is conducted based on existing literature.

In hypothesis 4a (Section 2.4.1), a direct impact of an information channel's social richness on System 1 information processing was assumed arguing – among other aspects – that social richness increases an information source's trustworthiness and represents a contextual cue that can be assimilated easily by the information seeker as a precondition of System 1 information processing. However, the interview transcripts suggest that perceived source credibility might act as a mediating variable with regard to the direct relationship between social richness and System 1 information processing.

The information source's credibility defined as "the extent to which an information source is perceived to be believable, competent, and trustworthy by information recipients" (Bhattacherjee and Sanford, 2006, p. 811) is reported to serve as an important contextual cue, i. e. high degrees of source credibility can act as a substitution mechanism suppressing the systematic scrutiny of information. Following this line of argumentation, high degrees of source credibility can replace effortful thinking processes because the information conveyed to the recipient is thought to be correct and valid as it was produced by a trustworthy party, e. g. an expert (Bhattacherjee and Sanford, 2006, p. 812). Consequently, source credibility as a peripheral information cue triggers System 1 information processing by providing an important and easily accessible indication of the quality of the retrieved information (Sussman and Siegal, 2003).

The positive emotional effects induced by a medium's increased social richness and the intensified trust perceptions translate into higher degrees of perceived source credibility. Social richness, not only represented by contextual information about the information source's identity and background, but also by group consensus information and personal recommendations was reported to convey an impression of confidence and assurance to the recipient that is not entailed in the factual information transmitted (Cross et al., 2001; Gefen and Straub, 2004; Sussman and Siegal, 2003). Consequently, the *source credibility* construct is added as a mediating variable into the research model, resulting in an adaptation of

Table 4.3.: Operationalization of the Construct *Perceived source credibility*

ID	Indicator	Source

ID	Indicator	Source
Perceived source credibility refers to the combined influence of an information source's believability, competence and trustworthiness.		
SC1	The information provided for solving the task was trustworthy.	Based on McComas and Trumbo (2001)
SC2	The information provided for solving the task was accurate.	Based on McComas and Trumbo (2001)
SC3	The information provided for solving the task was fair.	Based on McComas and Trumbo (2001)
SC4	The information provided for solving the task tells the whole story.	Based on McComas and Trumbo (2001)
SC5	The information provided for solving the task was unbiased.	Based on McComas and Trumbo (2001)

hypothesis 4a[3] and the introduction of hypothesis 4c (a summary view of the research model is given in Figure 4.3):

> *Hypothesis 4a*: The higher an information channel's social richness, the higher the degree of source credibility.*

> *Hypothesis 4c: The higher the degree of source credibility, the higher the degree of System 1 information processing.*

The measurement model used for operationalizing the source credibility construct was taken from McComas and Trumbo (2001) in the form of five indicator variables measured on a seven point Likert scale as listed in Table 4.3.

4.4. Summary

In the first part of this chapter, the web-based laboratory environment was pre-tested with a sample of 11 persons in order to identify problems the subjects encountered while using the software. Minor spelling mistakes were corrected immediately. Furthermore, the high number of tasks the subjects had to solve

---

3 The adaptation of hypothesis 4a is marked by a star (*) throughout the rest of the study.

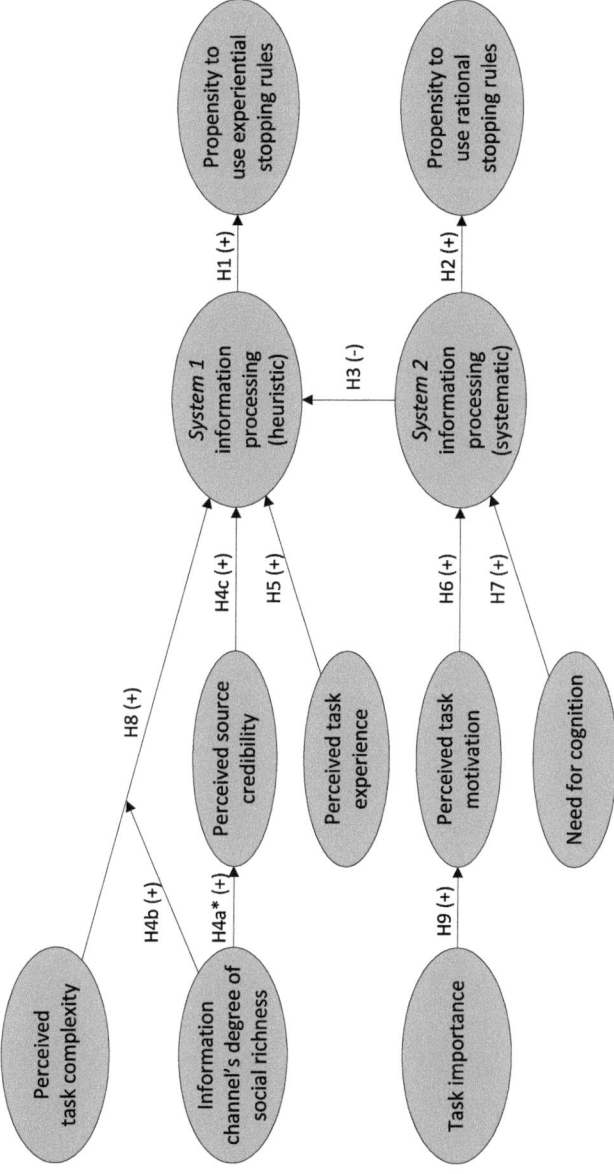

Figure 4.3.: Refined Explanatory Model of Information Seeking Stopping Behavior (*adapted version of hypothesis 4a)

during the experiment was criticized by several participants. Consequently, two tasks were selected for the main study. In order to induce high variance with regard to perceived task complexity, those tasks were selected that had the lowest and the highest score on the corresponding measurement scale. Additionally, heart rate variability data supported the selection process by giving insights into immediate, non-controllable body-reactions of the participants while solving the various tasks.

In the second part of the chapter, the findings from retrospective interviews were presented. These interviews had been conducted with every subject immediately after completing the experiments. Most subjects reported differences with regard to perceived source credibility depending on the degree of social richness they observed. Due to the small sample size, a coherent pattern could not be identified. Therefore, the construct "perceived source credibility" was integrated into the nomological network underlying this study by deducing cause-effect relationships based on existing literature on the variable.

The refined research model will be validated in the next chapter. For this reason, the laboratory environment software will be used to collect data on information seeking and stopping behavior of 132 subjects, each solving two independent tasks.

5. Empirical Validation

In Chapter 3, the research methodology for validating the study's research model on information seeking and stopping behavior was introduced. Subsequently, the laboratory environment software for collecting the required questionnaire data was pre-tested and refined in Chapter 4. This chapter elaborates on the validation of the research model itself in a laboratory experiment with 132 participants.

5.1. Experimental Design and Experimental Procedure

The experimental design used in the main study is similar to that developed in Chapter 4. A major change was made with regard to the number of tasks each participant has to solve: While subjects had to deal with six information seeking tasks in the pre-test, participants of the main study's experiment only receive two different tasks in order to reduce potential fatigue effects. Furthermore, a *training task* is included in the experimental work flow, so that subjects can familiarize with the software environment before the actual data collection process starts. The resulting experimental design is summarized in Figure 5.1.

The order of the two tasks presented to every subject during the experiment was pseudo-randomized resulting in eight different experimental conditions that reflect all possible combinations of the two variables that were manipulated in the laboratory experiment environment plus the varying degrees of task complexity that were measured via an appropriate set of indicators during the experiment. An overview of these conditions and the properties of the corresponding tasks is presented in Table 5.1. A detailed list of experiment and task descriptions as well as information provided during the experiment is summarized in Appendix C.

The experiment was conducted in May 2012 in a tutorial session on a lecture for Business Administration students at a German University. The students had been assigned randomly to 14 different tutorial sessions that took place once a week.

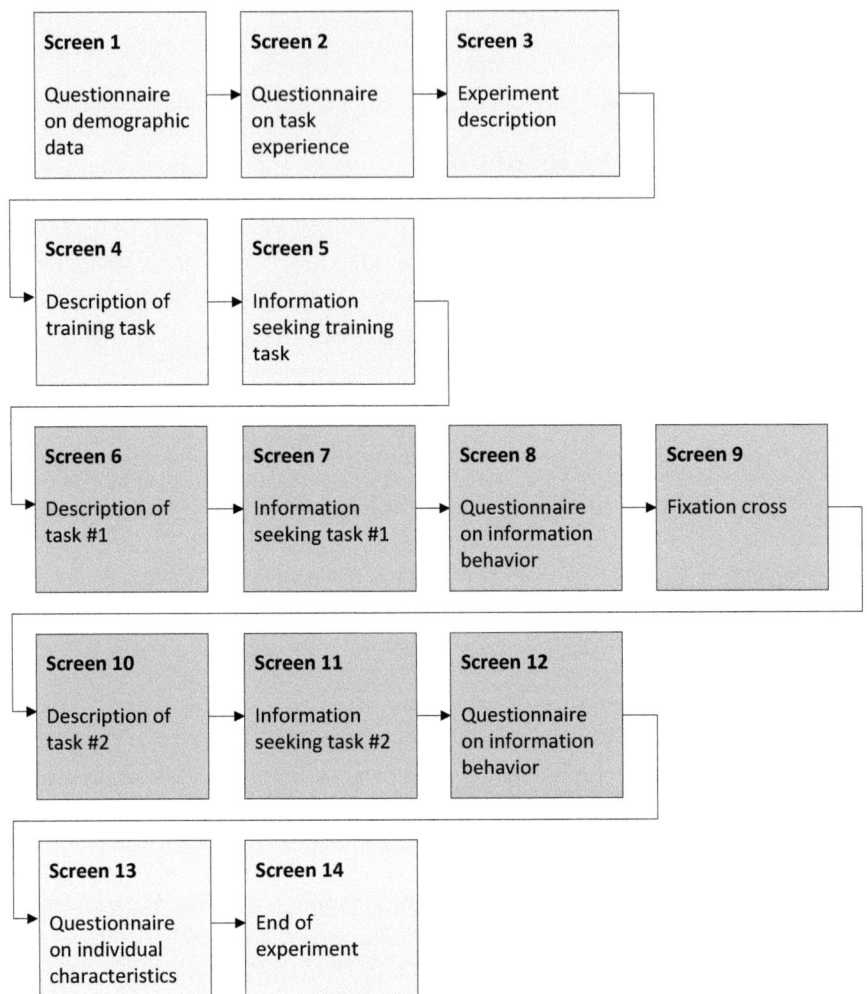

Figure 5.1.: Experimental Design in Main Study

Table 5.1.: Overview of Experimental Conditions (TI = Task Importance, SR = Social Richness, TC = Task Complexity)

Condition	TI	SR Task 1	SR Task 2	TC Task 1	TC Task 2
C1	High	High	Low	Low	High
C2	High	Low	High	Low	High
C3	High	High	Low	High	Low
C4	High	Low	High	High	Low
C5	Low	High	Low	Low	High
C6	Low	Low	High	Low	High
C7	Low	High	Low	High	Low
C8	Low	Low	High	High	Low

As every student had access to a computer, it was possible to let the subjects take part in the experiment simultaneously. All members of one tutorial session were assigned to one of the eight experimental conditions listed in Table 5.1.

In total, 174 persons were present in the 14 tutorial sessions (see Table 5.2). About 16 of these persons decided not to participate in the experiment because they either did not have interest or because they arrived too late when the other subjects had already completed the experiment. 25 of the 158 subjects originally taking part in the experiment decided not to complete the experiment. Several subjects aborting the experiment were asked for reasons and replied that they could not invest the required time because of other obligations. One participant was more than ten standard deviations older than the other participants. The data set of this person was removed manually from the sample as the subject did not meet the requirement of equal age. Finally, 132 students completed the experiments (75.9% of the original sample), each answering questionnaires on two different tasks, so that 264 data sets are available for the validation of the research model. A manual inspection of the response data confirmed that all participants have sufficient command of the German language, i. e. they clearly understood both the information they received during the experiment and the questions they had to answer. Consequently, no data set had to be deleted from the list of those participants that completed the experiment.

Table 5.2.: Participation in the Experiment

Category	Absolute	Relative
Original sample	174	100%
No interest or no time	16	9.2%
Incomplete experimental sessions	25	14.4%
Manually removed from sample	1	0.5%
Completed experimental sessions	132	75.9%

5.2. Data Analysis and Findings

In this section, the subjects' behavior with regard to information seeking and stopping will be analyzed based on both questionnaire results and interaction data captured in the laboratory environment software. In a first step, descriptive statistics are provided to give fundamental insights into various sample characteristics and to visualize differences with respect to information seeking and stopping behavior. In a second step, the research model underlying this study is estimated and validated.

5.2.1. Descriptive and Basic Inferential Statistics

5.2.1.1. Demographics and Educational Background

The sample is highly homogeneous with regard to *gender* and *age*, thus reducing biasing effects of these factors. As indicated by Table 5.3, the sample comprises 70 women (53%) and 62 men (47%). For both groups, the mean age is 22.4 years with a SD of 1.5 years for the women and 1.2 years for the men. No person is older than 28 years or younger than 21 years.

Also the probability of *cultural influences* on the information seeking and stopping behavior can be assumed to be reasonably low since 85.0% of the participants stated to be German (see Figure 5.2). Ten subjects mentioned six additional nationalities and nine participants did not report their nationality. As already outlined before, an analysis of the qualitative information the subjects had to

Table 5.3.: Age of Subjects

Gender	Number of subjects		Age [years]			
	Abs.	Rel.	M	SD	Min.	Max.
Female	70	53.0%	22.4	1.5	21	28
Male	62	47.0%	22.4	1.2	21	26

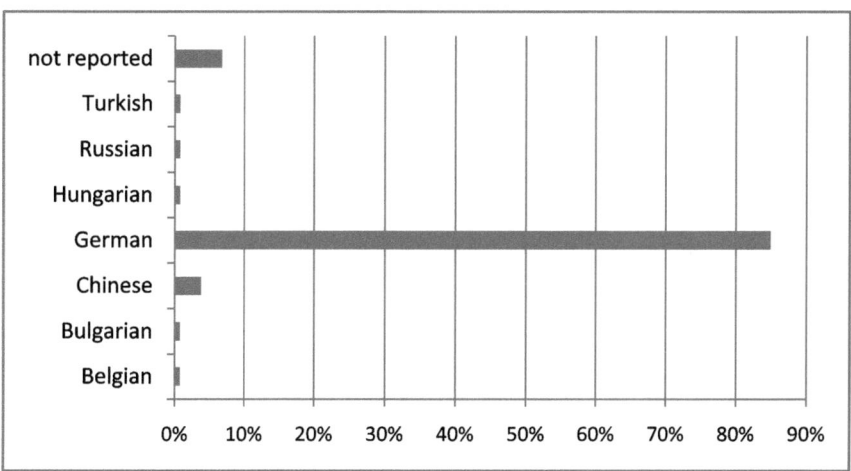

Figure 5.2.: Nationality of Subjects

enter in German language during the experiment suggests that all subjects understood the instructions shown during the experiment. Furthermore, there were no participants complaining about language problems after the experiment.

As a consequence of the fact that the experiment was conducted in a course mainly attended by *Business Administration students*, most subjects (89%) reported to study Business Administration. Seven of the remaining 13 subjects are enrolled in study programs closely related to Business Administration.

5.2.1.2. Information Seeking and Stopping Behavior

On average, subjects needed 16:33 minutes to complete the entire experiment which equals 50% of the time that was needed in the pre-test. The largest amount

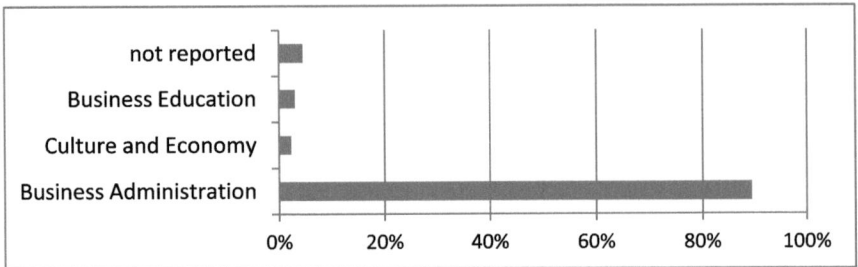

Figure 5.3.: Education Background of Subjects

of time was spent on filling in several questionnaires in the initial and final phase of the experiment and after every information seeking task as well. The seeking tasks themselves were finished in about one minute in case of the low complexity task and about 01:17 minute in case of the high complexity task (see Figure 5.4).

The higher task complexity of task 2 is also reflected by the number of *information chunks that were requested* by the subjects: as described in Section 3.4.1, subjects had to request information in chunks of 150 characters until they felt confident of being able to finish the task. In the complex task, participants requested about ten information chunks on average versus nine in the low complexity task (see Figure 5.5). This observation is in line with the prediction that increased task complexity poses higher demands on the information seeker's information processing capabilities (Speier and Morris, 2003; Todd and Benbasat, 1992).

5.2.1.3. Individual Characteristics

Since the students were assigned to groups in a largely randomized way, probabilistic equivalence of major individual characteristics is assured. In order to further corroborate this assumption, box plots of the three most important individual characteristics were created. Figures 5.6 to 5.8 show the results for *extraversion* scores, *maximizer tendency* scores and *need for cognition* scores calculated as average values of the measurement instruments' item scores. The figures visualize the corresponding median for all eight different experimental conditions listed in Table 5.1. Additionally, the interquartile range is shown comprising 25%

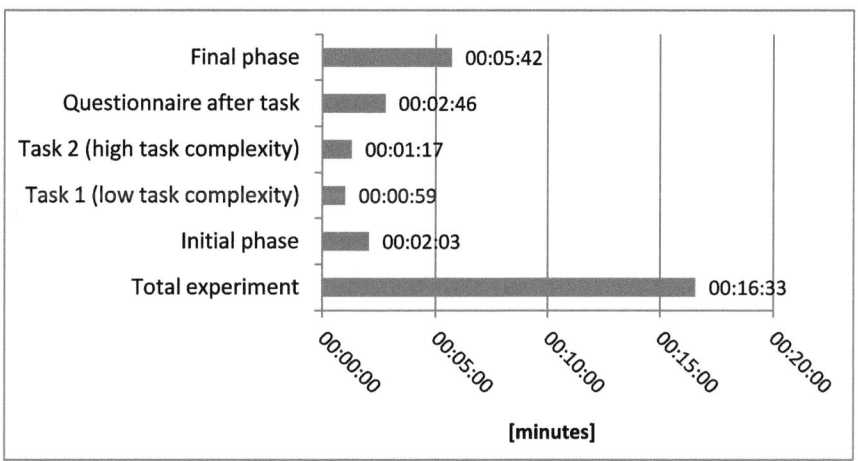

Figure 5.4.: Duration of Experiments and Sub-Tasks

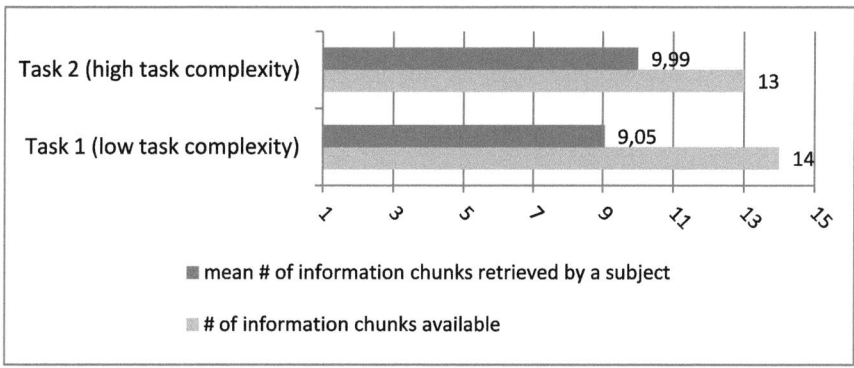

Figure 5.5.: Number of Information Chunks Retrieved by versus Available to a Subject

of values smaller and 25% of values larger than the median. Finally, the figures contain information about the smallest and the largest values observed in the sample symbolized by so-called "whiskers" (outliers are ignored).

The box plots show that the subjects do not differ substantially with respect to maximizer tendency and need for cognition scores among the eight conditions. Compared to the aforementioned scores, the median of extraversion scores fluctuates more intensively among the eight groups. Nevertheless, also with regard to extraversion, there are no obvious patterns indicating that members of the eight conditions substantially differ in their extraversion scores. This observation is also supported by the results of an analysis of variance (ANOVA) testing the null hypothesis of equal means among several groups. Thus, a p-value larger than .05 (rejection of the alternative hypothesis) suggests that the means of several groups do not differ significantly.

Before an ANOVA can be conducted, several assumptions have to be checked (Field, 2009): (1) The observations in the groups that are compared have to be independent, (2) the data has to be normally distributed and (3) the data in the different groups should have similar variances (homogeneity of variance). Conditions (2) and (3) were checked with a Kolmogorov-Smirnov test and a Levene test, respectively. As data were not normally distributed in case of extraversion scores, a non-parametric Kruskal-Wallis test was conducted. For all three variables, the tests returned non-significant results, indicating that the groups do not differ significantly ($F(7, 124) = 0.403$, $p = .899$ for maximizing tendencies, $F(7, 124) = 0.191$, $p = .144$ for need for cognition and $H(7) = 11.363$, $p = .110$ for extraversion).

To summarize the results reported above, participants in the eight experimental conditions did not show significant differences with respect to individual characteristics relevant in the context of this study. Consequently, it can be assumed that probabilistic equivalence among groups is given.

5.2.2. Model Estimation and Evaluation

In Section 3.3.2.2, it was pointed out that a component-based PLS approach is best suited for estimating this study's research model. Subsequently, the results

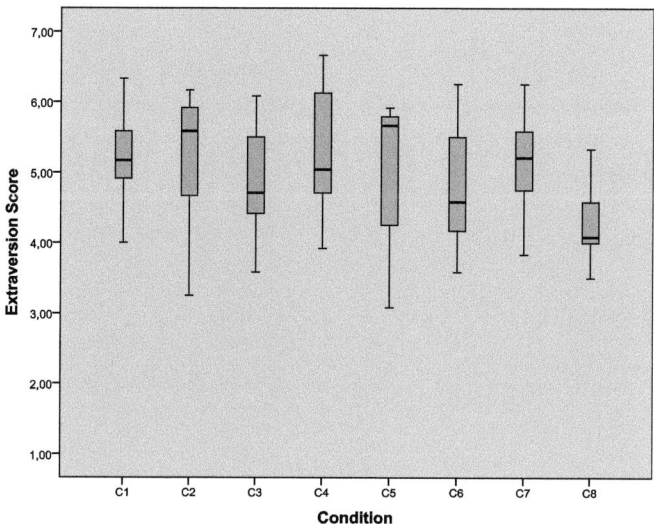

Figure 5.6.: Box plot of *Extraversion Scores* in Eight Experimental Conditions (Median, Interquartile Range, Min. and Max.)

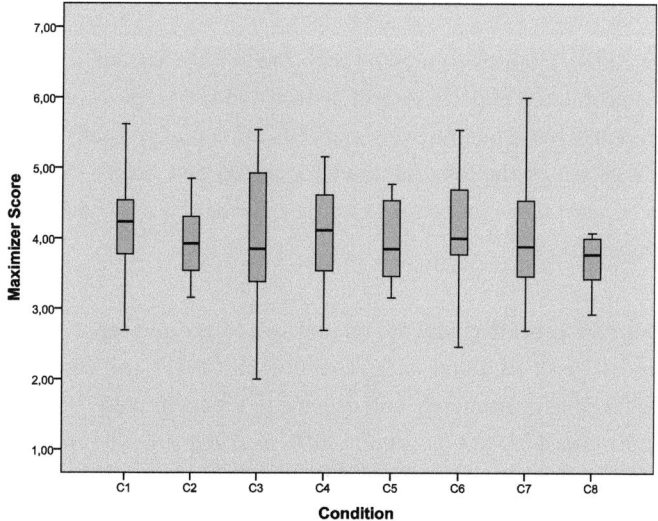

Figure 5.7.: Box plot of *Maximizer Tendency Scores* in Eight Experimental Conditions (Median, Interquartile Range, Min. and Max.)

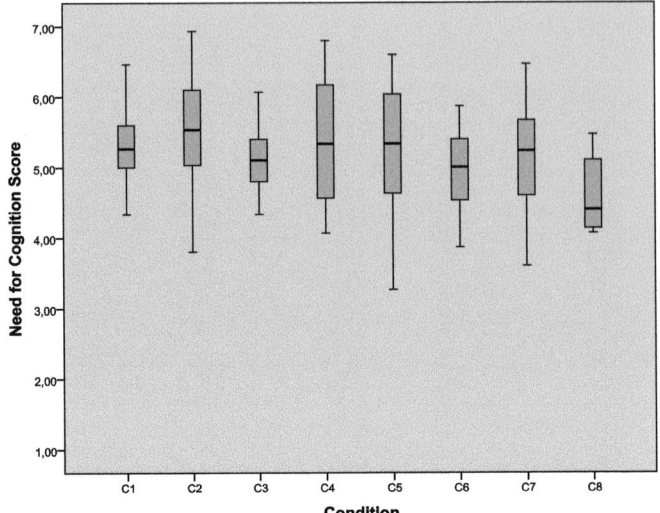

Figure 5.8.: Box plot of *Need for Cognition Scores* in Eight Experimental Conditions (Median, Interquartile Range, Min. and Max.)

of the quantitative analysis conducted with SmartPLS, Version 2.0.M3[1] are presented. The postulated hypotheses will be tested in two steps since the dependent variables were measured qualitatively and thus cannot be processed in SmartPLS. Therefore, a subset of the research model is tested first before the respondents' statements on why they stopped seeking for information are coded and included into the analysis.

Several authors provide guidelines on how to analyze and report data following the component-based PLS approach. Gefen et al. (2011) give condensed recommendations on which parameters and aspects to report in both component-based and covariance-based SEM. Götz et al. (2010) similarly describe steps that should be taken when analyzing data with PLS. As these articles can be regarded as state-of-the-art publications, they are used for structuring the following sections.

---

1 Ringle, C. M.; Wende, S.; Will A. (2005): SmartPLS 2.0 (beta), http://www.smartpls.de.

5.2.2.1. Measurement Model Evaluation

Based on the above-mentioned guidelines by Götz et al. (2010) and Gefen et al. (2011), *indicator reliability, construct reliability, convergent validity, discriminant validity* and *content validity* are reported besides several additional descriptive statistical measures.

Indicator reliability represents the share of an indicator's variance that can be explained by the latent variable it reflects ranging from zero to one. Usually, 50% of the variance should be explained by the latent variable resulting in less than 50% of the variance being caused by measurement error. Consequently, factor loadings of at least 0.7 are recommended by some authors, while others regard 0.6 as a sufficient value (Chin, 1998a) or even suggest to eliminate items only when factor loadings fall below 0.4 (Homburg and Baumgartner, 1998). Since the latent variables' scores are calculated on the basis of linear combinations of their indicators, a weight is attached to every indicator. These weights should be distributed equally over all indicators of a latent variable.

Table 5.4 contains the factor loadings, significance levels (based on bootstrapping with 500 samples), weights, means and standard deviations. In order to make sure that all factor loadings at least exceed a value of 0.6, some indicators with lower loadings had to be deleted sequentially (TC3, SC5 and TE2_2). With regard to well-validated measurement instruments of the constructs *maximizer tendencies, extraversion* and *need for cognition*, several items had to be deleted. Similar findings were reported in past literature on personality measures, e. g. in Matzler et al. (2008). All values shown in Table 5.4 represent the recalculated values after the elimination of items.

Table 5.4.: Indicator Reliability (**** / *** / ** / *: significant at 0.1% / 1% / 5% / 10% level; $p < .001$: $t = 3.107$, $p < .01$: $t = 2.334$, $p < .05$: $t = 1.648$, $p < .1$: $t = 1.283$)

Construct	Indicator	Loading		Weight	M	SD
Extraversion (Ext)	Ex1	0.661	****	0.156		
	Ex2	0.689	****	0.321		
	Ex4	0.668	***	0.081	5.5	1.0
	Ex8	0.874	****	0.367		
	Ex9	0.783	****	0.383		
Gender	Gen	1.000		1.000		
Maximizer tend. (Max)	Max11	0.847	****	0.319	5.5	1.3
	Max12	0.974	****	0.749		
Need for cognition (NFC)	NFC1	0.793	****	0.452		
	NFC2	0.664	****	0.313	5.5	0.9
	NFC5	0.811	****	0.394		
	NFC12	0.629	****	0.182		
Social richness	SR	1.000		1.000		
Source credibility (SC)	SC1	0.710	****	0.348		
	SC2	0.719	****	0.281	4.1	1.1
	SC3	0.808	****	0.321		
	SC4	0.815	****	0.359		
System 1 proc. (Sys1)	Sys1_1	0.869	****	0.427		
	Sys1_2	0.750	****	0.319	4.1	1.3
	Sys1_3	0.923	****	0.423		
System 2 proc. (Sys2)	Sys2_1	0.874	****	0.370		
	Sys2_2	0.929	****	0.360	4.4	1.4
	Sys2_3	0.924	****	0.371		
Task complexity (TC)	TC1	0.740	****	0.348		
	TC2	0.765	****	0.276	3.0	1.2
	TC4	0.849	****	0.626		
Task experience (TE)	TE1_1	0.952	****	0.509		
	TE1_2	0.862	****	0.261		
	TE1_3	0.865	****	0.336	4.1	1.4
	TE2_1	0.733	****	0.224		
	TE2_3	0.984	****	0.850		
Task importance	TI	1.000		1.000		
Task motivation (TM)	TM1	0.897	****	0.498		
	TM2	0.757	****	0.300	3.8	1.3
	TM3	0.843	****	0.387		

In addition to the requirement of sufficient indicator reliabilities, it has to be ensured that all indicators of a latent construct *in combination* properly reflect the latent variable's score. In this context, *Construct reliability* measures "the *internal consistency* of a latent variable, [i. e.] the degree to which several measurement items that reflect it are inter-correlated" (Gefen, 2003, p. 28). *Convergent validity* examines the correlation between "different methods of measuring the same construct" conceptualizing latent variables' reflective indicators as sufficiently different methods (Götz et al., 2010, p. 696). Three metrics are commonly used in extant literature and are both described and reported subsequently: (1) Cronbach's alpha, (2) composite reliability and (3) average variance extracted (Chin, 1998b; Götz et al., 2010). Cronbach's alpha is calculated according to Formula 5.1, while N indicates the number of items, σ_i^2 the variance of item i and σ_t^2 the variance of the sum of item values (Cronbach, 1951, p. 299). Composite reliability and average variance extracted are determined by the Formulas 5.2 and 5.3 (Götz et al., 2010, pp. 694–696, Fornell and Larcker, 1981, pp. 45–46). λ_i represents the factor loading of item i, ϵ_i is defined as the measurement error of item i. All measures usually range between zero and one, while Cronbach's alpha can also result in negative values (in case of negative average covariance among items, Chin 1998b).

$$\text{Cronbach's alpha: } \alpha = \left(\frac{N}{N-1}\right) * \left(1 - \frac{\sum_{i=1}^{N} \sigma_i^2}{\sigma_t^2}\right) \tag{5.1}$$

$$\text{Composite reliability: } \rho = \frac{(\sum_i \lambda_i)^2}{(\sum_i \lambda_i)^2 + \sum_i var(\epsilon_i)} \tag{5.2}$$

$$\text{Average variance extracted: } AVE = \frac{\sum_i \lambda_i^2}{\sum_i \lambda_i^2 + \sum_i var(\epsilon_i)} \tag{5.3}$$

In order to fulfill the construct reliability and convergent validity criteria, literature commonly recommends a Cronbach's alpha of at least 0.7, a composite reliability of at least 0.6 and an average variance extracted of at least 0.5 (Chin, 1998a; Homburg and Baumgartner, 1998). Table 5.5 summarizes the reliability and validity measures for the model constructs and confirms that all results range comfortably above the recommended critical values.

Table 5.5.: Construct Reliability and Convergent Validity

Construct	Cronbach's alpha	Composite reliability	Average variance extracted
Extraversion (Ext)	0.811	0.857	0.547
Gender (Gen)	1.000	1.000	1.000
Maximizer tendency (Max)	0.828	0.909	0.834
Need for cognition (NFC)	0.712	0.817	0.531
Social richness (SR)	1.000	1.000	1.000
Source credibility (SC)	0.762	0.849	0.584
System 1 processing (Sys1)	0.807	0.886	0.723
System 2 processing (Sys2)	0.895	0.935	0.827
Task complexity (TC)	0.727	0.829	0.618
Task experience_1 (TE_1)	0.877	0.923	0.799
Task experience_2 (TE_2)	0.749	0.856	0.752
Task importance (TI)	1.000	1.000	1.000
Task motivation (TM)	0.784	0.872	0.696

Discriminant validity examines if the shared variance between a latent variable and its assigned indicators is larger than the shared variance of these indicators with any other construct in the model, i. e. discriminant validity ensures that the selected indicators measure the constructs they are intended to measure. In PLS, discriminant validity is evaluated by applying the following calculations and tests: (1) The constructs' average variance extracted should be larger than the corresponding construct's squared correlation with any other model construct (Fornell and Larcker, 1981; Gefen and Straub, 2005; Götz et al., 2010). In this case, the ratio of variance explained by the construct's indicators is larger than that explained by other constructs. (2) In a confirmatory factor analysis, the items should load strongly on the constructs they are assigned to and weakly on all other constructs (Chin, 1998b; Gefen and Straub, 2005).

Both tests were conducted on the questionnaire data. Table 5.6 contains the squared correlations between latent variables and the AVEs printed in italic indicating that the AVE is always much higher than the corresponding squared correlations. The confirmatory factor analysis also provides positive results as the item loadings on their underlying constructs are consistently higher than the loadings on any other construct. Consequently, discriminant validity is ensured. Furthermore, as each item loads highest on the construct it is assigned to, the criterion of unidimensionality and thus, *content validity* is fulfilled (Gefen and Straub, 2005).

After the metrics for validating the measurement model's overall quality could be shown to comply with the quality criteria defined in extant literature, the structural model is analyzed next.

5.2.2.2. Structural Model Evaluation

Following the guidelines developed by Götz et al. (2010) and Gefen et al. (2011), the structural model is analyzed in terms of the dependent variables' share of explained variance (R^2), the validity of the proposed hypotheses including an investigation of significance levels and effect sizes (f^2) and an evaluation of the model's predictive power based on the Stone-Geisser test criterion Q^2. In a first step, quantitative questionnaire responses are analyzed with regard to information seeking behavior. In the next Section (5.2.2.3), this perspective is extended by the qualitative data concerning the information seeking stopping behavior exhibited by the experiment participants.

Analysis of the share of explained variance. Compared to covariance-based techniques, in the component-based PLS approach metrics for determining the estimated model parameters' goodness of fit cannot be calculated. Hence, the dependent variables' share of explained variance (R^2) is commonly used as a quality measure of the inner model. As a standardized measure, the values range between zero and one, while higher values of R^2 correspond with higher overall model quality. However, there are no clear recommendations available with regard to acceptable values of R^2, but this level highly depends on the respective study it is calculated for (Chin, 1998b; Götz et al., 2010).

The two dependent variables *System 1 information processing* and *System 2 information processing* achieve estimated R^2 values of 0.257 and 0.497 respectively. Consequently, about 26% of the first dependent variable's variance and approximately 50% of the second variable's variance can be explained by the constructs hypothesized in the research model. Considering the enormous complexity of human information processing on a biological level – i. e. with regard to processes

Table 5.6.: Discriminant Validity: Squared Correlations Between Model Constructs (Average Variance Extracted is Printed in Italic)

	Ext	Gen	Max	NFC	SR	SC	Sys1	Sys2	TC	TE_1	TE_2	TI	TM
Ext	*0.547*												
Gen	0.031	*1.000*											
Max	0.003	0.009	*0.834*										
NFC	0.007	0.008	0.082	*0.531*									
SR	0.000	0.000	0.000	0.000	*1.000*								
SC	0.000	0.007	0.000	0.006	0.075	*0.584*							
Sys1	0.028	0.078	0.009	0.046	0.001	0.001	*0.723*						
Sys2	0.009	0.030	0.000	0.129	0.007	0.012	0.176	*0.827*					
TC	0.029	0.002	0.007	0.019	0.001	0.004	0.073	0.003	*0.618*				
TE_1	0.001	0.261	0.001	0.082	0.000	0.004	0.022	0.051	0.000	*0.799*			
TE_2	0.001	0.095	0.000	0.010	0.000	0.000	0.027	0.087	0.002	0.262	*0.752*		
TI	0.008	0.027	0.001	0.053	0.000	0.003	0.003	0.018	0.000	0.048	0.011	*1.000*	
TM	0.014	0.047	0.000	0.050	0.007	0.021	0.050	0.451	0.003	0.046	0.055	0.027	*0.696*

taking place in the person's brain – and the overall lack of profound knowledge in this field, the R^2 values reported before are highly encouraging when comparing them with the results of similar studies: Johnson (2005) investigates individuals' processing behavior with regard to risk information. Based on extant literature, he identifies several independent variables that potentially influence an individual's propensity to use heuristic as opposed to systematic information processing in the context of risk information. R^2 values between 0.12 and 0.20 are reached (p. 642). Hilbig (2008) analyzes the impact of individual differences, especially *extraversion* on the use of fast-and-frugal decision making heuristics, reporting an R^2 value of 0.14 (p. 1643). In a study by Novak and Hoffman (2009), rational versus experiential thinking styles are conceptualized as independent variables predicting individuals' task performance in standardized rational and experiential tasks. In this case, R^2 values between 0.090 and 0.328 are reported (p. 64). In summary, a lower bound of 0.2 appears to be acceptable for studies explaining systematic versus heuristic information processing behavior or its impact on dependent variables.

Test of hypotheses. The path coefficients calculated by SmartPLS represent β-coefficients of the underlying partial least square algorithm. Path coefficients range between minus one and plus one, have to be significantly different from zero and have to show the proposed sign (+ or –) in order to support the corresponding hypothesis. In this study, the bootstrapping routine as a resampling method is used with a sample size of 500 in order to calculate T statistics and significance levels. Furthermore, effect sizes are calculated to verify that the constructs have a substantial impact on dependent variables, which is indicated by effect sizes that are considerably larger than zero. For this reason, the structural model is calculated both with and without the independent variables being present. Thereafter, Formula 5.4 is used to determine the effect size f^2 (Chin, 1998b; Götz et al., 2010). Consequently, the larger the f^2 value, the more variance of the dependent variable is exclusively explained by the corresponding independent variable and thus, underlines the independent variable's explanatory power.

An overview of the research model's path coefficients and levels of significance is given in Table 5.7 complemented by information about the corresponding effect sizes listed in Table 5.8 and a graphical illustration in Figure 5.9.

$$\text{Effect size: } f^2 = \frac{R_{incl}^2 - R_{excl}^2}{1 - R_{incl}^2} \qquad (5.4)$$

Table 5.7.: Impacts on System 1 and System 2 Information Processing (**** / ***
/ ** / *: significant at 0.1% / 1% / 5% / 10% level; $p < .001$: $t = 3.107$,
$p < .01$: $t = 2.334$, $p < .05$: $t = 1.648$, $p < .1$: $t = 1.283$)

Hypothesis	Relationship	Path co-efficient	T value		Supported
H3 (−)	Sys2 → Sys1	-0.403	7.247	****	yes
H4a* (+)	SR → SC	-0.274	5.109	****	no
H4c (+)	SC → Sys1	0.091	1.472	*	yes
H5 (+)	TE_1 → Sys1	-0.057	0.840	n.s.	no
	TE_2 → Sys1	0.019	0.256	n.s.	no
H6 (+)	TM → Sys2	0.622	15.622	****	yes
H7 (+)	NFC → Sys2	0.221	4.316	****	yes
H8 (+)	TC → Sys1	0.248	4.952	****	yes
H9 (+)	TI → TM	0.165	2.709	***	yes

With regard to *System 1 information processing*, the hypotheses H3, H4c and
H8 are supported. The impact of perceived task complexity and System 2 information processing is highly significant on a $p < .001$ level whereas the impact
of source credibility has to be considered weak based on a small effect size and
a weak significance on a $p < .1$ significance level. The results imply that increased levels of task complexity result in heuristic information processing while
high levels of systematic information seeking attenuate the activity of System 1
information processing.

In terms of *System 2 information processing*, both perceived task motivation
and need for cognition have a significant impact ($p < .001$) on the dependent
variable, thus supporting the hypotheses H6 and H7. Especially a high task
motivation seems to be an important predictor of systematic information seeking. Need for cognition as a rather time-invariant personality predisposition also

Table 5.8.: Effect Sizes of Constructs Influencing Dependent Variables

Construct	R^2 for model including the construct	R^2 for model not including the construct	Effect size f^2
Dependent variable *System 1 information processing*			
Task complexity	0.257	0.196	0.082
Source credibility	0.257	0.249	0.011
System 2 information processing	0.257	0.113	0.194
Dependent variable *System 2 information processing*			
Task motivation	0.497	0.128	0.734
Need for cognition	0.497	0.451	0.092

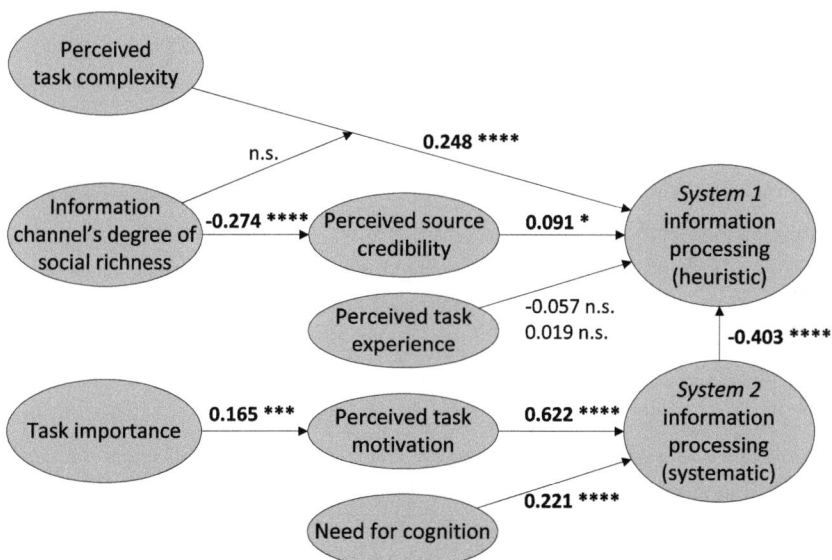

Figure 5.9.: Results of Partial Model (**** / *** / ** / *: significant at 0.1% / 1% / 5% / 10% level; $p < .001$: $t = 3.107$, $p < .01$: $t = 2.334$, $p < .05$: $t = 1.648$, $p < .1$: $t = 1.283$)

strongly activates System 2 information processing, though showing a lower effect size.

The effect of the experimental manipulations was also significant on the .001 and .01 level, thus supporting hypotheses H4a* and H9. As hypothesized, a higher task importance leads to an increased motivation to fulfill the assigned task accurately by processing issue-relevant information in an effortful way. However, in contrast to the assumption that an increase of an information channel's degree of social richness will result in higher perceived source credibility, the corresponding path coefficient is found to be negative. This deviation from theoretical reasoning will be discussed in detail in Chapter 6.

From an experimental perspective, the corresponding path coefficients represent the *main effects* of social richness and task motivation respectively on the specific dependent variables. This means that in the factorial design setting, the values of one variable are consistently larger (or smaller) between the two experimental conditions for all levels of the other variable manipulated in the experiment (Field and Hole, 2003; Trochim and Donnelly, 2008). Figure 5.10 visualizes this situation by indicating that the reported task motivation scores increase when task importance is high – no matter if the social richness condition is present or not (figure on the left). A similar interpretation can be derived from the impact of social richness on source credibility (figure on the right). The main effects were further analyzed via two-way ANOVA confirming the findings reported above with task importance having a significant impact on task motivation ($F(1, 260) = 6.875$, $p = .009$) and social richness having a significant impact on source credibility ($F(1, 260) = 27.017$, $p = .000$). In both cases, interaction effects between the two independent variables could not be observed ($F(1, 260) = 0.185$, $p = .668$ and $F(1, 260) = 0.826$, $p = .364$). Levene tests on homogeneity of variances did not reject the null hypothesis of equal variances. The assumption of normally distributed data was slightly violated in one subgroup according to Shapiro-Wilk tests, skewness however, was smaller than the critical value of 0.5 (Field, 2009; Harwell et al., 1992).

Stone-Geisser test criterion for assessing a model's predictive relevance. The Stone-Geisser test criterion reveals how well the collected data can be predicted based on the model and the parameters calculated by the PLS algorithm (Götz et al., 2010, p. 702). For this reason, SmartPLS' blindfolding method

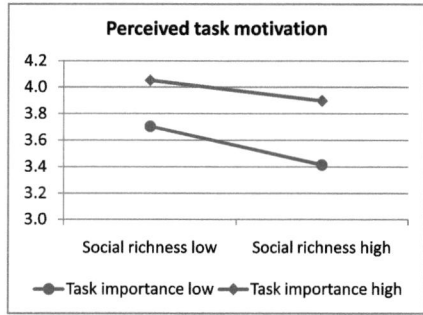 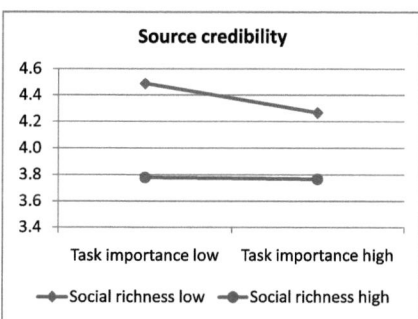

Figure 5.10.: Main and Interaction Effects of Variables Manipulated in the Experiment; Left: Impact of Task Importance on Task Motivation, Right: Impact of Social Richness on Source Credibility

was used with an omission distance (D) of seven. Hence, in seven iterations, all D data points are omitted, i. e. in a matrix of I indicators and C cases, all data points at position one and multiples of D *plus one* are deleted. In the second iteration, the second data point and all multiples of D *plus two* are deleted and so forth. Finally, the Stone-Geisser test criterion is calculated according to Formula 5.5 with SSE_D representing the squared error that results from a prediction of the omitted data points based on the estimated parameters (Henseler et al., 2009, p. 303, Chin 1998a, pp. 317–318, Götz et al. 2010, pp. 702–703). SSO_D indicates the squared error resulting from a comparison of the observed values with a prediction calculated based on the mean of the non-omitted data points ("trivial prediction error", Götz et al. 2010, p. 703).

$$\text{Stone-Geisser: } Q^2 = 1 - \frac{\sum_D SSE_D}{\sum_D SSO_D} \tag{5.5}$$

Q^2 values larger than zero support a model's predictive relevance because in this case, the squared error of the difference between predicted and observed data is smaller than the squared error of the difference between mean and observed data. Q^2 of this study is 0.15 and thus satisfies the aforementioned criterion.

Moderator and control variables. In Section 2.4.1, additional moderator and control hypotheses were defined, which are analyzed next. Basically, there are two different ways of evaluating moderator effects in PLS, namely (1) the calculation of product terms and (2) the assessment of group comparisons. While the former is applicable for continuous variables, the latter is especially used when the moderator variable is categorical (Henseler and Fassott, 2010). As the independent variable *Information channel's degree of social richness* is of categorical origin, the second approach is followed. Therefore, the sample data set is divided into two groups representing the cases in which low levels of social richness were induced and those cases in which high levels of social richness were induced. Second, the research model is estimated in SmartPLS once with the data of each group (bootstrapping with 500 cases) and the results are compared based on Formulas 5.6 and 5.7 (Huber et al., 2007, p. 118).

$$t = \frac{p_1 - p_2}{s\sqrt{\frac{1}{m} + \frac{1}{n}}} \tag{5.6}$$

$$\text{with } s = \sqrt{\frac{(m-1)^2}{(m+n-2)}(\sigma(p_1))^2 + \frac{(n-1)^2}{(m+n-2)}(\sigma(p_2))^2} \tag{5.7}$$

In the above equations, p_1 and p_2 indicate the estimates of the path coefficients in group 1 and group 2. $\sigma(p_1)$ and $\sigma(p_2)$ represent the standard errors in both groups while m and n symbolize the number of observations in group 1 and group 2, respectively. Following this logic, hypothesis H4b assuming a positive impact of social richness on the influence of *task complexity* on System 1 information processing has to be rejected, i. e. a moderator effect could not be found.

The construct *maximizing tendency* does not have a significant impact on System 2 information processing either. However, a post-hoc analysis revealed a significant correlation between maximizing tendency and need for cognition (path coefficient: 0.327, $p < .001$) indicating that seeking a global optimum is not necessarily bound to systematic information seeking but still reflects a person's general intention to embrace cognitively demanding tasks.

As predicted by hypothesis H11, a subject's *extraversion* score has a positive impact on System 1 information processing ($p < .01$). Thus, extraverted persons pay more attention to contextual information without actively investing significant amounts of effort into the underlying seeking activities.

Table 5.9.: Impacts on System 1 and System 2 Information Processing – Moderator and Control Variables (**** / *** / ** / *: significant at 0.1% / 1% / 5% / 10% level; $p < .001$: $t = 3.107$, $p < .01$: $t = 2.334$, $p < .05$: $t = 1.648$, $p < .1$: $t = 1.283$)

Hypothesis	Relationship	Path co-efficient	T value		Supported
H4b (+)	SR → H8	/	0.298	n.s.	no
H10 (+)	Max ↛ Sys2	-0.065	1.266	n.s.	no
H11 (+)	Ext → Sys1	0.145	2.373	***	yes
H12a	Gen → Sys1	0.232	3.624	****	no
H12b	Gen ↛ Sys2	-0.009	0.199	n.s.	yes

With regard to *gender differences*, the results are ambiguous: While gender – as predicted by hypothesis H12b – does not have a significant impact on System 2 information seeking, hypothesis H12a is not supported. On the contrary, female persons show significant overall tendencies to process information heuristically ($p < .001$).

All results concerning the impact of moderator and control variables are summarized in Table 5.9.

5.2.2.3. Analysis of Stopping Behavior

The subjects' information seeking stopping behavior is assessed based on qualitative statements given by the participants immediately after the termination of a seeking activity. In Section 3.5.3, several advantages of this procedure were discussed, such as reduction of common-method bias, reduction of demand effects and the identification of "new" stopping rules.

In order to be able to analyze the subjects' stopping behavior, the textual statements have to be coded and assigned to one of the two categories "Propensity to use rational stopping rules" and "Propensity to use experiential stopping rules". Browne et al. (2007) developed five cognitive stopping rules (see Table 2.2). Two of these rules, namely the *mental list rule* and the *single criterion rule* clearly represent such rules that require the information seeker to actively process information content-wise and to extract issue-relevant information (Nickles et al., 1995). Consequently, these stopping rules can be regarded as rational stopping rules in the sense of the construct definition given in Table 2.5.

Exemplary statements that were coded as rational stopping rules are listed below:

- *"The two most important criteria were mentioned in the text."* (mental list)

- *"Search for key words. As soon as the corresponding information had been retrieved I stopped."* (mental list)

- *"I stopped because the criteria that had to be taken into consideration were fulfilled by the acquired information."* (mental list)

- *"The criterion that was relevant for this task had been mentioned in the text."* (single criterion)

- *"I stopped after the criterion 'video quality' had been mentioned."* (single criterion

All stopping behavior statements in which a clear reasoning referring to issue-relevant information was absent and the subjects stopped seeking for reasons that clearly go beyond the factual content of the acquired information were classified as *experiential stopping rules*. A post-coding analysis of the statements assigned to the aforementioned construct revealed two sub-categories: (1) *Spontaneous stopping*: The subjects reported that they suddenly had the feeling of having obtained a sufficient amount of information. Others stopped because they were overwhelmed by too much information at a specific point of time or they simply lost interest in acquiring additional information. (2) *Dissonance-induced stopping*: Several subjects stopped seeking for information as a spontaneous reaction to the impression they formed concerning the source of information, e. g. based on an accumulation of aspects they either perceived as credible or not suitable in the given context.

Example codings are listed below:

- *"Did not have interest in seeking any more, too much information. Stopped spontaneously."* (Spontaneous stopping)

- *"Spontaneously, based on a gut feeling."* (Spontaneous stopping)

- *"Based on an unspecific feeling."* (Spontaneous stopping)

- *"Because the information represented a very subjective opinion with low credibility."* (Dissonance-induced stopping)

- *"Because many disadvantages were mentioned so that I decided not to continue reading."* (Dissonance-induced stopping)

- *"Information too detailed and from a non-trustworthy source."* (Dissonance-induced stopping)

In accordance with the coding scheme presented above, 119 statements could be assigned either to the rational or to the experiential stopping rule category. Thus, the dependent variables are conceptualized as *binary constructs*, indicating if the subject stopped using a rational or an experiential stopping rule. Since the PLS algorithm implemented in SmartPLS estimates the model parameters in form of linear regressions, dichotomous dependent variables cannot be included into the model (Cleary and Angel, 1984). Therefore, an alternative approach has to be used in order to validate the hypotheses H1 and H2 assuming a positive impact of System 1 information processing on the use of experiential stopping rules and System 2 information processing on rational stopping rules: In a first step, a Mann-Whitney U-test is conducted in order to pre-validate the above-mentioned relationships. Thereafter – following state-of-the-art statistical approaches – a binary logistic regression analysis is performed (Cleary and Angel, 1984; Field, 2009).

A Mann-Whitney U-test is conducted because a parametric t-test cannot be used as – based on a Kolmogorov-Smirnov test – the data violate the normal distribution requirement. Subjects relying on experiential stopping rules show significantly higher scores in System 1 information processing ($Mdn = 5.00$) than subjects using experiential stopping rules ($Mdn = 4.00$), $z = 3.066$, $p = .002$. Conversely, subjects using rational stopping rules report significantly higher System 2 information processing scores ($Mdn = 5.00$) than those applying experiential stopping rules ($Mdn = 4.00$), $z = 2.764$, $p = .006$.

In addition to the Mann-Whitney U-test, the binary logistic regression analysis offers insights into the strength of the relationships underlying the hypotheses H1 and H2. In contrast to linear regression models in which the dependent variable score is predicted as a weighted combination of the independent variables, in logistic regression, the *probability* of a binary outcome is predicted. Hence, the β-coefficients resulting from linear regression models are not directly comparable to the results of a logistic regression. Furthermore, there is no consensus yet with respect to an equivalent to the R^2 parameter used in linear regression models as a model fit parameter. Instead, the so-called *odds ratio, Exp(B)* is used to analyze the strength of relationships. This ratio describes the probability of a positive event (coded as "1") divided by the probability of the negative outcome (coded as "0"). Hence, an odds ratio larger than one represents a positive relationship between an independent and its dependent variable while the opposite is true in case of an odds ratio smaller than one (Cleary and Angel, 1984; Field, 2009; Newbold et al., 2010).

Before a logistic regression can be conducted, it has to be checked if the continuous independent variable is related to the dependent variable in a linear way. For this reason, an interaction term of the independent variable with its log values is regressed against the dependent variables. In both cases, i. e. for System 1 information processing and for System 2 information processing, this requirement is met (non-significant interaction effects with $p = .289$ and $p = .326$).

With respect to the impact of System 1 information processing on the use of experiential stopping rules, the logistic regression analysis resulted in $Exp(B) = 1.575$ (lower and upper boundaries of 95% confidence interval: 1.151 and 2.156), $\chi^2(1) = 8.045$, $p = .005$. Hence, there is a significantly positive impact, supporting hypothesis H1. The odds ratio of 1.575 can be interpreted in the following way: after an increase of the independent variable "System 1 information processing" by one unit, the probability of experiential stopping rule use will be 1.575 times higher than before (Field, 2009, pp. 288–289).

Also hypothesis H2 proposing a positive impact of System 2 information processing on rational stopping rule use is supported. The logistic regression analysis returned $Exp(B) = 1.479$ (lower and upper boundaries of 95% confidence interval: 1.112 and 1.968), $\chi^2(1) = 7.236$, $p = .007$, again suggesting a significantly positive impact of the predictor variable on the dependent variable.

5.3. Summary

In this chapter, the research model developed in Section 2.4.1 was validated based on a laboratory experiment. The major results of the model estimation are summarized in Figure 5.11 comprising all proposed relationships except for control variables, which will be shortly described below before they are discussed in more detail in Chapter 6.

The results strongly support the overall assumption of a combined impact of task, technology and individual characteristics on the way human beings process information and decide to stop information acquisition. Furthermore, the study indicates that in addition to rational stopping rules, which have been well-researched in the past, a significant portion of human behavior in information seeking is impulsive and not grounded in the comprehensive scrutiny of task-relevant information, thus resulting in non-rational, i. e. experiential stopping.

The model suggests that an increase in perceived task motivation and need for cognition positively influences systematic information seeking and rational stopping. On the contrary, perceived task complexity is identified as a main driver of effortless, intuitive information processing and experiential stopping. The attenuation effect of System 2 on System 1 information processing as proposed by Chaiken and Maheswaran (1994) and Evans (2003) is also supported, corroborating existing theories in an IT-related context.

The role of task importance in relation to perceived task motivation could also be demonstrated based on the empirical data. Interestingly, however, the presence of social cues did not have the proposed positive impact on perceived source credibility, but was found to have the opposite effect. This finding is not in line with ex-ante expectations, but might offer new insights into the mechanisms underlying source credibility assessments in online settings.

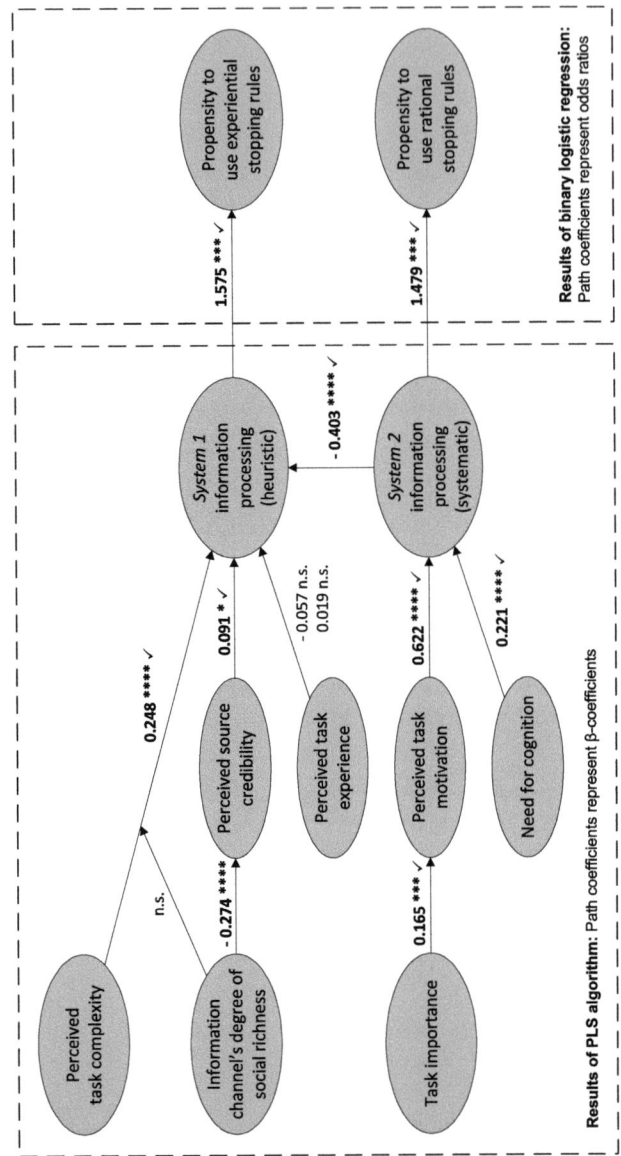

Figure 5.11.: Model Results (**** / *** / ** / *: significant at 0.1% / 1% / 5% / 10% level; $p < .001$: $t = 3.107$, $p < .01$: $t = 2.334$, $p < .05$: $t = 1.648$, $p < .1$: $t = 1.283$, ✓: hypothesis is supported by empirical data)

6. Discussion

The objective of the present study consists in the development and validation of a mid-range theory for explaining and predicting human information seeking and stopping behavior. Thus, it aims at providing insights into the variables influencing the aforementioned behavior and hence answers questions regarding *when* and *why* individuals stop seeking for information. By combining dual-process theories (Cacioppo et al., 1996; Chaiken, 1980; Petty and Cacioppo, 1986), social presence theory (Short et al., 1976; Straub and Karahanna, 1998) and the effort-accuracy framework of cognition (Payne, 1982; Wang and Benbasat, 2009), the study's research model extends existing stopping behavior research by explicitly taking into account that human information seekers do not necessarily process information in a purely rational way. On the contrary, the use of spontaneous, experiential stopping rules is proposed based on research in the field of heuristic choice and decision making (Aschenbrenner et al., 1984; Gigerenzer and Goldstein, 1999; Gigerenzer et al., 1999).

In this chapter, the major results of the laboratory experiment presented in the previous chapter are discussed. Following an interpretation of the empirical data collected in the experiment sessions, the study's theoretical contributions are demonstrated and complemented by managerial implications. Finally, the specific limitations of this research project are described, before opportunities for future research are outlined.

6.1. Interpretation of Results

The results of the empirical investigation strongly support the existence of two fundamentally different categories of reasons why humans stop seeking for information in online settings: Whereas one group of experiment participants clearly described specific pieces of information they were looking for before terminating the information acquisition (*rational stopping*), another group of people did not follow a dedicated strategy but stopped seeking for information spontaneously (*experiential stopping*). In both cases, the stopping behavior was preceded by a specific information processing style suggesting that systematic information processing primarily results in rule-based stopping, whereas heuristic information processing primarily results in spontaneous stopping. Consequently, the study extends the scope of traditional dual-process theories by showing that these theories cannot only be used to predict information processing activities, but also help to explain stopping behavior which is closely tied to the information processing phase. The findings indicate that information seekers do not necessarily define a stopping rule ex ante, i. e. before they start seeking for information, but their behavior can be strongly influenced and shaped by the *process of acquiring information*. Thus, the study adds to the discussion about the direction of causality in stopping behavior research (Browne et al., 2007) by asserting that the selection of a specific stopping rule *before* the start of the information seeking process is not a mandatory step in information seeking tasks. Rather, especially in cases in which the information seeker processes information holistically (System 1 information processing), the stopping behavior evolves from the information seeking context.

Furthermore, another effect proposed by dual-process theories could be confirmed by the empirical results: High levels of System 2 information processing resulted in a decrease of System 1 information processing, hence *attenuating automatic, intuitive information processing*. Nevertheless, the subjects did not report to rely on System 1 information processing exclusively, but their behavior was governed by the concurrent activation of both processing modes, which is in line with recent results on the parallelism of cognitive processes (Evans, 2003; Lieberman, 2003; Novak and Hoffman, 2009).

With regard to the determinants of information seeking and stopping behavior, it can be stated that the majority of hypotheses deduced in Section 2.4.1 was supported by the empirical results. *Perceived task complexity* had a significantly positive impact on System 1 information processing, thus supporting the assumption of the effort-accuracy framework of cognition asserting that human problem-solvers constantly try to minimize the cognitive effort they experience when solving a task (Payne, 1982). This effect could also be observed in the pre-study using heart rate variability measurement: Subjects solving complex tasks showed significantly higher mental stress levels at the beginning compared to the end of the task, thus adding to the assumption that in high task complexity scenarios, subjects refrain from scrutinizing all available information but switch to an information processing mode in which they are guided by impressions and past experiences and which is less effortful to perform.

Perceived source credibility also had the predicted positive impact on System 1 information processing indicating that source credibility indeed serves as a trigger for trusting the provided information without processing it systematically and in detail (Bhattacherjee and Sanford, 2006; Sussman and Siegal, 2003). However, the rather weak path coefficient and significance level underline that source credibility only had a minor effect on information processing. This might be due to experimental conditions as source credibility levels were only indirectly manipulated via the information channel's *degree of social richness*. In the high social richness treatment condition, subjects received additional contextual information about the person who was said to have provided the corresponding information. Since the subjects did not know these persons, their perception of source credibility might be biased and result in less variance on part of the perceived source credibility construct.

Surprisingly, however, the presence of social cues did not lead to an increase in source credibility and trust as assumed by social presence theory, but the opposite effect was observed. That is, even though the factual information provided to the subjects in the high versus low social richness treatment groups was identical, subjects getting *additional* positive contextual cues reported lower source credibility levels than those receiving the same information *without* these contextual information about the information source. This finding is counter-intuitive and represents an *information pathology* which will be discussed in more detail in Section 6.2. Nevertheless, the impact of social richness on source credibility was significant indicating that social cues were processed by the subjects either consciously or subconsciously. This is an important finding because in the pre-test phase, many participants reported that the presence of social cues did not have any impact on their behavior. This self-perception is clearly negated by the experiment data.

The non-significant relationship between *perceived task experience* and System 1 information processing is not in line with existing dual-process research since the latter suggests that people experienced in a specific field can easily access this knowledge when solving similar tasks in the future (Lieberman, 2000; Smith and DeCoster, 2000). A possible explanation for this hypothesis not being supported by the empirical data might be the observation that experience can also result in seeking for information in a goal-directed way because the person knows how to disseminate the problem (Browne et al., 2007). Thus, additional mechanisms seem to influence the impact of task experience on information processing leading to different outcomes that should be investigated in future research projects.

With regard to System 2 information processing, *perceived task motivation*, i. e. the subject's willingness to perform well in a task, could be identified as the main driver. In terms of the effort-accuracy framework of cognition, this finding suggests that people are willing to invest cognitive effort especially when their major objective consists in increasing the accuracy and quality of the task outcome, e. g. a decision they have to make (Wang and Benbasat, 2009). Furthermore, during the experiments, it was possible to influence the perceived task motivation indirectly by manipulating the *task's importance*. The latter was basically achieved by variations in the formulation of task descriptions. Since the subjects did not receive any immediate benefits from taking part in the experiment, this effect was primarily due to increased levels in intrinsic motivation.

Extrinsic motivators such as financial benefits might have an even stronger impact on the subjects' motivation to perform well. Thus, it could be shown that a person's use of systematic information processing strategies can be stimulated actively and that by doing so, the use of heuristics is suppressed. This is an important finding since System 1 information processing, i. e. the use of cognitive shortcuts (heuristics), can also result in good solutions without time-consuming argument scrutiny (Kahneman, 2003; Novak and Hoffman, 2009). From an organizational perspective, suppressing the use of such heuristics by introducing extrinsic motivators would have negative consequences as it would lead to a reduced overall efficiency.

The fact that people reporting high *need for cognition* levels processed information more systematically is in line with past research in the field of dual-process theories (Petty and Cacioppo, 1986; Thompson et al., 1993). Consequently, people high in need for cognition also show a tendency to use rational instead of experiential stopping rules in information seeking tasks. From an IS perspective, this finding is highly important as need for cognition represents a rather stable personality predisposition. Such predispositions, however, did not receive substantial attention in past research even though they obviously have a significant impact on human behavior (Huber, 1984). Information technology taking these differences with regard to its users' personality profiles into account has the potential to efficiently support or to actively influence behavior and will be discussed in more detail in Section 6.5.

6.2. Theoretical Contributions

As outlined in Chapter 2, research on the relationship between human beings and the entity *information* in computer-based scenarios is largely fragmented. Against this background, the study at hand integrates several theoretical lenses to explain and predict human information seeking stopping behavior by assuming that people do not act in a purely rational way when acquiring information. Thus, it extends and complements existing research and provides several theoretical contributions that are elaborated in the following sections.

Providing a richer understanding of the mechanisms influencing information seeking and stopping behavior from a human task technology fit perspective. The quantity of information made accessible via modern technologies such as the Internet and mobile devices significantly exceeds any human information processing capabilities. Hence, the question of *why and when people stop seeking for information* becomes increasingly important in order to satisfy information needs in an adequate way (Browne and Parsons, 2012; Browne et al., 2007; Davern et al., 2012b). Several decades of research in the information seeking and decision making domain were dominated by the assumption of persons acting rationally when solving problems. Additionally, a large share of publications concentrated on the mathematic-axiomatic deduction of optimal, i. e. normative stopping rules (Connolly and Gilani, 1982; Connolly and Thorn, 1987; Klein and Ford, 2003; Kogut, 1990; Spetzler and Stael Von Holstein, 1975; Stigler, 1961).

This study extends the extant view by integrating an idea originally proposed in the context of choice problem research: Many information seekers do not follow a precise plan prescribing how to seek for information in a computer-based system, but are *guided by intuition and subtle past experiences* (Gigerenzer et al., 1999; Hausmann and Lage, 2008; Metzger et al., 2010). Consequently, when being asked for the reasons why they stopped seeking for information, they are not able to argue in terms of issue-relevant information they just acquired, but admit to have stopped spontaneously, e. g. based on diffuse gut feelings. Identifying determinants influencing the information seeking and stopping behavior of IS users represents the core of this study. To accomplish this goal, stopping behavior is assumed to be strongly tied to information seeking behavior. By introducing dual-process theories differentiating between effortless, automatic information processing on the one hand and effortful, systematic information processing on the other hand, a well-established and validated theoretical framework is transferred to the IS domain (Chaiken, 1980; Epstein, 1994; Evans and Chi, 2008). The results indicate that the aforementioned theory represents an adequate means for examining the duality underlying information seeking and stopping behavior in online scenarios.

However, dual-process theories do not make specific assumptions about *technological artifacts* providing information to its users or *organizational tasks* underlying the observed information acquisition patterns. Consequently, this study is among the first to combine the basic idea of dual-process theories with the *impact of technology characteristics and characteristics of an organizational task* resulting in a human task technology fit (HTTF) model. Thus, a further major contribution is made by developing a *novel nomological network* predicting the interplay between task, technology and the individual with regard to the combined effect on information seeking and stopping behavior.

The holistic evaluation of these major contingency factors in *one model* can only be realized by extending the study's theory base by integrating the social presence theory (Short et al., 1976; Straub and Karahanna, 1998) and the effort-accuracy framework of cognition (Payne, 1982; Wang and Benbasat, 2009). For the first time, it is now possible to quantify the strength by which predictor variables originating from three different categories influence information processing and stopping modes. It becomes clear, that the task and technology characteristics analyzed in this study, have a dominant impact on System 1 information processing and experiential stopping, whereas individual characteristics predominantly influence System 2 information processing and rational stopping. This finding is especially important considering that individual characteristics have not received much attention in the IS domain after Huber (1983) reported the absence of a significant effect of individual differences in cognitive style on MIS success (Davern et al., 2012a). In summary, this study both significantly enhances extant knowledge regarding two fundamentally different types of information seeking stopping behavior and provides comprehensive insights into its determinants. By taking a HTTF perspective and introducing new causal relationships such as the impact of task complexity or social cues on System 1 information processing, it is now possible to predict, which combinations of task, technology and individual characteristics will result in an experiential versus a rational termination of information seeking activities (Whetten, 1989). Thus, the study bridges a highly relevant gap between past rational choice research and research in the field of fast and frugal heuristics eventually resulting in the design of information systems that reflect the reciprocal interdependencies between organizational tasks, information technology and the users of this technology. Only by considering variables originating from the three aforementioned dimensions in one research model, the complex interaction between individuals and the entity information can be addressed adequately.

Furthermore, the study informs two additional IS research streams, namely *cognitive fit theory* (Vessey and Galletta, 1991) and research in the field of the *actual use of information systems* (Burton-Jones and Straub, 2006). The former concentrates on the match between the internal (cognitive) and the external representation of a problem and claims that problem-solving performance increases when internal and external representation are congruent. The present study extends this view by differentiating between two fundamentally different information processing modes. In terms of the *cognitive fit concept*, the results suggest that – in order to realize the aforementioned congruency – detailed information should be presented in a structured way if the IS user is highly motivated and has a high need for cognition. Symbolic representations might be preferable if task complexity increases and holistic information processing is dominant.

Research in the field of *actual system use* focuses on the extent by which information and information technology is utilized by individual users to solve given tasks. Information seeking stopping behavior has not been analyzed in past studies on system use. This study's findings on experiential stopping behavior provide valuable insights into the determinants of the spontaneous termination of information seeking activities in computer-mediated contexts. Thus, the understanding of system use is improved with regard to the intensity by which the provided information is evaluated on a cognitive level.

New insights into the direction of causality in information seeking stopping behavior. In their article on information search in online tasks, Browne et al. (2007) raise the question if the selection of a specific search strategy determines the use of related stopping rules or vice versa. The results of the study at hand clearly speak in favor of the assumption that the information processing mode influences the decision when and based on which criteria an information acquisition process should be terminated, i. e. the search strategy significantly influences the stopping behavior.

Two reasons support this interpretation: (1) The presence of social cues had a significant effect on the evaluation of a source's credibility and subsequently on the activation of System 1 information processing. Source credibility assessments, however, cannot be made *before* the search process is initiated (Metzger et al., 2010). (2) The results of the heart rate variability measurements revealed that in complex tasks, subjects show high cognitive loads at the beginning and low stress levels before they terminate the seeking activity which is in line with predictions about adaptive decision makers (Payne, 1982; Payne et al., 1993). That is, information seekers regularly switch between effortful and effortless information processing modes as soon as they realize that a specific task exceeds their cognitive capacities. Accordingly, a priori selected stopping rules are potentially "overridden" in the process of acquiring information, e. g. in order to be able to cope with a high information load.

Hence, this study refines extant research on information seeking stopping behavior in the IS discipline by not only focusing on the stopping behavior itself, but also taking upstream cognitive processes into account. Thus, an important theoretical contribution consists in the observation that information seeking and stopping behavior is not predetermined and static. On the contrary, it changes dynamically depending on characteristics of the task environment such as properties of the technological artifacts used by the information seeker for acquiring information.

Identification of information pathologies. As mentioned earlier, this research extends the body of knowledge concerning *information pathologies*. Information pathologies represent inadequacies and deficiencies in the production, transmission, acquisition and use of information and have a significant impact on individual and organizational performance (Scholl, 1999; Wilensky, 1967). Literature distinguishes between two major antecedents of information pathologies: on the one hand, power exerted by influential persons in organizations is believed to restrict the amount and the quality of information produced and distributed within a company. On the other hand, limitations regarding the information receivers' cognitive capacities (Kahneman et al., 1982; Simon, 1982) result in sub-optimal information acquisition and processing strategies and related phenomena such as information overload (Eppler and Mengis, 2004) or the use of over-simplified heuristics (Scholl, 1999).

This study's empirical results provide evidence for a *technology-induced information pathology* that was not predicted by extant research on para-social presence. Recent derivatives of social presence theory assume a positive link between perceived social presence of a web site and the degree of trust visitors experience (Cyr et al., 2009; Fogg, 2003; Gefen and Straub, 2004). Surprisingly, however, in the information seeking tasks of this study, *the presence of social cues had a negative effect on perceived source credibility.* That is, if the subjects received factual information that was enriched by information about the person who "produced" the content they read and a positive group judgment of the information quality was present, information seekers reported *low* levels of source credibility. If the *identical factual information* was presented to members of the control group, who did *neither* receive additional information about the information source nor any group judgments of information quality, *higher* source credibility levels were reported.

A possible explanation for this phenomenon is the fact that information seekers regularly judge single opinions by individual social actors as fake testimonials (Metzger et al., 2010), resulting in lower source credibility assessments as reported in this study. However, if the identical information is provided without social cues and without additional positive contextual information, there is no reason to believe that the information seeker would rate its source more credible as he *did not obtain any hints* about the source's credibility. Hence, the fact that subjects reported higher source credibility values when *additional positive* social cues were absent, must be regarded as dysfunctional, because it indicates a highly unreflected assessment of information that *appears* to have been provided by an official source as opposed to an individual actor.

As these surprising findings are in contrast with recent social presence research, they should foster the critical discourse about potentially detrimental effects of a web site's perceived social presence on information seeking and stopping behavior. Consequently, this study is among the first falsifying the prevailing assumption that social presence *in general* has a positive effect on user satisfaction and the users' judgment of source credibility and web site trustworthiness. This finding is particularly important as in recent years, the number of interactive web sites conveying the impression of a personal interaction with other persons has increased substantially (Bawden and Robinson, 2009; Mudambi and Schuff, 2010). However, without having a clear understanding of the contingencies influencing technology-induced source credibility assessments, a goal-directed support of information search activities and organizational decision making heavily relying on information search is difficult to realize (Metzger et al., 2010).

Figure 6.1 summarizes the above discussion in a simplified format and adds to the literature on social information processing by assuming that source credibility is not higher *in general* if social cues are present in online media, but only if a sufficient number of convincing testimonials is present – an effect which has been called "social information pooling" in past research (Metzger et al., 2010, p. 420). Consequently, websites containing social cues activate source credibility assessment patterns that are largely ignored if contextual information is not available. In the latter case, i. e. in the absence of social cues, subjects pathologically show a higher propensity to accept message content without critically calling it into question if the number of testimonials is low.

The analysis of the empirical data collected during the experiments resulted in a *second observation* that can be interpreted as an information pathology under specific conditions: As predicted by dual-process theories, *higher task importance positively influences perceived task motivation* and finally the propensity to pursue systematic information seeking (Bhattacherjee and Sanford, 2006; Chaiken, 1980). At the same time, a person's willingness to engage in heuristic information processing is reduced significantly. Hence, it can be summarized that an

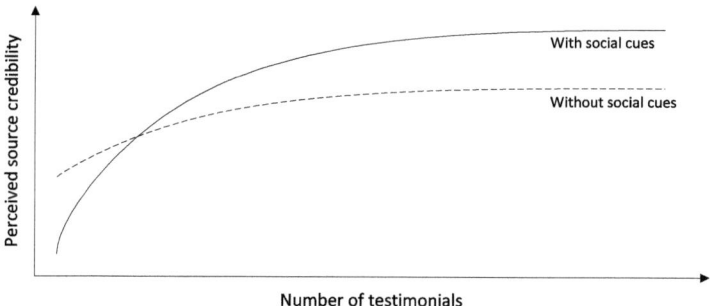

Figure 6.1.: Assumed Impact of the Number of Testimonials on Perceived Source Credibility (based on Metzger et al., 2010)

external increase of task importance both on an extrinsic and an intrinsic level enforces System 2 information processing at the expense of System 1 information processing. However, this phenomenon can have an adverse effect on a person's performance in terms of his operational efficiency. This is the case when a person, highly experienced in a specific domain, is given incentives to scrutinize information even though – due to past experience – a highly accurate solution could also be found based on intuition (Kahneman, 2003; Novak and Hoffman, 2009).

In this context, the study adds to extant knowledge by not only confirming existing assumptions about the effect of external motivators but also providing insights into micro-level cognitive processes that mediate the effect of task importance on stopping behavior. Hence, this study might serve as a theoretical blueprint for future investigations into the impact of organizational incentives on knowledge worker productivity by analyzing dysfunctional patterns of human information behavior.

Assessment of the research model's increase in explanatory power resulting from the use of a triangulation approach. A further major contribution of this study consists in the novel research design which integrates several research methods in a staged process. The combination of quantitative and qualitative research methods in one study provides alternative explanations that would otherwise remain undetected such as the mediated impact of social cues on System 1 information processing which has been identified based on qualitative data and which has later been supported by a quantitative analysis. Furthermore, undesired effects such as common-method bias and demand effects are reduced. Consequently, by adopting a triangulation approach, it is possible to extend existing knowledge with regard to information processing and stopping on the one hand and to explain and predict the interplay of technology, task and individual characteristics on the other hand. Thus, new insights into the duality of information seeking and stopping behavior in computer-mediated contexts could be obtained that have not been reported in past, traditional research relying on single data collection methods.

Especially heart rate variability measurements as an instance of psychophysiological approaches have rarely been used in past IS research. Thus, the study also adds to a rather new sub-discipline called "NeuroIS" (Dimoka et al., 2011; Riedl et al., 2010a) which aims at employing both neuroimaging tools such as fMRI and Electroencephalography (EEG) and psychophysiological tools such as ECG or Galvanic Skin Response (GSR). Dimoka et al. (2011) describe "seven opportunities that IS researchers can use to inform IS phenomena" (p. 687). Two of these opportunities, namely "capturing hidden mental processes" and "complementing existing sources of IS data with brain data" (Dimoka et al., 2011, p. 687) are particularly pursued in this study, hence increasing the research model's explanatory power as specific effects could not have been measured with traditional approaches such as questionnaires or interviews.

With regard to the first opportunity mentioned above, it was possible to get deeper insights into hidden mental processes guiding information seeking activities. By analyzing real-time HRV data captured in fine granularity during the information seeking tasks, the prediction by Payne (1982) could be confirmed assuming that people try to reduce mental load when being exposed to complex tasks. Whereas a post-hoc questionnaire on information seeking is able to capture behavioral drivers at *one* point in time, HRV makes this behavior more transparent and also helps in identifying stimuli triggering a change in behavioral outcomes.

An even more important contribution was made with regard to the second opportunity concerning the *extension of traditional data collection methods*. In this context, it could be shown that psychophysiological data can support the design of tasks in experimental settings by identifying significant differences with respect to parasympathetic activation when solving various kinds of tasks. Thus, it was possible to select two experimental tasks that did not only differ with respect to *perceived*, i. e. self-reported task complexity, but also in terms of uncontrollable and immediate body reactions. Consequently, a more accurate empirical evaluation of the research model could be conducted in the main study phase by ensuring sufficient degrees of variation in the *perceived task complexity* construct.

Integration of fragmented IS research on human information behavior with the objective of demonstrating the necessity of a cumulative research trajectory in HCIB. In addition to the specific contributions with regard to information seeking stopping behavior, this study also adds to the creation of a cumulative research trajectory in human computer-based information behavior. A comprehensive literature review and categorization of IS articles on HCIB in Chapter 2 revealed a substantial fragmentation of extant research. IS articles dealing with HCIB-related topics regularly focus on isolated steps in the computer-mediated information acquisition process and do not integrate strong cross-references to similar articles that had been published in IS outlets before.

This development is astonishing as research on the relationship between human information seekers and the entity information in computer-mediated contexts should be one of the IS discipline's cores. Only by having a clear understanding of evolutionary-shaped behavioral patterns individuals show when interacting with information and information technology, the IS discipline can give well-informed recommendations on how to design technological artifacts that efficiently and effectively support its users in solving organizational tasks. Hence, by categorizing existing IS research along a cyclical model of human computer-based information behavior in Figure 2.1, it becomes obvious that information acquisition is a complex process that can not be investigated in one isolated research project, but requires the combined effort of many researchers. Consequently, another important contribution consists in the identification of a highly relevant research trajectory that had not been investigated coherently in past IS research. Derived contributions that go beyond the scope of the IS domain are illustrated in the next section.

Creation of inter-textual coherence. The IS discipline commonly borrows knowledge from adjacent domains, thus necessarily acting as a boundary spanner with the objective of creating new knowledge. Since a *native IS theory* on human information behavior does not exist yet (Hemmer and Heinzl, 2011; Straub, 2012), another contribution of this study consists in the development of a *multi-theoretical research model* integrating several research streams that are commonly not cited together, hence yielding inter-textual coherence (Locke and Golden-Biddle, 1997).

Consequently, the corresponding reference theories are validated and corroborated by showing their overall applicability in new contexts. From a philosophy of science perspective, this approach *strengthens the underlying theories* as long as they resist falsification attempts (Chalmers, 1999). With regard to *dual-process theories* and the *effort-accuracy framework of cognition*, key assumptions could be confirmed not only by applying traditional data collection approaches but also by relying on novel methods such as heart rate variability measurement (Berntson et al., 1997).

Furthermore, early versions of dual-process and social presence theories were developed long *before* most of today's modern information technologies were available. Therefore, it is encouraging to realize that the theories also hold in modern settings that reflect the today's situation better with regard to the availability of complex information technology.

To summarize, the findings represent an important theory feedback into the field of psychology and *bridge the gap* between this discipline and research in the IS domain by stressing the interdependencies between individual characteristics on the one hand and technology and task characteristics on the other hand.

6.3. Managerial and Practical Implications

From a practical perspective, this study makes several contributions for various stakeholders within organizations and among information technology end-users. These implications are described and discussed next.

Implications for managers and system designers. Computer-based information search is a core activity in the daily working life of persons on any hierarchy level in modern organizations. As the amount of information accessible for every user increases constantly, it is crucial to understand the mechanisms that influence information processing and the decision to stop acquiring information (Browne et al., 2007). On a more general level, the *information processing capacity of a firm* is still restricted by the bounded rationality of its individual employees as information technology is intended to serve its users and should not be regarded as an end in itself (Sviokla, 1989).

Especially *managers* being responsible for the portfolio of software applications that are accessible for the employees of their company should be well-aware of the impacts these technologies have on human information behavior. Applications like social search, microblogging and social networks have been shown to have many positive impacts on employee satisfaction and productivity (Andriole, 2010; Morris et al., 2010). The results of this study, however, also suggest that a higher density of social cues in the set of information a person acquires can evoke distrust and finally result in *ignoring and avoiding information* that might be nevertheless important. Hence, in scenarios in which it is important that employees scrutinize information and make informed decisions, software applications that make cautious use of social cues should be used.

Apart from technology characteristics, managers should also be aware of the effect *reward systems* implemented in a company have on the information processing behavior of their employees. This study indicates that extrinsic and intrinsic motivators strongly activate systematic information processing and attenuate the use of heuristics. Consequently, in scenarios in which it is desirable that employees act intuitively and do not invest too much time into information acquisition, information should be presented in such a way that it is not immediately amenable to systematic processing, e. g. by using continuous text instead of tables with catchwords.

Designers of modern information technology should be especially aware of the fact that they develop software for a wide range of users that potentially differ significantly in various individual characteristics. *Need for cognition* was identified as an important individual characteristic in this study positively influencing System 2 information processing (Cacioppo et al., 1996). However, there are also *situation-specific differences* that might have an impact on information behavior. For example, a person's emotional arousal can have negative effects on an information seeker's behavior and performance. Already today, there are devices that warn a stock broker, for example if he is in an emotional state which does not allow him to make wise decisions[1].

Software designers should think about ways how to sense a user's information processing mode and react in real-time in terms of adaptive user interfaces that for example vary the degree of social richness a web site conveys to a user or remind the user of the current task's importance in order to activate systematic information processing. Furthermore, the perceived task complexity could be reduced in real-time by providing various different modes of information presentation (text, table or graphics) that help the user to reduce his cognitive workload and concentrate on issue-relevant information (Hong et al., 2004b; Vessey and Galletta, 1991).

Implications for operators of e-commerce web sites. In the context of e-commerce web sites, impulsive buying behavior is desirable in many scenarios. Hence, for operators of e-commerce platforms, it is important to understand how they can *influence the customers' information seeking and especially their stopping behavior* in such a way that the search finally results in buying goods. The results of this study show that providing information that is not available in a highly structured format evokes heuristic information processing. However, the availability of social cues did not have the expected positive impact on System 1 information processing. Hence, convincing information produced by other users of the platform should be combined with such sources of information that convey the impression to originate from a trusted and independent third party.

Furthermore, the in-depth analysis of buying behavior based on log files might allow for the identification of customers' basic information seeking and stopping behavior. This knowledge could be used to adapt the user interface dynamically in future transactions. For example, users who regularly scrutinized large amounts of information before making a buying decision in the past could be exposed to a user-interface which satisfies the need for systematic information processing but additionally contains credible heuristic cues. Thus, the attenuating effect of System 2 on System 1 information processing could be reduced, hence increasing the chance for experiential information seeking stopping behavior.

---

1 c. f. for example the *"Rationalizer"* project on http://www.design.philips.com

Implications for educational institutions. The importance of information technology both in young people's working and private life is growing constantly. Hence, these persons have to develop skills supporting them in making efficient and effective use of the large amount of information they have to process regularly. The results of this study point out that people might have problems judging the credibility and trustworthiness of information correctly, depending on contextual information they get about the information source.

Particularly the fact that many subjects trusted anonymous sources they did not get any information about should be reflected critically by educational institutions and should result in adaptations of the way competencies in the field of information technology are taught to young persons. Fundamental education in the field of information technology should not be restricted to the design and operational use of those systems, but should also focus on the *entity information*. In this study, two dimensions of the entity information were considered: (1) The *quantity of information* available via the Internet exceeds human information processing capacities and results in coping strategies such as ignoring huge portions of the available information. Even though this strategy can lead to beneficial outcomes (Novak and Hoffman, 2009), information seekers have to develop an idea about when this approach is applicable and how the relevant pieces of information – which should not be ignored – can be identified. (2) The *quality of information* accessible via the Internet is difficult to judge. The study revealed that simple contextual cues can bias the recipients' perception of a source's credibility and thus can also bias the assessment of the information's overall quality. The fact that the Internet is an open medium everybody can easily contribute to, bears the risk of goal-directed manipulations that remain undetected if the users are not sensitized to potential sources of fraud.

A third dimension that was not discussed in this study but should also be considered by educational institutions is the *high degree of accessibility of information* via modern mobile technologies such as smartphones. These devices might change the way information is produced in terms of compressing information so that it fits the small screens and quickly attracts the users' attention as these devices often compete with secondary tasks.

To summarize, modern information technology has the potential to provide information more effectively and increase information processing efficiency. However, information technology might also produce new information pathologies that have a detrimental effect on overall task performance. Education systems should counteract these negative effects and teach people in all age groups how to cope with high information load, how to assess information quality and how to deal with the fact that information is ubiquitously available via mobile technology.

6.4. Limitations

The research at hand has several limitations that are worth noting and should be taken into consideration when interpreting the results and drawing conclusions.

Following the reasoning in Section 3.2, a *laboratory experiment* design was considered an appropriate *research methodology* for answering the study's research questions. However, as shown by Bonoma (1985), every research methodology has the potential to fulfill a different degree of internal and external validity while both dimensions cannot be optimized at the same time. In laboratory experiment designs, internal validity is high as the factors influencing the experimental setting can be controlled. External validity, though, is rather low because subjects might behave differently in non-artificial settings. In order to increase external validity, the experimental tasks were designed in a way that they are close to every-day problems in organizational scenarios and the information accessible for the subjects was taken from actual web applications, i. e. it was not developed artificially. Nevertheless, subjects did not have the chance to use a wide range of traditional information channels such as search engines or company web sites they would probably have used under real-life conditions. Hence, the results of this study give insights into information seeking and stopping behavior on a micro level, not taking the users' selection of different information channels into account holistically.

Even though the experiment in this study was designed rigorously, some trade-off decisions had to be made. For example, in order not to stretch the processing time beyond an acceptable level of about 15-20 minutes, only two tasks could be solved by every subject. Hence, the *task type* – information seeking in a hypothetical organizational context – could not be varied. Consequently, this construct might also have an impact on information processing and stopping behavior that was not captured by the research model (Byström and Järvelin, 1995), e. g. information seeking and stopping behavior in hedonic contexts when seeking information about a new movie might follow a different logic (van der Heijden, 2004). Another *threat to the generalizability* of the findings consists in the fact that all participants of the study are in a similar age group and have a similar education background. These research boundaries (Weber, 2012), i. e. excluding age and education background from the scope of variables being investigated, had to be defined in order to keep the model parsimonious and to focus on the major determinants deduced from past research.

Furthermore, in the high social richness condition, only *positive social cues were used*, i. e. pictures of persons who had been rated to have a competent outward appearance, positive star ratings by other users and positive evaluations of the information content based on a group rating shown below the textual product description. This approach was chosen because one of the study's objectives consisted in demonstrating that the presence of social cues can – in the best case – positively influence the assessment of an information source's credibility compared to a control condition in which no social cues are shown at all. The impact of dissonant or negatively connoted social cues might also have a measurable impact on information processing, but represents a second research step after the basic impact of the presence of social cues could be verified.

Another category of potential limitations is concerned with the *data collection procedure*. First, the sample size of 132 persons in the main study solving 264 tasks in total meets the requirements for using the PLS structural equation modeling approach (Chin, 1998a) and is comfortably in accordance with the rule of thumb recommending a sample size that is at least ten times larger than the "number of structural paths directed at a particular latent construct in the structural model" (Hair et al., 2011, p. 144). However, additional participants would have increased *statistical power*, i. e. the probability of not committing a Type II error (Cohen, 1988) which is difficult to estimate based on the aforementioned rule of thumb (Henseler et al., 2009). By increasing the sample size substantially, it will also be possible to manipulate several variables that were measured but not manipulated in this study. Furthermore, in the pre-test phase, a *heart rate variability measurement* was conducted. Literature recommends to analyze segments comprising at least two to five minutes of heart rate data (Berntson et al.,

1997). In the present study, shorter segments had to be used since many subjects needed less than two minutes to complete the task. Hence, the heart rate variability data should be interpreted cautiously as they only show a fundamental *tendency* regarding autonomous nervous system activity.

Finally, this study's major objective consists in the *explanation and prediction of human behavior* in relation to the entity information. Consequently, it does not make statements about the impact of specific information seeking and stopping strategies on *performance variables*, e. g. economic measures such as employee productivity or the quality of task outcomes (Cramme, 2005). Hence, the results have to be interpreted against the background of specific scenario-dependent requirements. For example – as outlined above – the use of rational stopping rules might be preferable in the context of organizational decision making, but might be less desirable with regard to consumers' buying activities. Thus, the reader has to decide critically which class of stopping behavior is more preferable in a specific situation in order to be able to quantify the independent variables' influence on dependent performance variables.

6.5. Avenues for Future Research

The contributions and limitations described in the previous sections provide numerous opportunities for extending this study. First, the study should be replicated outside the laboratory, e. g. by conducting *field studies* examining the information seeking and stopping behavior of various stakeholders such as managers on different levels, employees or end-users of public web applications (examples are given in Browne et al. 2005; Zach 2005). This would open the door for investigating the interdependencies that emerge from the *selection of different information channels* throughout a search process (c. f. Figure 2.1). For instance, the stopping behavior might be different if the information seeker retrieves structured and convincing information first and then moves to textual information rich in social cues or vice versa (see also Browne et al. 2007). Variations in stopping behavior might result from *information avoidance strategies* that are often used when new information contradicts the assumptions of a person's existing mental model (van Zuuren and Wolfs, 1991).

A fruitful starting point for doing research in this area might be the stream of research on *communication media choice* because computer-based information seeking can be regarded as a communication process between a person and an artificial information system (Hemmer and Heinzl, 2012). Consequently, variables influencing the selection of communication media might also have an impact on the selection of information channels in information search. For example, the *Media Synchronicity Theory* differentiates between *convergence* and *conveyance processes* (Dennis et al., 2008). Whereas in the former, a person has to combine several potentially contradictory pieces of information, in the latter, the focus is on the transmission of large amounts of raw information. In their article, the authors propose various attributes of a communication medium that support convergence and conveyance processes to different degrees. This logic could be transferred to the question of information channel choice tasks in order to better understand why individuals prefer specific information channels in different stages of an information seeking task.

Second, this research gives a broad introduction into *human-computer based information behavior* and holistically stresses the combined impact of task, technology and individual characteristics on the use of information technology (Burton-Jones and Straub, 2006) and resulting information seeking and stopping behavior. Thus, a broad research framework is created which should be *further validated, refined and extended* in the future as the importance of the entity information for both society and organizations is growing constantly. Hence, it appears to be essential for IS researchers, IS designers and managers to get a clear understanding of cognitive processes and evolutionary-shaped behavioral patterns underlying the acquisition and processing of computer-based information in order to be able to develop technology that effectively supports individuals or helps to structure and guide behavior. Subsequently, important research questions with regard to human computer-based information seeking and stopping behavior are described.

Task characteristics. In future research, information seeking and stopping behavior should be investigated in many different contexts. Whereas in this study, the focus was set on information acquisition in organizational settings using web interfaces, information seeking behavior should also be analyzed with respect to organizational tasks in which *time pressure* is present as this is often the case in business contexts. Furthermore, from the perspective of search engine, e-commerce web site and social network operators, it is important to understand the behavior of persons who act outside an organization, thus use the technology for private reasons. For these persons, the aspect of hedonism is a strong behavioral driver (van der Heijden, 2004). Consequently, especially the operators of social networks and search engines earning money predominantly by placing advertisements on their web sites, have to find ways in which they can increase the "stickiness" of their applications. That is, they want to postpone the users' information seeking stopping decision as long as possible (Browne et al., 2007, p. 99).

Technology characteristics. In addition to the information channel choice theme that was introduced above, a closer investigation of the *presence or absence of social cues* appears to be fruitful (Gefen and Straub, 2004; Kumar and Benbasat, 2002; Short et al., 1976). Whereas in this study, the impact of positive social cues was analyzed, future studies should also include negative cues or shed light on the impact of dissonant information (e. g. textual information that conveys a positive impression of the underlying subject matter combined with negative social cues such as an unattractive picture of the person who wrote the text and vice versa). Especially the *source credibility* construct as a mediating variable should be explored in more detail as there seems to be a lack of research with regard to source and information credibility assessments in computer-based contexts (McComas and Trumbo, 2001; Metzger et al., 2010). This might be due to the fast pace of modern technology intruding into the society.

Individual characteristics. Since today's information technology evolved over a period of only a few decades, the first generation that grew up entirely "networked" is currently entering the job market. As opposed to "*digital immigrants*" who did not have the chance to interact with information technology when they were young, the aforementioned "*digital natives*" had access to these technologies from the beginning (Vodanovich et al., 2010, p. 711). Consequently, digital natives are believed to be less resistant to technological innovations and differentiate less strictly between business and private life (Jones et al., 2010; Vodanovich et al., 2010). With regard to information processing, Prensky (2001, p. 2) states that "today's students think and process information fundamentally differently from their predecessors" and even assumes that brain structures change when people are exposed to information technology already in early years.

As a consequence, it is worth investigating the impact of continuous information technology exposure on the strategies that are employed for efficiently acquiring and evaluating information. Hence, theories like the dual-process theories and the social-presence theory used in this research should be replicated in future studies on computer-based information behavior (c. f. Majchrzak and Jarvenpaa 2010; Yu et al. 2011) in order to make sure that their propositions and hypotheses – that were largely developed with regard to the behavior of persons who are unexperienced in using modern information technology – are transferable to digital natives. Changes in behavioral patterns that are characteristic of digital natives should be reflected critically and result in the adaptation of organizational information infrastructures that better reflect the respective needs and cognitive habits.

As information acquisition is usually not an end in itself, the link between information seeking stopping behavior and downstream processes such as decision making should be investigated in the future. Hence, the research reported in this study could be extended by economic variables that represent the relative benefits of using specific technological artifacts when supporting individuals in solving organizational tasks with certain characteristics.

Third, more attention should be paid to the phenomenon of *information pathologies* on the part of the recipients in computer-mediated contexts. This study revealed two pathologies that potentially have a detrimental effect on overall task performance. Many additional pathologies might be observable, e. g. reduced attention spans in information acquisition as people are ubiquitously exposed to several information channels in parallel (Koufaris, 2002). Another example would be the fact that individuals increasingly receive information which is condensed to a few characters so that it can be consumed more easily. Information overload and the resulting potentially inefficient coping strategies are also under-investigated in the IS domain (Eppler and Mengis, 2004). In this context, adaptive user interfaces might be part of a solution by sensing when the user's mental workload exceeds specific limits. As mental workload is difficult to measure with traditional approaches such as questionnaires, modern psychophysiological approaches might help in capturing the user's cognitive load in real-time by measuring immediate, uncontrollable and less-biased physiological body reactions (Dimoka et al., 2012, 2011; Riedl et al., 2010a).

Finally, this study took the perspective of the *information consumer*. Future research should also consider the opposite stance and shed light on the *production of information*, e. g. investigate the factors that make organizations and private persons share information on public web sites such as social networks (Mesmer-Magnus and DeChurch, 2009). Hence, the mechanisms driving the entire information supply chain comprising the producer of information, the technology that offers the information and the consumer of information will become more transparent and will reveal opportunities for future improvements.

7. Conclusion

This study was motivated by the identification of a significant research gap concerning the relationship between users of modern information technology and the entity information, a phenomenon which was termed "human computer-based information behavior". At the same time, it was found that during the last decades, several technological advances resulted in a situation in which information is ubiquitously available in an almost unlimited amount. Furthermore, it appeared that content provided via modern media such as the Internet is increasingly and visibly produced by other private users.

The aforementioned observations guided the formulation of two research questions addressing a critical phase in any information acquisition process, namely the question *why* people stop seeking for information in computer-mediated settings and *which factors* influence this decision. It was shown that information seeking is a crucial step in many organizational decision making and sense making processes and that terminating seeking activities too early or too late has detrimental effects on the information seeker's overall task performance.

An analysis of extant literature on information seeking stopping behavior revealed that most publications deal with strategies for terminating information acquisition activities in choice tasks. Only a few studies decidedly addressed stopping behavior in which the sufficiency of information was of primary concern. Additionally, there was no research coherently integrating rational, systematic seeking and stopping behavior on the one hand and spontaneous, impulsive seeking and stopping behavior on the other hand.

Hence, a comprehensive research model was developed explaining the combined effect of task, technology and individual characteristics on information seeking and stopping behavior. The model's refinement and evaluation was conducted in a two-staged process using a web-based laboratory environment in order to be able to control for the impact of several variables that might otherwise bias the results. The data collected in the main study comprising the answers of 132 participants solving 264 tasks in total clearly support most of the hypotheses that were deduced from dual-process theories, social presence theory and the effort-accuracy framework of cognition. In line with the theories' predictions, task complexity was identified as the major determinant of effortless, heuristic information processing and stopping, activating coping mechanisms for reducing mental stress. This effect could also be demonstrated based on heart rate variability data, measuring the participants' immediate body reactions while they were solving various tasks. Likewise, the participants' motivation to perform well in the tasks could be shown to represent a major determinant of systematic information seeking and stopping behavior that can be activated externally by manipulating the task's importance.

Interestingly, a counter-intuitive finding emerged with respect to the impact of social richness on information seeking and stopping behavior. In contrast to the prediction by social presence theory and derivatives, the availability of social cues did not have a positive impact on the participants' judgment of perceived source credibility. This peculiarity adds to the knowledge in the field of information pathologies and can be regarded as an important starting point for additional research on the impact of social cues on the information behavior of persons in various age groups.

In summary, this study does not only provide a framework for explaining and predicting human information behavior and thus adds to a research stream that was largely neglected by IS researchers in the past. It also applies theories that were partly developed before modern information technologies were widely adopted by organizational and private users. Thus, it makes important contributions in terms of theory development and theory corroboration and increases various stakeholders' awareness of individual and technology-induced differences with regard to human information processing. Future studies should build on the given insights in order to better reflect evolutionary-shaped behavioral tendencies in the design of person-centered information technology.

Appendices

A. Literature on Human Computer-Based Information Behavior in the IS Community

In Section 2.2 an overview over IS research on human computer-based information behavior was given. Table A.1 contains a list of all reviewed articles including information about the research approach adopted, the research method used and the level of analysis investigated in the article (c. f. Hemmer and Heinzl, 2011). Furthermore, an analysis of the article's relevance was conducted. For this reason, every journal's h index was calculated based on citation data published in Thomson Reuters' Web of Knowledge as the most renowned source for citation data (Meho and Yang, 2007).

In its traditional form, a researcher has an index h, if h of his papers are cited at least h times each and the remaining papers of this author have less citations (Hirsch, 2005). In the table below, the above-mentioned logic is transferred to the articles published in various IS outlets in order to get an h index for every journal on a yearly basis. This allows for the judgment of an article's relevance by comparing its total number of citations with the publishing journal's h index in the specific year.

Impact factors for EJIS and some older articles could not be calculated due to missing data. EJIS: European Journal of Information Systems, ISJ: Information Systems Journal, ISR: Information Systems Research, JAIS: Journal of AIS, JMIS: Journal of MIS, MISQ: MIS Quarterly

Table A.1.: Research Addressing Information Behavior-related Aspects in the IS Domain

Journal	Study	Information need	Choice among comp.-based info channel	Information request	Information delivery	Information assim. and evaluation	Interpretive	Positivist	Conceptual	Mathematical / axiomatic	Survey / interview	Case study	Lab. experiment	Individual	Group	Organization	Journal's H-Index (Y)	Average # of citations	# of article citations
		Stages in information acquisition process					Empirical		Non empirical		Research method			Level of analysis			Impact		
MISQ	(Ives, 1982)				x				x					x			/	/	/
MISQ	(Robey and Taggart, 1982)		x		x	x			x					x			14	34	166
MISQ	(Huber, 1984)				x				x						x		17	40	40
MISQ	(El Sawy, 1985)	x			x	x		x			x			x			14	32	8
MISQ	(Specht, 1986)	x						x				x		x			/	/	/
JMIS	(Sviokla, 1989)	x					x					x				x	/	/	/
Total	**Total 1980–1989**	**3**	**1**	**0**	**4**	**2**	**1**	**2**	**3**	**0**	**1**	**2**	**0**	**4**	**1**	**1**			
MISQ	(Watson, 1990)	x	x		x	x		x			x			x			16	24	35
ISR	(Vessey and Galletta, 1991)				x	x		x					x	x			/	/	/
MISQ	(Wetherbe, 1991)	x			x				x					x			22	62	38
ISR	(Morris et al., 1992)				x	x		x					x	x			/	/	/
MISQ	(Todd and Benbasat, 1992)					x					x			x			21	52	92
ISR	(De et al., 1993)			x						x							/	/	/
EJOIS	(Hertzum et al., 1993)				x				x			x					/	/	/
EJOIS	(Jones et al., 1993)		x									x					/	/	/
JMIS	(Chen, 1995)				x	x			x					x			17	63	97
MISQ	(Dennis, 1996)				x	x							x		x		/	/	/
EJOIS	(Rudy, 1996)																9	12	23
ISR	(Vandenbosch and Higgins, 1996)	x			x	x		x			x			x			16	39	34
MISQ	(Choudhury and Sampler, 1997)			x					x							x	18	70	46

Journal	Study	Information need	Choice among comp.-based info channel	Information request	Information delivery	Information assim. and evaluation	Interpretive	Positivist	Conceptual	Mathematical / axiomatic	Survey / interview	Case study	Lab. experiment	Individual	Group	Organization	Journal's H-Index (Y)	Average # of citations	# of article citations
		Stages in information acquisition process					Research approach — Empirical		Non empirical		Research method			Level of analysis			Impact		
ISR	(Moore et al., 1997)	x		x		x				x				x			15	47	6
MISQ	(Vandenbosch and Huff, 1997)	x				x		x				x		x			18	70	47
ISR	(Mendelson and Pillai, 1998)					x		x			x					x	17	50	41
JMIS	(Mennecke and Valacich, 1998)		x		x								x		x		/	/	/
ISR	(Gordon and Moore, 1999)			x		x		x					x	x			15	42	2
JMIS	(Grisé and Gallupe, 1999)				x	x							x	x			11	24	21
JMIS	(Lin et al., 1999)				x	x							x	x			11	24	15
Total	Total 1990-1999	5	3	4	9	11	0	9	4	3	4	2	6	12	2	2			
ISR	(Bordetsky and Mark, 2000)	x				x			x				x	x			15	46	8
EJOIS	(Edwards et al., 2000)								x					x			6	17	5
ISR	(Lim et al., 2000)				x			x					x	x			15	46	14
ISR	(Krishnan et al., 2001)			x	x	x		x					x	x			16	59	8
JMIS	(Stenmark, 2001)			x	x	x	x					x		x			21	45	27
ISR	(Miranda and Saunders, 2003)		x	x	x	x	x					x		x	x		16	62	49
ISJ	(Rafaeli and Ravid, 2003)			x	x	x								x			10	12	12
ISR	(Hong et al., 2004a)	x		x	x	x		x					x	x	x		16	45	31
JMIS	(Hong et al., 2004b)			x	x	x		x					x	x			17	19	31
ISR	(Jones et al., 2004)		x	x	x	x		x				x		x			16	45	67
MISQ	(Kumar and Benbasat, 2004)				x	x		x					x	x			20	73	10
JMIS	(Browne and Pitts, 2004)				x	x		x					x	x			17	19	12
ISR	(Schultze and Orlikowski, 2004)						x		x		x						16	45	54
JMIS	(Chung et al., 2005)			x	x				x			x					17	17	26
ISR	(Jiang et al., 2005)			x	x												14	30	3
JMIS	(Nelson et al., 2005)							x			x		x	x			17	17	48
JAIS	(Wang and Benbasat, 2005)	x				x		x						x			/	/	/
EJOIS	(Hovorka and Larsen, 2006)	x				x	x					x		x			11	9	2
MISQ	(Kuechler and Vaishnavi, 2006)				x								x			x	21	31	6

Journal	Study	Information need	Choice among comp.-based info channel	Information request	Information delivery	Information assim. and evaluation	Interpretive	Positivist	Conceptual	Mathematical / axiomatic	Survey / interview	Case study	Lab. experiment	Individual	Group	Organization	Journal's H-Index (Y)	Average # of citations	# of article citations
		Stages in information acquisition process					Research approach (Empirical / Non empirical)				Research method			Level of analysis			Impact		
JMIS	(Liang et al., 2006)	x			x	x		x					x	x			14	11	17
JAIS	(Li and Kettinger, 2006)			x	x	x			x								9	6	4
JMIS	(Liang et al., 2006)	x		x	x	x		x					x	x			14	11	17
EJOIS	(Scheepers, 2006)				x				x			x				x	11	9	4
MISQ	(Tam and Ho, 2006)				x	x		x				x	x	x			21	31	20
MISQ	(Arazy and Woo, 2007)				x			x					x	x			15	22	2
MISQ	(Browne et al., 2007)			x		x		x					x	x			15	22	10
MISQ	(Watson-Manheim and Bélanger, 2007)		x			x		x				x		x			15	22	28
MISQ	(Nadkarni and Gupta, 2007)	x			x			x					x	x			15	22	13
MISQ	(Dennis et al., 2008)		x			x			x				x	x			12	13	37
ISR	(Forman et al., 2008)	x			x	x		x			x	x		x			8	6	37
ISJ	(Melville and Ramirez, 2008)	x			x		x				x	x			x		8	5	4
JMIS	(Ren et al., 2008)			x	x			x			x				x		11	7	9
ISR	(Storey et al., 2008)			x	x				x			x					8	6	3
JAIS	(Zhang and Watts, 2008)					x		x			x			x			6	4	0
MISQ	(Wang and Benbasat, 2009)		x		x	x		x					x	x			8	4	4
MISQ	(Dou et al., 2010)	x			x	x		x					x	x			3	1	1
MISQ	(Mani and Barua, 2010)	x			x	x		x			x					x	3	1	2
MISQ	(Riedl et al., 2010)				x	x		x					x	x			3	1	3
Total	**Total 2000-2010**	12	6	14	26	20	5	23	7	1	4	10	20	28	3	3			
Sum	**Sum 1980-2010**	20	10	18	39	33	6	34	14	4	9	14	26	44	6	6			

B. Architecture of Laboratory Experiment Environment Software

Since this study aims at examining human information seeking and stopping behavior in *online environments*, a major requirement with regard to the laboratory experiment software consisted in imitating the classical user interface of today's web applications. Thus, the experiment's external validity can be increased.

Furthermore, the software not only had to be able to present the experimental tasks to the subjects, but also to seamlessly integrate questionnaire functionality and tracking features for recording and analyzing the participants' information seeking and stopping behavior.

In order to fulfill the above-mentioned requirements, a web-based experiment environment was developed in the programming language PHP[1] and complemented by JavaScript code for capturing user interactions in real time. Cascading Style Sheets[2] were employed to format the HTML content displayed on the screen.

The platform itself was installed on a Apache web server supporting PHP (version 5.2) and connecting to a MySQL[3] database (version 5.0.84) for storing and retrieving data relevant in the context of the experiments. The database configuration was realized via the phpMyAdmin[4] front end (version 3.3.5.1) also running on the Apache web server.

The database model underlying the laboratory experiment software is summarized in Figure B.1 showing all tables, columns, data types and relationships between tables that are necessary to provide the required functionality.

---

1 http://www.php.net
2 http://www.w3.org/Style/CSS/Overview.en.html
3 http://www.mysql.com
4 http://www.phpmyadmin.net

The software was optimized for the Firefox[5] web browser and tested extensively in combination with various versions of the product. The target screen resolution was 1024 x 768 pixels using full screen browser windows and hidden tool bars in order to minimize visual distractors on the screen and provide identical sets of information to every experiment participant.

5 http://www.mozilla.org

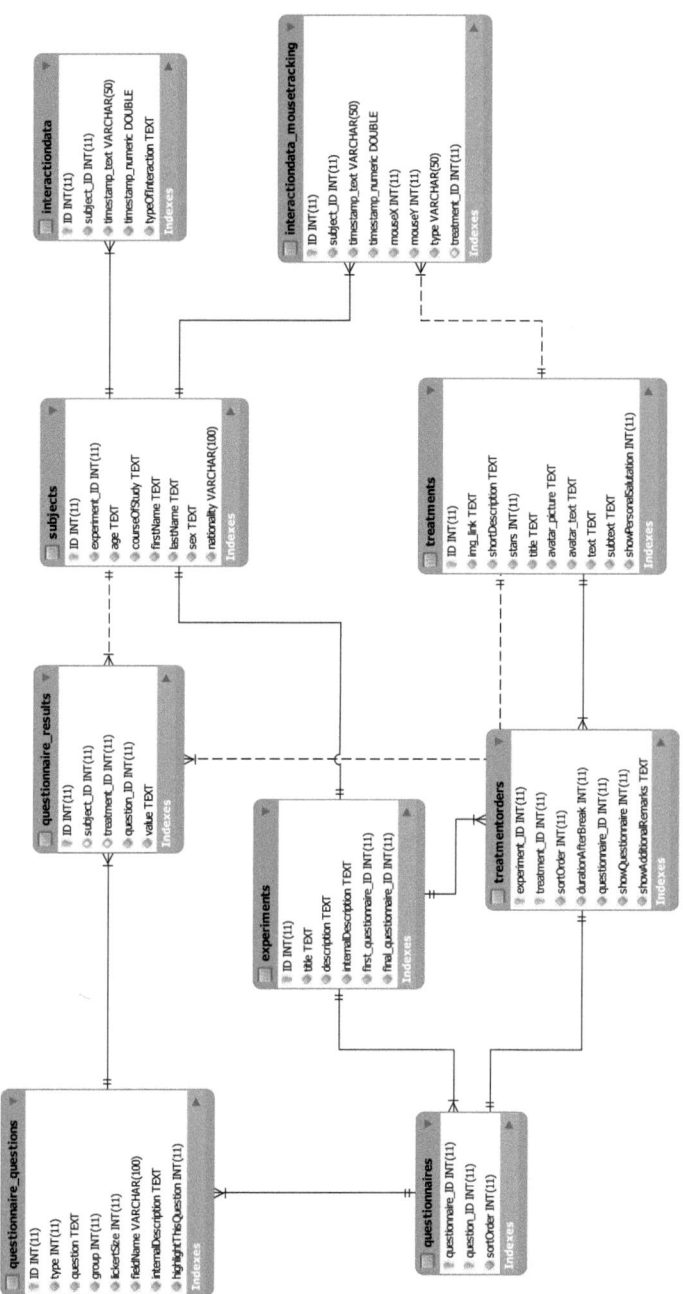

Figure B.1.: Database Model

C. Detailed Description of the Laboratory Experiment

In Chapter 4 and Chapter 5, the results of two laboratory experiments were presented. After in Appendix B, the laboratory environment software was described from a technical perspective, this chapter provides detailed insights into the experimental manipulations (Section C.1) and the experiment protocol that was used in the pre-test phase to standardize the data collection process (Section C.2).

C.1. Task Design

In the main experiment phase, every subject had to solve two different tasks. The participants were assigned randomly to different treatment groups. Members of the high task importance group received the following experiment and task descriptions (in German language since the majority of participants consisted of native German speakers).

Experiment description (high task importance):

"Das Ziel des nachfolgenden Experiments besteht darin, das Verhalten von Menschen im Umgang mit Informationssystemen zu untersuchen und diese Erkenntnisse für die Entwicklung einer Anwendung zu nutzen, die zukünftig in mehreren Großunternehmen eingesetzt wird. Sie gehören zu einem kleinen Kreis an Probanden, so dass ihr authentisches Verhalten wichtig für den Erfolg des Projekts ist.

Nachfolgend werden Sie in zwei Teilaufgaben gebeten, sich in die Rolle unterschiedlicher Unternehmensvertreter zu versetzen und verschiedene Produkte zu evaluieren, die für den Einsatz im Unternehmen vorgeschlagen werden. Nach jeder Aufgabe werden Sie aufgefordert, einen kurzen Fragebogen auszufüllen. Danach erfolgt eine kurze Pause, während der Sie ein schwarzes Kreuz auf Ihrem Monitor sehen. Bitte blicken Sie auf dieses Kreuz, um Ihre Aufmerksamkeit anschließend auf die folgende Aufgabe zu richten.

Es gibt keine richtigen oder falschen Antworten. Sie werden während des Experiments nicht beobachtet und werden gebeten, so zu handeln, wie Sie es in Situationen außerhalb der Experimentalumgebung gewohnt sind.

Falls Sie während des Experiments Fragen haben, versuchen Sie bitte, diese selbst zu klären. Während des Experiments sollte nicht gesprochen werden."

Task Description – Task 1 (high task importance):

"Sie sind verantwortlich für die IT-Systeme eines Großunternehmens im Ingenieursbereich und wurden mit der Aufgabe betraut, alle Mitarbeiter mit neuen Monitoren auszustatten. Dabei ist insbesondere von Bedeutung, dass die Monitore energiesparend arbeiten und zudem eine hohe Bildqualität liefern.

Bewerten Sie anhand der Informationen auf der nächsten Bildschirmseite (nach einem Klick auf 'Weiter'), ob der dort erwähnte Monitor 'Monitor A' für diesen Zweck geeignet ist. Bei Monitor A handelt es sich um den einzigen aktuell lieferbaren Monitor.

Fordern Sie durch Klicks auf 'Weiterlesen' so viele Informationen an, bis Sie bereit sind, eine Empfehlung auszusprechen. Klicken Sie auf der nächsten Bildschirmseite auf 'Weiter', sobald Sie die Empfehlung aussprechen und im Experiment fortfahren möchten."

Task Description – Task 2 (high task importance):

"Sie arbeiten als CIO in einem Großunternehmen. Zukünftig sollen alle Mitarbeiter mit einem eigenen Tintenstrahl-Drucker ausgestattet werden.

Bewerten Sie anhand der Informationen auf der nächsten Bildschirmseite (nach einem Klick auf 'Weiter'), ob der dort erwähnte Drucker 'Drucker A' für diesen Zweck geeignet ist.

Fordern Sie durch Klicks auf 'Weiterlesen' so viele Informationen an, bis Sie bereit sind, eine Empfehlung auszusprechen. Klicken Sie auf der nächsten Bildschirmseite auf 'Weiter', sobald Sie die Empfehlung aussprechen und im Experiment fortfahren möchten."

Members of the low task importance group received the following experiment and task descriptions:

Experiment description (low task importance):

"Das Ziel des nachfolgenden Experiments besteht darin, das Verhalten von Menschen im Umgang mit Informationssystemen zu untersuchen und diese Erkenntnisse für die Entwicklung einer Anwendung zu nutzen, die zukünftig in kleinen Unternehmen eingesetzt wird. Neben Ihnen nehmen zahlreiche weitere Personen an dem Experiment teil, so dass Ihre individuelle Leistung aufgrund der Bildung eines Durchschnittswertes nachträglich nicht mehr ermittelt werden kann.

Nachfolgend werden Sie in zwei Teilaufgaben gebeten, diverse Produkte zu evaluieren, die für den Einsatz in einem Unternehmen vorgeschlagen werden. Nach jeder Aufgabe werden Sie aufgefordert, einen kurzen Fragebogen auszufüllen. Danach erfolgt eine kurze Pause, während der Sie ein schwarzes Kreuz auf Ihrem Monitor sehen. Bitte blicken Sie auf dieses Kreuz, um Ihre Aufmerksamkeit anschließend auf die folgende Aufgabe zu richten.

Es gibt keine richtigen oder falschen Antworten. Sie werden während des Experiments nicht beobachtet und werden gebeten, so zu handeln, wie Sie es in Situationen außerhalb der Experimentalumgebung gewohnt sind.

Falls Sie während des Experiments Fragen haben, versuchen Sie bitte, diese selbst zu klären. Während des Experiments sollte nicht gesprochen werden."

Task Description – Task 1 (low task importance):

"Sie sind verantwortlich für die IT-Systeme eines Kleinunternehmens im Ingenieursbereich und wurden mit der Aufgabe betraut, einen Mitarbeiter mit einem neuen Monitor auszustatten. Dabei ist insbeson-

dere von Bedeutung, dass der Monitor energiesparend arbeitet und zudem eine hohe Bildqualität liefert.

Bewerten Sie anhand der Informationen auf der nächsten Bildschirmseite (nach einem Klick auf 'Weiter'), ob der dort erwähnte Monitor 'Monitor A' für diesen Zweck geeignet ist. Bei Monitor A handelt es sich um den einzigen aktuell lieferbaren Monitor.

Fordern Sie durch Klicks auf 'Weiterlesen' so viele Informationen an, bis Sie bereit sind, eine Empfehlung auszusprechen. Klicken Sie auf der nächsten Bildschirmseite auf 'Weiter', sobald Sie die Empfehlung aussprechen und im Experiment fortfahren möchten."

Task Description – Task 2 (low task importance):

"Sie arbeiten als technischer Leiter in einem Kleinunternehmen. Zukünftig sollen zwei Mitarbeiter mit einem eigenen Tintenstrahl-Drucker ausgestattet werden.

Bewerten Sie anhand der Informationen auf der nächsten Bildschirmseite (nach einem Klick auf 'Weiter'), ob der dort erwähnte Drucker 'Drucker A' für diesen Zweck geeignet ist.

Fordern Sie durch Klicks auf 'Weiterlesen' so viele Informationen an, bis Sie bereit sind, eine Empfehlung auszusprechen. Klicken Sie auf der nächsten Bildschirmseite auf 'Weiter', sobald Sie die Empfehlung aussprechen und im Experiment fortfahren möchten."

The information accessible during the experiment for solving the tasks was taken from the Amazon web site[1] in January 2012 and is presented below. The best-ranked user comments were adopted in order to ensure a sufficient quality level. Thus, the external validity of the experiment results can be increased.

Task 1 (high social richness)

"Wir nutzen 'Monitor A' seit längerer Zeit in all unseren Büros - er erweist sich regelmäßig als ein optischer Hingucker und ist absolut zu empfehlen! Die flache Bauweise dieses kompakten Monitors wird durch die eingesetzte LED-Technologie ermöglicht. So wirkt dieser TFT-LED Monitor schlicht und elegant zugleich. Die innovative

---

1 http://www.amazon.com

LED Technologie ermöglicht nicht nur eine minimalistische Bauweise. Dank des Einsatzes des stromsparenden White LED Backlights verbraucht der Monitor in unserem täglichen Betrieb bis zu 40 Prozent weniger Energie als herkömmliche Monitore. Besonderer Clou: Über das On Screen Display können wir genau nachverfolgen, was wir in einem bestimmten Zeitraum an Strom und CO_2 eingespart haben. Trotz all dieser Energieeffizienz glänzt dieser Multimedia Monitor selbstverständlich auch in Punkto Bildqualität: Features wie Reaktionszeit von nur 5 ms, dynamisches Kontrastverhältnis von 5.000.000:1 und der Bildoptimierungs-Chip sorgen dafür, dass die Inhalte stets optimal dargestellt werden. Das 16:9 Breitbildformat und Schwenkarm- sowie Wandhalterungsvorrichtungen sorgen für den perfekten Benutzerkomfort.

Gelegentlich benötigen wir gestochen scharfe Kontraste und daneben sattes Schwarz - dazu können wir mit Hilfe der LED Backlight Technologie die Hintergrundbeleuchtung des 'Monitor A' vollkommen abdunkeln. Außerdem ist der LED Monitor mit einer Energieeinsparung von bis zu 40 Prozent äußerst effizient und durch den Verzicht auf Halogen und Quecksilber besonders umweltfreundlich.

Aus mehrwöchiger Erfahrung lässt sich sagen, dass höchste Präzision und beste Qualität in der Darstellung in allen Bereichen - ob für Filme, Computerspiele oder Multimedia- und Office-Anwendungen - garantiert sind. Pixel für Pixel stellt dieser Monitor mit einer kurzen Reaktionszeit von 5 ms (ISO), großem Blickwinkel von bis zu 170° und einer maximalen Auflösung von 1920x1080 die Bilder genauso dar, wie sie die Quelle liefert. Das sorgt für eine reibungslose Wiedergabe und garantiert extrem scharfe und kristallklare Bilder, die selbst bei bewegungsreichen Inhalten nicht ins Ruckeln geraten.

Diesen Monitor würden wir jederzeit erneut kaufen."

Task 2 (high social richness)

"Nach intensiven Tests habe ich festgestellt, dass der Tintenstrahldrucker 'Drucker A' für einen Ausdruck in extra feiner Schriftsatzqualität

deutlich länger als ein Farblaser braucht. Als tintenbasierender Multifunktionsdrucker erbringt er aber sehr gute Leistungen.

Die Inbetriebnahme gestaltete sich etwas mühselig, weil erst sehr viele blaue Plastikklebestreifen überall am und im Gerät abgezogen sowie etliche Styropor- und massive Plastikteile aus dem Innern des Druckers entfernt werden mussten. Hat man alles nach Anleitung entfernt und die Verbrauchsmaterialien eingesetzt, geht es los - mit Warten. Der Drucker braucht einige Zeit, bis er sich konfiguriert hat.

Das Display ist meines Erachtens zur weiteren Ersteinrichtung dringend nötig, um aus einer zunächst unübersichtlich großen Auswahl an Möglichkeiten den Drucker so einzurichten, dass Ergebnisse erzielt werden, wie man sie bevorzugt. Nach Ersteinrichtung und Treiberkonfiguration geht es komfortabel ans Werk. Die Farben sind insbesondere auf Spezialpapier mit höchstmöglicher Auflösung sehr gut.

Der Drucker liefert nach meinen Tests sowohl auf $100g/m^2$ Inkjetpapier als auch auf günstigem Multifunktionspapier mit $80g/m^2$ saubere Ergebnisse, auch beidseitig. Das ist auf dem preiswerten Papier ein erstaunliches Ergebnis. Lediglich die Einstellungen für Druckdichte und Trocknungszeit der Tinte sind zu variieren.

Bei der Faxfunktion gelang es mir bisher nicht, eine verkleinerte Kopie der ersten, gesendeten Seite mit den Übermittlungsdaten ausdrucken zu können, wie das z.B. viele S/W-Laser-Faxkombinationsdrucker automatisch machen.

Die Kurzwahlfunktion fürs Fax wäre am Gerät leicht und schnell eingerichtet - wenn da nicht die üble Tipperei pro Taste wäre, bis man den jeweils richtigen Buchstaben erwischt hat. Das hätte man mit einer vom Handy gewohnten Displaytastatur besser lösen können.

Die Duplexfunktion arbeitet bisher fehlerfrei."

Task 1 (low social richness)

"'Monitor A' ist in jedem Büro ein optischer Hingucker. Die durch LED mögliche flache Bauweise dieses kompakten Monitors ermöglicht das extrem schlanke und moderne Design. So wirkt dieser TFT-LED

*Monitor schlicht und elegant zugleich. Die innovative LED Techno-
logie ermöglicht nicht nur eine minimalistische Bauweise. Dank des
Einsatzes des stromsparenden White LED Backlights verbraucht der
Monitor bis zu 40 Prozent weniger Energie als herkömmliche Monitore. Besonderer Clou: Über das On Screen Display können Sie genau
nachverfolgen, was Sie in einem bestimmten Zeitraum an Strom und
CO2 eingespart haben. Trotz all dieser Energieeffizienz glänzt dieser
Multimedia Monitor selbstverständlich auch in Punkto Bildqualität:
Features wie Reaktionszeit von nur 5 ms, dynamisches Kontrastverhältnis von 5.000.000:1 und der Bildoptimierungs-Chip sorgen dafür,
dass die Inhalte stets optimal dargestellt werden. Das 16:9 Breitbildformat und Schwenkarm- sowie Wandhalterungsvorrichtungen sorgen
für den perfekten Benutzerkomfort.*

*Dank der intelligenten LED Backlight Technologie lässt sich die Hin-
tergrundbeleuchtung des Monitor A vollkommen abdunkeln, so dass
gestochen scharfe Kontraste, eine erstaunliche Bildtiefe und ein sattes
Schwarz entstehen. Außerdem ist der LED Monitor mit einer Energieeinsparung von bis zu 40 Prozent äußerst effizient und durch den
Verzicht auf Halogen und Quecksilber besonders umweltfreundlich.*

*Höchste Präzision und beste Qualität in der Darstellung sind in al-
len Bereichen - ob für Filme, Computerspiele oder Multimedia- und
Office-Anwendungen - garantiert. Pixel für Pixel stellt dieser Monitor
mit einer kurzen Reaktionszeit von 5 ms (ISO), großem Blickwinkel
von bis zu 170° und einer maximalen Auflösung von 1920x1080 die
Bilder genauso dar, wie sie die Quelle liefert. Das sorgt für eine reibungslose Wiedergabe und garantiert extrem scharfe und kristallklare
Bilder, die selbst bei bewegungsreichen Inhalten nicht ins Ruckeln geraten."*

Task 2 (low social richness)

*"Für einen Ausdruck in extra feiner Schriftsatzqualität braucht der
Tintenstrahldrucker 'Drucker A' deutlich länger als ein Farblaser.
Als tintenbasierender Multifunktionsdrucker erbringt er aber sehr gute
Leistungen.*

Die Inbetriebnahme gestaltet sich etwas mühselig, weil zunächst sehr viele blaue Plastikklebestreifen überall am und im Gerät abgezogen sowie etliche Styropor- und massive Plastikteile aus dem Innern des Druckers entfernt werden müssen. Wurde alles nach Anleitung entfernt und die Verbrauchsmaterialien eingesetzt, benötigt der Drucker einige Zeit, bis er sich konfiguriert hat.

Das Display ist zur weiteren Ersteinrichtung dringend nötig, um aus einer zunächst unübersichtlich großen Auswahl an Möglichkeiten den Drucker so einzurichten, dass Ergebnisse erzielt werden, wie sie benötigt werden. Nach Ersteinrichtung und Treiberkonfiguration geht es komfortabel ans Werk. Die Farben sind insbesondere auf Spezialpapier mit höchstmöglicher Auflösung sehr gut.

Der Drucker liefert sowohl auf 100g/m^2 Inkjetpapier als auch auf günstigem Multifunktionspapier mit 80g/m^2 saubere Ergebnisse, auch beidseitig. Das ist auf dem preiswerten Papier ein erstaunliches Ergebnis. Lediglich die Einstellungen für Druckdichte und Trocknungszeit der Tinte sind zu variieren.

Bei der Faxfunktion ist es nicht möglich, eine verkleinerte Kopie der ersten, gesendeten Seite mit den Übermittlungsdaten ausdrucken zu können, wie das z.B. viele S/W-Laser-Faxkombinationsdrucker automatisch machen.

Die Kurzwahlfunktion fürs Fax wäre am Gerät leicht und schnell eingerichtet - jedoch müssen über Zifferntasten die Buchstaben ausgewählt werden. Das hätte mit einer vom Handy gewohnten Displaytastatur besser gelöst werden können.

Die Duplexfunktion arbeitet fehlerfrei."

C.2. Experiment Protocol

In order to ensure a standardized data collection procedure during the pre-test phase (including heart rate variability data), a experiment protocol was used which is presented in Table C.1.

Table C.1.: Protocol Used to Prepare the Experiment Sessions during the Pre-test Phase

Activity category	Details
Before a sequence of experiments	
Synchronize clocks	Experiment computer (with web server), heart rate monitor watch
Put a "Do not disturb" sign on the door of the laboratory	/
Prepare experiment computer	Start web browser with laboratory environment, start video software for showing baseline videos, start software used for conducting interviews after every experiment
Before every experiment	
Check experiment computer	Is the web browser containing the laboratory environment available? Is the video software for showing baseline videos available? Is the software for recording interviews available?
Subject should go to the toilet	/
Inform the subject about the experiment	Roughly describe the experiment (without disclosing the research objectives underlying the experiment), inform the subject about anonymous data collection

Activity category	Details
Ask the subject if he wants to take part in the experiment	/
Attach heart rate monitor sensor	Clean the spot on the chest where the sensor is attached, then install the sensor and activate the watch
Start of the experiment	
Perform the measurement of the subject's basal heart rate	Start videos, take notes on the time when the baseline recording starts
Leave the room	/
Enter the room after five minutes	Deactivate the videos, start the experiment environment in the web browser and maximize the window
Leave the room and wait	/
Enter the room after the subject finished the experiment	/
After the experiment	
Deactivate software and heart rate monitor watch and detach the sensor	/
Activate the audio recording software and conduct the interview	/
Debriefing	Explain the research objectives and how the collected data is analyzed

D. Operationalization of Constructs (German)

In Section 3.5, the instruments for measuring the latent variables of this study's research model were introduced. As the participants of the study's experiment are native German speakers, measurement items were presented in German language in order to reduce language biases. All indicators are listed below.

Table D.1.: Operationalization of the Construct *Perceived task complexity* (German)

Item	Indicator	Source
Perceived task complexity refers to the combined influence of task structure and task variability on the difficulty a person feels while solving a task.		
TC1	Die Aufgabe war mental anspruchsvoll.	Based on Maynard and Hakel (1997)
TC2	Die Aufgabe erforderte viel Nachdenken und Problemlösen.	Based on Maynard and Hakel (1997)
TC3	Die Aufgabe war gut strukturiert.*	Based on Haerem and Rau (2007)
TC4	Während der Lösung der Aufgabe bin ich auf Probleme gestoßen, die mich verunsichert haben.	Based on Haerem and Rau (2007)

*Inversely coded item

Table D.2.: Operationalization of the Construct *Perceived task experience* (German)

Item	Indicator	Source
Perceived task experience refers to the extent of the information seeker's prior knowledge with respect to a given task (buying and using *monitors, p*=1 and *printers, p*=2).		
TE1_1, TE2_1	Ich verfüge über Erfahrung in Bezug auf den Kauf und die Nutzung von <Produktkategorie>.	Developed for this study
TE1_2, TE2_2	Ich habe schon häufig <Produktkategorie> gekauft.	Developed for this study
TE1_3, TE2_3	Ich verfüge nur über ein sehr eingeschränktes Verständnis von <Produktkategorie>*.	Developed for this study

*Inversely coded item

Table D.3.: Operationalization of the Construct *Perceived task motivation* (German)

Item	Indicator	Source
Perceived task motivation refers to the level of information seeker's involvement in a task as a function of the task's relevance and importance for the recipient.		
TM1	Ich war motiviert, die Aufgabe so gewissenhaft wie möglich zu bearbeiten.	Based on Maynard and Hakel (1997)
TM2	Die Aufgabe erschien mir interessant.	Based on Maynard and Hakel (1997)
TM3	Ich habe viel Energie investiert, um die bestmögliche Antwort zu finden.	Based on Maynard and Hakel (1997)

Table D.4.: Operationalization of the Construct *Need for Cognition* (German),
Adopted from Bless et al. (1994)

Item	Indicator
	Need for cognition refers to an individual predisposition with regard to an "individual's tendency to engage in and enjoy effortful cognitive endeavors" (Cacioppo et al., 1996, p. 197).
NFC1	Die Aufgabe, neue Lösungen für Probleme zu finden, macht mir wirklich Spaß.
NFC2	Ich würde lieber eine Aufgabe lösen, die Intelligenz erfordert, schwierig und bedeutend ist, als eine Aufgabe, die zwar irgendwie wichtig ist, aber nicht viel Nachdenken erfordert.
NFC3	Ich setze mir eher solche Ziele, die nur mit erheblicher geistiger Anstrengung erreicht werden können.
NFC4	Die Vorstellung, mich auf mein Denkvermögen zu verlassen, um es zu etwas zu bringen, spricht mich nicht an.*
NFC5	Ich finde es besonders befriedigend, eine bedeutende Aufgabe abzuschließen, die viel Denken und geistige Anstrengung erfordert hat.
NFC6	Ich denke lieber über kleine, alltägliche Vorhaben nach, als über langfristige.*
NFC7	Ich würde lieber etwas tun, das wenig Denken erfordert, als etwas, das mit Sicherheit meine Denkfähigkeit herausfordert.*
NFC8	Ich finde wenig Befriedigung darin, angestrengt und stundenlang nachzudenken.*
NFC9	In erster Linie denke ich, weil ich muss.*
NFC10	Ich trage nicht gerne die Verantwortung für eine Situation, die sehr viel Denken erfordert.*
NFC11	Denken entspricht nicht dem, was ich unter Spaß verstehe.*
NFC12	Ich versuche Situationen vorauszuahnen und zu vermeiden, in denen die Wahrscheinlichkeit groß ist, dass ich intensiv über etwas nachdenken muss.*
NFC13	Ich habe es gern, wenn mein Leben voller kniffliger Aufgaben ist, die ich lösen muss.
NFC14	Ich würde komplizierte Probleme einfachen Problemen vorziehen.
NFC15	Es genügt mir, einfach die Antwort zu kennen, ohne die Gründe für die Antwort eines Problems zu verstehen.*
NFC16	Es genügt, dass etwas funktioniert, mir ist es egal, wie oder warum.*

*Inversely coded item

Table D.5.: Operationalization of the Construct *Extraversion* (German), Adopted
from Borkenau and Ostendorf (2008)

Item	Indicator
Extraversion refers to a dispositional character trait representing the degree of an information seeker's sociability and need for social relationships.	
Ex1	Ich habe gerne viele Leute um mich herum.
Ex2	Ich bin leicht zum Lachen zu bringen.
Ex3	Ich halte mich nicht für besonders fröhlich.*
Ex4	Ich unterhalte mich wirklich gern mit anderen Menschen.
Ex5	Ich bin gern im Zentrum des Geschehens.
Ex6	Ich ziehe es gewöhnlich vor, Dinge allein zu tun.*
Ex7	Ich habe oft das Gefühl, vor Energie überzuschäumen.
Ex8	Ich bin ein fröhlicher, gut gelaunter Mensch.
Ex9	Ich bin kein gut gelaunter Optimist.*
Ex10	Ich führe ein hektisches Leben.
Ex11	Ich bin ein sehr aktiver Mensch.
Ex12	Lieber würde ich meine eigenen Wege gehen, als eine Gruppe zu führen.*

*Inversely coded item

Table D.6.: Operationalization of the Construct *Maximizer tendency* (German), Adopted from Schwartz et al. (2002)

Item	Indicator
	Maximizer tendencies refers to the a person's attempt to solve tasks in an optimal way by considering all information available in a specific context.
Max1	Wenn ich Fernseh schaue, wechsle ich häufig zwischen den verfügbaren Programmen, sogar wenn ich versuche, ein bestimmtes Programm zu schauen.
Max2	Wenn ich im Auto Radio höre, wechsle ich häufig zu anderen Sendern, um zu prüfen, ob dort etwas besseres gespielt wird, auch wenn ich relativ zufrieden mit der Musik bin, die ich aktuell höre.
Max3	Beziehungen sind für mich wie Kleider: Ich versuche möglichst viel auszuprobieren, bevor ich die perfekte Beziehung eingehe.
Max4	Unabhängig davon, wie zufrieden ich mit meinem Job bin, erscheint es mir logisch, nach besseren Möglichkeiten Ausschau zu halten.
Max5	Ich fantasiere häufig darüber, in einer Art und Weise zu leben, die ziemlich stark von meinem tatsächlichen Leben abweicht.
Max6	Ich mag Listen, die Dinge in eine Rangfolge bringen (die besten Filme, die besten Sänger, die besten Athleten, die besten Romane etc.)
Max7	Ich finde es häufig schwer, ein Geschenk für einen Freund zu kaufen.
Max8	Wenn ich einkaufe, fällt es mir schwer Kleider zu finden, die mir wirklich gefallen.
Max9	Videos auszuleihen ist wirklich schwierig. Ich ringe immer mit mir selbst, um das beste auszuwählen.
Max10	Ich finde, dass Schreiben wirklich schwer ist, auch wenn es nur ein Brief an einen Freund ist, weil es so schwierig ist, die richtigen Worte zu finden. Auch bei einfachen Sachverhalten erstelle ich häufig mehrere Entwürfe.
Max11	Egal was ich tue, ich habe die höchsten Erwartungen mir selbst gegenüber.
Max12	Ich gebe mich nie mit dem Zweitbesten zufrieden.
Max13	Wann immer ich eine Auswahlentscheidung treffen muss, versuche ich mir alle anderen Möglichkeiten vorzustellen, sogar solche, die aktuell nicht verfügbar sind.

Table D.7.: Operationalization of the Constructs *System 1 information processing* and *System 2 information processing* (German), Adopted from Novak and Hoffman (2009)

Item	Indicator
System 1 information processing refers to the degree to which information is processed in an effortless, associative way, taking past experiences into account and following simple information cues.	
Sys1_1	Während der Bearbeitung der Aufgabe habe ich mich auf mein Bauchgefühl verlassen.
Sys1_2	Mein erster Eindruck hat die Bearbeitung der Aufgabe bestimmt.
Sys1_3	Während der Bearbeitung der Aufgabe bin ich meiner Intuition gefolgt.
System 2 information processing refers to the degree to which information is processed in an effortful, logical way, sequentially following specific rules of reasoning.	
Sys2_1	Während der Bearbeitung der Aufgabe habe ich sorgfältig nachgedacht.
Sys2_2	Ich habe diese Aufgabe systematisch bearbeitet.
Sys2_3	Während der Bearbeitung der Aufgabe habe ich alles logisch durchdacht.

Table D.8.: Operationalization of the Constructs *Propensity to use experiential / rational stopping rules* (German), Adopted from Browne et al. (2007)

ID	Indicator
Propensity to use experiential stopping rules refers to the tendency to rely on affect and intuition when making the decision to terminate the information seeking process, while *Propensity to use rational stopping rules* refers to the endency to decide consciously to stop seeking for information based on a content-wise analysis of issue-relevant information.	
Stop1	Warum haben Sie die Aufnahme von Informationen zu einem bestimmten Zeitpunkt beendet?
Stop2	Wie haben Sie entschieden, die Suche nach Informationen zu beenden?

Table D.9.: Operationalization of the Construct *Perceived source credibility* (German)

ID	Indicator	Source
	*Perceived source credibility* refers to the combined influence of an information source's believability, competence and trustworthiness.
SC1	Die zur Lösung der soeben bearbeiteten Aufgabe bereitgestellten Informationen waren vertrauenswürdig.	Based on McComas and Trumbo (2001)
SC2	Die zur Lösung der soeben bearbeiteten Aufgabe bereitgestellten Informationen waren korrekt.	Based on McComas and Trumbo (2001)
SC3	Die zur Lösung der gerade gelösten Aufgabe bereitgestellten Informationen waren angemessen.	Based on McComas and Trumbo (2001)
SC4	Die zur Lösung der gerade gelösten Aufgabe bereitgestellten Informationen waren vollständig.	Based on McComas and Trumbo (2001)
SC5	Die zur Lösung der gerade gelösten Aufgabe bereitgestellten Informationen waren nicht verzerrt.	Based on McComas and Trumbo (2001)

Bibliography

[Alexander et al. 2011] ALEXANDER, Patricia ; PIETERSE, Vreda ; LOTRIET, Hugo: A Comparison of Computing and non-Computing Students' Personalities Based on the Five-Factor Model. In: *Proceedings of the European Conference on Information Systems*, 2011

[Andriole 2010] ANDRIOLE, Stephen J.: Business Impact of Web 2.0 Technologies. In: *Communications of the ACM* 53 (2010), No. 12, pp. 67–79

[Angst and Agarwal 2009] ANGST, Corey M. ; AGARWAL, Ritu: Adoption of Electronic Health Records in the Presence of Privacy Concerns: The Elaboration Likelihood Model and Individual Persuasion. In: *Management Information Systems Quarterly* 33 (2009), No. 2, pp. 339–370

[Arazy and Woo 2007] ARAZY, Ofer ; WOO, Carson: Enhancing Information Retrieval Through Statistical Natural Language Processing: A Study of Collocation Indexing. In: *Management Information Systems Quarterly* 31 (2007), No. 3, pp. 525–546

[Areni et al. 2000] ARENI, Charles S. ; FRERRELL, M. E. ; WILCOX, James B.: The Persuasive Impact of Reported Group Opinions On Individuals Low vs. High in Need for Cognition: Rationalization vs. Biased Elaboration? In: *Psychology & Marketing* 17 (2000), No. 10, pp. 855–875

[Aschenbrenner et al. 1984] ASCHENBRENNER, K. M. ; ALBERT, Dietrich ; SCHMALHOFER, Franz: Stochastic choice heuristics. In: *Acta Psychologica* 56 (1984), No. 1-3, pp. 153–166

[Avison and Elliot 2006] AVISON, David ; ELLIOT, Steve: Scoping the Discipline of Information Systems. In: KING, John L. (Ed.) ; LYYTINEN, Kalle (Ed.): *Information Systems: The State of the Field*. 1. Chichester : Wiley, 2006

[Backs 1998] BACKS, Richard W.: A comparison of factor analytic methods of obtaining cardiovascular autonomic components for the assessment of mental workload. In: *Ergonomics* 41 (1998), No. 5, pp. 733–745

[Bagozzi et al. 1999] BAGOZZI, Richard P. ; GOPINATH, Mahesh ; NYER, Prashanth U.: The Role of Emotions in Marketing. In: *Journal of the Academy of Marketing Science* 27 (1999), No. 2, pp. 184–206

[Baron et al. 1996] BARON, Robert S. ; VANDELLO, Joseph A. ; BRUNSMAN, Bethany: The Forgotten Variable in Conformity Research: Impact of Task Importance on Social Influence. In: *Journal of Personality and Social Psychology* 71 (1996), No. 5, pp. 915–927

[Bawden and Robinson 2009] BAWDEN, David ; ROBINSON, Lyn: The dark side of information: overload, anxiety and other paradoxes and pathologies. In: *Journal of Information Science* 35 (2009), No. 2, pp. 180–191

[Beach and Strom 1989] BEACH, Lee R. ; STROM, Eric: A toadstool among the mushrooms: Screening decisions and image theory's compatibility test. In: *Acta Psychologica* 72 (1989), No. 1, pp. 1–12

[Bearden et al. 2006] BEARDEN, J. N. ; AMNON, Rapoport ; MURPHY, Ryan O.: Sequential Observation and Selection with Rank-Dependent Payoffs: An Experimental Study. In: *Management Science* 52 (2006), No. 9, pp. 1437–1449

[Bearden et al. 2005] BEARDEN, J. N. ; MURPHY, Ryan O. ; RAPOPORT, Amnon: A multi-attribute extension of the secretary problem: Theory and experiments. In: *Journal of Mathematical Psychology* 49 (2005), No. 5, pp. 410–422

[Belkin 1980] BELKIN, Nicholas J.: Anomalous states of knowledge as a basis for information retrieval. In: *The Canadian journal of information science* 5 (1980), pp. 133–143

[Benbasat 2010] BENBASAT, Izak: HCI Research: Future Challenges and Directions. In: *AIS Transactions on Human-Computer Interaction* 2 (2010), No. 2, pp. 16–21

[Berntson et al. 1997] BERNTSON, Gary G. ; BIGGER JR., Thomas ; ECKBERG, Dwain L. ; GROSSMAN, Paul ; KAUFMANN, Peter G. ; MALIK, Marek ; NA-GARAJA, Haikady N. ; PORGES, Stephen W. ; SAUL, J. P. ; STONE, Peter H. ; MOLEN, Maurits W. d.: Heart rate variability: Origins, methods, and interpretive caveats. In: *Psychophysiology* 34 (1997), No. 6, pp. 623–648

[Berntson et al. 1993] BERNTSON, Gary G. ; CACIOPPO, John T. ; QUIGLEY, Karen S.: Respiratory sinus arrhythmia: Autonomic origins, physiological mechanisms, and psychophysiological implications. In: *Psychophysiology* 30 (1993), No. 2, pp. 183–196

[Berntson et al. 1990] BERNTSON, Gary G. ; QUIGLEY, Karen S. ; JANG, Jaye F. ; BOYSEN, Sarah T.: An Approach to Artifact Identification: Application to Heart Period Data. In: *Psychophysiology* 27 (1990), No. 5, pp. 586–598

[Berryman 2008] BERRYMAN, Jennifer M.: Judgements during information seeking: a naturalistic approach to understanding the assessment of enough information. In: *Journal of Information Science* 34 (2008), No. 2, pp. 196–206

[Bhattacherjee 2012] BHATTACHERJEE, Anol: *Social Science Research: Principles, Methods, and Practices*. 2. Zurich : Global Text Project, 2012

[Bhattacherjee and Sanford 2006] BHATTACHERJEE, Anol ; SANFORD, Clive: Influence Processes for Information Technology Acceptance: An Elaboration Likelihood Model. In: *Management Information Systems Quarterly* 30 (2006), No. 4, pp. 805–825

[Bitzer et al. 2007] BITZER, Jürgen ; SCHRETTL, Wolfram ; SCHRÖDER, Philipp J. H.: Intrinsic motivation in open source software development. In: *Journal of Comparative Economics* 35 (2007), No. 1, pp. 160–169

[Bless et al. 1990] BLESS, Herbert ; BOHNER, Gerd ; SCHWARZ, Norbert ; STRACK, Fritz: Mood and Persuasion: A Cognitive Response Analysis. In: *Personality and Social Psychology Bulletin* 16 (1990), No. 2, pp. 331–345

[Bless et al. 1994] BLESS, Herbert ; WÄNKE, Michaela ; BOHNER, Gerd ; FELLHAUER, Roland F. ; SCHWARZ, Norbert: Need for Cognition: Eine Skala zur Erfassung von Engagement und Freude bei Denkaufgaben. In: *Zeitschrift für Sozialpsychologie* 25 (1994), No. 2, pp. 147–154

[Bode 1997] BODE, Jürgen: Der Informationsbegriff in der Betriebswirtschaft-slehre. In: *Zeitschrift für betriebswirtschaftliche Forschung* 49 (1997), No. 5, pp. 449–468

[Bollen and Lennox 1991] BOLLEN, Kenneth ; LENNOX, Richard: Conventional Wisdom on Measurement: A Structural Equation Perspective. In: *Psychological Bulletin* 110 (1991), No. 2, pp. 305–314

[Bonoma 1985] BONOMA, Thomas V.: Case Research in Marketing: Opportunities, Problems, and a Process. In: *Journal of Marketing Research* 22 (1985), No. 2, pp. 199–208

[Bordetsky and Mark 2000] BORDETSKY, Alex ; MARK, Gloria: Memory-Based Feedback Controls to Support Groupware Coordination. In: *Information Systems Research* 11 (2000), No. 4, pp. 366–385

[Borkenau and Ostendorf 2008] BORKENAU, Peter ; OSTENDORF, Fritz: *NEO-FFI: NEO-Fünf-Faktoren-Inventar nach Costa und McCrae*. 2. Hogrefe, 2008

[Brickman 1972] BRICKMAN, Philip: Optional Stopping on Ascending and Descending Series. In: *Organizational Behavior and Human Performance* 7 (1972), No. 1, pp. 53–62

[Browne and Parsons 2012] BROWNE, Glenn J. ; PARSONS, Jeffrey: More Enduring Questions in Cognitive IS Research. In: *Journal of the Association for Information Systems* 13 (2012), No. 12, pp. 1000–1011

[Browne and Pitts 2004] BROWNE, Glenn J. ; PITTS, Mitzi G.: Stopping rule use during information search in design problems. In: *Organizational Behavior and Human Decision Processes* 95 (2004), No. 2, pp. 208–224

[Browne et al. 2005] BROWNE, Glenn J. ; PITTS, Mitzi G. ; WETHERBE, James C.: Stopping Rule Use During Web-Based Search. In: *Proceedings of the 38th Hawaii International Conference on System Sciences*, 2005

[Browne et al. 2007] BROWNE, Glenn J. ; PITTS, Mitzi G. ; WETHERBE, James C.: Cognitive Stopping Rules for Terminating Information Search in Online Tasks. In: *Management Information Systems Quarterly* 31 (2007), No. 1, pp. 89–104

[Burton-Jones 2009] BURTON-JONES, Andrew: Minimizing Method Bias Through Programmatic Research. In: *Management Information Systems Quarterly* 33 (2009), No. 3, pp. 445–471

[Burton-Jones and Straub 2006] BURTON-JONES, Andrew ; STRAUB, Detmar W.: Reconceptualizing System Usage: An Approach and Empirical Test. In: *Information Systems Research* 17 (2006), No. 3, pp. 228–246

[Busemeyer and Rapoport 1988] BUSEMEYER, Jerome R. ; RAPOPORT, Amnon: Psychological Models of Deferred Decision Making. In: *Journal of Mathematical Psychology* 32 (1988), No. 2, pp. 91–134

[Byström and Järvelin 1995] BYSTRÖM, K. ; JÄRVELIN, K.: Task Complexity Affects Information Seeking and Use. In: *Information Processing & Management* 31 (1995), No. 2, pp. 191–213

[Cacioppo and Petty 1982] CACIOPPO, John T. ; PETTY, Richard E.: The Need for Cognition. In: *Journal of Personality and Social Psychology* 42 (1982), No. 1, pp. 116–131

[Cacioppo et al. 1996] CACIOPPO, John T. ; PETTY, Richard E. ; FEINSTEIN, Jeffrey A. ; JARVIS, W. Blair G.: Dispositional Differences in Cognitive Motivation: The Life and Times of Individuals Varying in Need for Cognition. In: *Psychological Bulletin* 119 (1996), No. 2, pp. 197–253

[Cacioppo et al. 1984] CACIOPPO, John T. ; PETTY, Richard E. ; KAO, Chuan F.: The Efficient Assessment of Need for Cognition. In: *Journal of Personality Assessment* 48 (1984), No. 3, pp. 306–307

[Campbell 1988] CAMPBELL, Donald J.: Task Complexity: A Review and Analysis. In: *The Academy of Management Review* 13 (1988), No. 1, pp. 40–52

[Capurro and Hjorland 2003] CAPURRO, Rafael ; HJORLAND, Birger: The Concept of Information. In: *Annual Review of Information Science and Technology* 37 (2003), No. 1, pp. 343–411

[Case 2007] CASE, Donald O.: *Looking for information.* Emerald Group Publishing, 2007

[Chaiken 1980] CHAIKEN, Shelly: Heuristic Versus Systematic Information Processing and the Use of Source Versus Message Cues in Persuasion. In: *Journal of Personality and Social Psychology* 39 (1980), No. 5, pp. 752–766

[Chaiken and Maheswaran 1994] CHAIKEN, Shelly ; MAHESWARAN, Durairaj: Heuristic Processing Can Bias Systematic Processing: Effects of Source Credibility, Argument Ambiguity, and Task Importance on Attitude Judgment. In: *Journal of Personality and Social Psychology* 66 (1994), No. 3, pp. 460–473

[Chalmers 1999] CHALMERS, Alan F.: *What is this thing called Science?* 3. Maidenhead : Open University Press, 1999

[Chen 1995] CHEN, Minder: A Model-Driven Approach to Accessing Managerial Information: The Development of a Repository-Based Executive Information System. In: *Journal of Management Information Systems* 11 (1995), No. 4, pp. 33–63

[Chewning and Harrell 1990] CHEWNING, Eugene G. ; HARRELL, Adrian M.: The effect of information load on decision makers' cue utilization levels and decision quality in a financial distress decision task. In: *Accounting, Organizations and Society* 15 (1990), No. 6, pp. 527–542

[Chin 1998a] CHIN, Wynne W.: Issues and Opinion on Structural Equation Modeling. In: *Management Information Systems Quarterly* 22 (1998), No. 1, pp. vii–xvi

[Chin 1998b] CHIN, Wynne W.: The Partial Least Squares Approach to Structural Equation Modeling. In: MARCOULIDES, George A. (Ed.): *Modern Methods for Business Research*. Mahwah : Lawrence Erlbaum, 1998, pp. 295–336

[Chin 2010] CHIN, Wynne W.: How to Write Up and Report PLS Analyses. In: VINZI, Vincenzo E. (Ed.) ; CHIN, Wynne W. (Ed.) ; HENSELER, Jörg (Ed.) ; WANG, Huiwen (Ed.): *Handbook of Partial Least Squares: Concepts, Methods and Applications*. Berlin : Springer, 2010, pp. 691–711

[Chin and Newsted 1999] CHIN, Wynne W. ; NEWSTED, Peter R.: Structural Equation Modeling: Analysis with Small Samples Using Partial Least Squares. In: HOYLE, R. (Ed.): *Statistical Strategies for Small Sample Research*. Sage Publications, 1999, pp. 307–341

[Choudhury and Sampler 1997] CHOUDHURY, Vivek ; SAMPLER, Jeffrey L.: Information Specificity and Environmental Scanning: An Economic Perspective. In: *Management Information Systems Quarterly* 21 (1997), No. 1, pp. 25–53

[Chung et al. 2005] CHUNG, Wingyan ; CHEN, Hsinchun ; NUNAMAKER JR., Jay F.: A Visual Framework for Knowledge Discovery on the Web: An Empirical Study of Business Intelligence Exploration. In: *Journal of Management Information Systems* 21 (2005), No. 4, pp. 57–84

[Cinaz et al. 2011] CINAZ, Burcu ; ARNRICH, Bert ; LA MARCA, Roberto ; TRÖSTER, Gerhard: Monitoring of mental workload levels during an everyday life office-work scenario. In: *Personal and Ubiquitous Computing Online First* (2011), pp. 1–11

[Cleary and Angel 1984] CLEARY, Paul D. ; ANGEL, Ronald: The Analysis of Relationships Involving Dichotomous Dependent Variables. In: *Journal of Health and Social Behavior* 25 (1984), No. 3, pp. 334–348

[Cohen et al. 1955] COHEN, Arthur R. ; STOTLAND, Ezra ; WOLFE, Donald M.: An Experimental Investigation of Need for Cognition. In: *The Journal of abnormal and social psychology* 51 (1955), No. 2, pp. 291–294

[Cohen 1988] COHEN, Jacob: *Statistical power analysis for the behavioral sciences*. New Jersey : Lawrence Erlbaum Associates, 1988

[Connolly and Gilani 1982] CONNOLLY, Terry ; GILANI, Naveed: Information Search in Judgment Tasks: A Regression Model and Some Preliminary Findings. In: *Organizational Behavior and Human Performance* 30 (1982), No. 3, pp. 330–350

[Connolly and Thorn 1987] CONNOLLY, Terry ; THORN, Brian K.: Predecisional Information Acquisition: Effects of Task Variables on Suboptimal Search Strategies. In: *Organizational Behavior and Human Decision Processes* 39 (1987), No. 3, pp. 397–416

[Cramme 2005] CRAMME, Carsten: *Informationsverhalten als Determinante organisationaler Entscheidungseffizienz*. Mering : Hampp, 2005

[Creswell 2009] CRESWELL, John W.: *Research Design: Qualitative, Quantitative, and Mixed Methods Approaches*. 3. Thousand Oaks : SAGE Publications, 2009

[Cronbach 1951] CRONBACH, Lee J.: Coefficient Alpha and the Internal Structure of Tests. In: *Psychometrika* 16 (1951), No. 3, pp. 297–334

[Cross et al. 2001] CROSS, Rob ; RICE, Ronald E. ; PARKER, Andrew: Information seeking in social context: Structural influences and receipt of information benefits. In: *IEEE Transactions on Systems, Man, and Cybernetics, Part C* 31 (2001), No. 4, pp. 438–448

[Cyr et al. 2009] CYR, Dianne ; HEAD, Milena ; LARIOS, Hector ; PAN, Bing: Exploring Human Images in Website Design: A Multi-Method Approach. In: *Management Information Systems Quarterly* 33 (2009), No. 3, pp. 539–566

[Danneels 2004] DANNEELS, Erwin: Disruptive Technology Reconsidered: A Critique and Research Agenda. In: *Journal of Product Innovation Management* 21 (2004), No. 4, pp. 246–258

[Darley and Smith 1995] DARLEY, William K. ; SMITH, Robert E.: Gender Differences in Information Processing Strategies: An Empirical Test of the Selectivity Model in Advertising Response. In: *Journal of Advertising* 24 (1995), No. 1, pp. 41–56

[Davenport and Prusak 1998] DAVENPORT, Thomas H. ; PRUSAK, Laurence: *Wokring Knowledge: How Organizations Manage What They Know*. Boston, Massachusetts : Harvard Business School Press, 1998

[Davern et al. 2012a] DAVERN, Michael ; SHAFT, Teresa ; TE'ENI, Dov: Cognition Matters: Enduring Questions in Cognitive IS Research. In: *Journal of the Association for Information Systems* 13 (2012), No. Special Issue, pp. 273–314

[Davern et al. 2012b] DAVERN, Michael ; SHAFT, Teresa ; TE'ENI, Dov: More Enduring Questions in Cognitive IS Research: A Reply. In: *Journal of the Association for Information Systems* 13 (2012), No. 12, pp. 1012–1016

[David et al. 2007] DAVID, Prabu ; SONG, Mei ; HAYES, Andrew ; FREDIN, Eric S.: A cyclic model of information seeking in hyperlinked environments:

The role of goals, self-efficacy, and intrinsic motivation. In: *International Journal of Human-Computer Studies* 65 (2007), No. 2, pp. 170–182

[Davis 1989] DAVIS, Fred D.: Perceived Usefulness, Perceived Ease of Use, and User Acceptance of Information Technology. In: *Management Information Systems Quarterly* 13 (1989), No. 3, pp. 319–340

[Davis et al. 1989] DAVIS, Fred D. ; BAGOZZI, Richard P. ; WARSHAW, Paul R.: User Acceptance of Computer Technology: A Comparison of Two Theoretical Models. In: *Management Science* 35 (1989), No. 8, pp. 982–1003

[De et al. 1993] DE, Prabuddha ; JACOB, Varghese S. ; PAKATH, Ramakrishnan: A Formal Approach for Designing Distributed Expert Problem-solving Systems. In: *Information Systems Research* 4 (1993), No. 2, pp. 141–165

[Dennis et al. 2008] DENNIS, A. R. ; FULLER, R. M. ; VALACICH, J. S.: Media, Tasks, and Communication Processes: A Theory of Media Synchronicity. In: *Management Information Systems Quarterly* 32 (2008), No. 3, pp. 575–600

[Dennis 1996] DENNIS, Alan R.: Information Exchange and Use in Group Decision Making: You Can Lead a Group to Information, but You Can't Make It Think. In: *Management Information Systems Quarterly* 20 (1996), No. 4, pp. 433–457

[DeSanctis and Poole 1994] DESANCTIS, Gerardine ; POOLE, Marshall S.: Capturing the Complexity in Advanced Technology Use: Adaptive Structuration Theory. In: *Organization Science* 5 (1994), No. 2, pp. 121–147

[Devaraj et al. 2008] DEVARAJ, S. ; EASLEY, R. F. ; CRANT, J. M.: How Does Personality Matter? Relating the Five-Factor Model to Technology Acceptance and Use. In: *Information Systems Research* 19 (2008), No. 1, pp. 93–105

[Dibbern et al. 2004] DIBBERN, Jens ; GOLES, Tim ; HIRSCHHEIM, Rudy ; JAYATILAKA, Bandula: Information Systems Outsourcing: A Survey and Analysis of the Literature. In: *The DATA BASE for Advances in Information Systems* 35 (2004), No. 4, pp. 6–102

[Dibbern et al. 2001] DIBBERN, Jens ; GÜTTLER, Wolfgang ; HEINZL, Armin: Die Theorie der Unternehmung als Erklärungsansatz für das selektive Outsourcing der Informationsverarbeitung. In: *Zeitschrift für Betriebswirtschaft* 71 (2001), No. 6, pp. 675–700

[Dillman 2007] DILLMAN, Don A.: *Mail and Internet Surveys: The Tailored Design Method*. Second Edition. Hoboken, New Jersey : John Wiley & Sons, 2007

[Dimoka et al. 2012] DIMOKA, Angelika ; BANKER, Rajiv D. ; BENBASAT, Izak ; DAVIS, Fred D. ; DENNIS, Alan R. ; GEFEN, David ; GUPTA, Alok ; IS-CHEBECK, Anja ; KENNING, Peter H. ; PAVLOU, Paul A. ; MÜLLER-PUTZ, Gernot ; RIEDL, René ; BROCKE, Jan vom ; WEBER, Bernd: On the Use of Neurophysiological Tools in IS Research: Developing a Research Agenda for NeuroIS. In: *Management Information Systems Quarterly* 36 (2012), No. 3, pp. 679–702

[Dimoka et al. 2011] DIMOKA, Angelika ; PAVLOU, Paul A. ; DAVIS, Fred D.: NeuroIS: The Potential of Cognitive Neuroscience for Information Systems Research. In: *Information Systems Research* 22 (2011), No. 4, pp. 687–702

[Dou et al. 2010] DOU, Wenyu ; LIM, Kai H. ; SU, Chenting ; ZHOU, Nan ; CUI, Nan: Brand Positioning Strategy Using Search Engine Marketing. In: *Management Information Systems Quarterly* 34 (2010), No. 2, pp. 261–A4

[Dudezert and Leidner 2011] DUDEZERT, Aurélie ; LEIDNER, Dorothy E.: Illusions of control and social domination strategies in knowledge mapping system use. In: *European Journal of Information Systems* 20 (2011), pp. 574–588

[Edwards and Bagozzi 2000] EDWARDS, Jeffrey R. ; BAGOZZI, Richard P.: On the Nature and Direction of Relationships Between Constructs and Measures. In: *Psychological Methods* 5 (2000), No. 2, pp. 155–174

[Edwards et al. 2000] EDWARDS, JS ; DUAN, Y ; C, Robins P.: An analysis of expert systems for business decision making at different levels and in different roles. In: *European Journal of Information Systems* 9 (2000), No. 1, pp. 36–46

[Eisenhardt 1989] EISENHARDT, Kathleen M.: Making Fast Strategic Decisions in High-Velocity Environments. In: *The Academy of Management Journal* 32 (1989), No. 3, pp. 543–576

[El Sawy 1985] EL SAWY, Omar A.: Personal Information Systems for Strategic Scanning in Turbulent Environments: Can the CEO Go On-Line? In: *Management Information Systems Quarterly* 9 (1985), No. 1, pp. 53–60

[Engelmann et al. 2009] ENGELMANN, Jan B. ; DAMARAJU, Eswar ; PADMALA, Srikanth ; PESSOA, Luiz: Combined effects of attention and motivation on visual task performance: transient and sustained motivational effects. In: *Frontiers in Human Neuroscience* 3 (2009), No. 4, pp. 1–17

[Eppler and Mengis 2004] EPPLER, Martin J. ; MENGIS, Jeanne: The Concept of Information Overload: A Review of Literature from Organization Science, Accounting, Marketing, MIS, and Related Disciplines. In: *The Information Society* 20 (2004), pp. 325–344

[Epstein 1994] EPSTEIN, Seymour: Integration of the Cognitive and the Psychodynamic Unconscious. In: *American Psychologist* 49 (1994), No. 8, pp. 709–724

[Epstein et al. 1996] EPSTEIN, Seymour ; PACINI, Rosemary ; DENES-RAJ, Veronika ; HEIER, Harriet: Individual Differences in Intuitive-Experiential and Analytical-Rational Thinking Styles. In: *Journal of Personality and Social Psychology* 71 (1996), No. 2, pp. 390–405

[Evans and Chi 2008] EVANS, Brynn M. ; CHI, Ed H.: Towards a Model of Understanding Social Search. In: *Proceedings of the ACM conference on Computer supported cooperative work*, ACM, 2008, pp. 485–494

[Evans 2003] EVANS, Jonathan St. B. T.: In two minds: dual-process accounts of reasoning. In: *Trends in Cognitive Sciences* 7 (2003), No. 10, pp. 454–459

[Evans 2008] EVANS, Jonathan St. B. T.: Dual-Processing Accounts of Reasoning, Judgment, and Social Cognition. In: *Annual Review of Psychology* 59 (2008), No. 1, pp. 255–278

[Fiegenbaum et al. 1996] FIEGENBAUM, Avi ; HART, Stuart ; SCHENDEL, Dan: Strategic Reference Point Theory. In: *Strategic Management Journal* 17 (1996), No. 3, pp. 219–235

[Field 2009] FIELD, Andy: *Discovering Statistics Using SPSS*. 3. London : SAGE Publications, 2009

[Field and Hole 2003] FIELD, Andy ; HOLE, Graham: *How to Design and Report Experiments*. London : SAGE Publications, 2003

[Fogg 2003] FOGG, B. J.: *Persuasive Technology: Using Computers to Change What We Think and Do*. San Francisco : Morgan Kaufmann Publishers, 2003

[Forman et al. 2008] FORMAN, Chris ; GHOSE, Anindya ; WIESENFELD, Batia: Examining the Relationship Between Reviews and Sales: The Role of Reviewer Identity Disclosure in Electronic Markets. In: *Information Systems Research* 19 (2008), No. 3, pp. 291–313

[Fornell and Cha 1994] FORNELL, Claes ; CHA, Jaesung: Partial Least Squares. In: BAGOZZI, Richard P. (Ed.): *Advanced Methods of Marketing Research*. Cambridge, MA : Blackwell, 1994, pp. 52–78

[Fornell and Larcker 1981] FORNELL, Claes ; LARCKER, David F.: Evaluating Structural Equation Models with Unobservable Variables and Measurement Error. In: *Journal of Marketing Research* 18 (1981), No. 1, pp. 39–50

[Gefen 2003] GEFEN, David: Assessing Unidimensionality Through LISREL: An Explanation and an Example. In: *Communications of the Association for Information Systems* 12 (2003), No. 1, pp. 23–47

[Gefen et al. 2011] GEFEN, David ; RIGDON, Edward E. ; STRAUB, Detmar: An Update and Extension to SEM Guidelines for Administrative and Social Science Research. In: *Management Information Systems Quarterly* 35 (2011), No. 2, pp. iii–xiv

[Gefen and Straub 2004] GEFEN, David ; STRAUB, D. W.: Consumer trust in B2C e-Commerce and the importance of social presence: experiments in e-Products and e-Services. In: *Omega* 32 (2004), No. 6, pp. 407–424

[Gefen and Straub 2005] GEFEN, David ; STRAUB, Detmar: A Practical Guide to Factorial Validity Using PLS-Graph: Tutorial and Annotated Example. In: *Communications of the Association for Information Systems* 16 (2005), No. 1, pp. 91–109

[Gefen et al. 2000] GEFEN, David ; STRAUB, Detmar W. ; BOUDREAU, Marie-Claude: Structural Equation Modeling and Regression: Guidelines for Research Practice. In: *Communications of the Association for Information Systems* 4 (2000), No. 7, pp. 2–77

[Gemünden 1993] GEMÜNDEN, Hans G.: Informationsverhalten. In: HAUSCHILDT, Jürgen (Ed.) ; GRÜN, Oskar (Ed.): *Ergebnisse empirischer betriebswirtschaftlicher Forschung: Zu einer Realtheorie der Unternehmung.* Stuttgart : Schäffer-Poeschel, 1993

[Gigerenzer and Brighton 2009] GIGERENZER, Gerd ; BRIGHTON, Henry: Homo Heuristicus: Why Biased Minds Make Better Inferences. In: *Topics in Cognitive Science* 1 (2009), No. 1, pp. 107–143

[Gigerenzer and Goldstein 1996] GIGERENZER, Gerd ; GOLDSTEIN, Daniel G.: Reasoning the Fast and Frugal Way: Models of Bounded Rationality. In: *Psychological Review* 103 (1996), No. 4, pp. 650–669

[Gigerenzer and Goldstein 1999] GIGERENZER, Gerd ; GOLDSTEIN, Daniel G.: Betting on One Good Reason: Take The Best and Its Relatives. In: GIGERENZER, Gerd (Ed.) ; TODD, Peter M. (Ed.) ; GROUP, ABC R. (Ed.): *Simple Heuristics That Make Us Smart* Vol. 1. Oxford University Press, USA, 1999, pp. 75–95

[Gigerenzer and Goldstein 2011] GIGERENZER, Gerd ; GOLDSTEIN, Daniel G.: The recognition heuristic: A decade of research. In: *Judgment and Decision Making* 6 (2011), No. 1, pp. 100–121

[Gigerenzer et al. 1999] GIGERENZER, Gerd ; TODD, Peter M. ; GROUP, ABC R.: *Simple Heuristics That Make Us Smart.* 1. Oxford University Press, USA, 1999

[Gilovich et al. 2002] GILOVICH, Thomas ; GRIFFIN, Dale ; KAHNEMAN, Daniel: *Heuristics and Biases: The Psychology of Intuitive Judgment.* New York : Cambridge University Press, 2002

[Goodhue et al. 2012a] GOODHUE, Dale L. ; LEWIS, William ; THOMPSON, Ron: Comparing PLS to Regression and LISREL: A Response to Marcoulides, Chin, and Saunders. In: *Management Information Systems Quarterly* 36 (2012), No. 3, pp. 703–716

[Goodhue et al. 2012b] GOODHUE, Dale L. ; LEWIS, William ; THOMPSON, Ron: Does PLS Have Advantages for Small Sample Size or Non-Normal Data? In: *Management Information Systems Quarterly* 36 (2012), No. 3, pp. 981–1001

[Gordon and Moore 1999] GORDON, Michael D. ; MOORE, Scott A.: Depicting the Use and Purpose of Documents to Improve Information Retrieval. In: *Information Systems Research* 10 (1999), No. 1, pp. 23–37

[Gregor 2006] GREGOR, Shirley: The Nature of Theory in Information Systems. In: *Management Information Systems Quarterly* 30 (2006), No. 3, pp. 611–642

[Grisé and Gallupe 1999] GRISÉ, Mary-Liz ; GALLUPE, R. B.: Information Overload: Addressing the Productivity Paradox in Face-to-Face Electronic Meetings. In: *Journal of Management Information Systems* 16 (1999), No. 3, pp. 157–185

[Grunert 1984] GRUNERT, Klaus G.: The Consumer Information Deficit: Assessment and Policy Implications. In: *Journal of Consumer Policy* 7 (1984), No. 3, pp. 359–388

[Götz et al. 2010] GÖTZ, Oliver ; LIEHR-GOBBERS, Kerstin ; KRAFFT, Manfred: Evaluation of Structural Equation Models Using the Partial Least Squares (PLS) Approach. In: VINZI, Vincenzo E. (Ed.) ; CHIN, Wynne W. (Ed.) ; HENSELER, Jörg (Ed.) ; WANG, Huiwen (Ed.): *Handbook of Partial Least Squares: Concepts, Methods and Applications.* Berlin : Springer, 2010, pp. 691–711

[Haerem and Rau 2007] HAEREM, Thorvald ; RAU, Devaki: The Influence of Degree of Expertise and Objective Task Complexity on Perceived Task Complexity and Performance. In: *Journal of Applied Psychology* 92 (2007), No. 5, pp. 1320–1331

[Haines and Mann 2011] HAINES, Russell ; MANN, Joan Ellen C.: A new perspective on de-individuation via computer-mediated communication. In: *European Journal of Information Systems* 20 (2011), No. 2, pp. 156–167

[Hair et al. 2011] HAIR, Joe F. ; RINGLE, Christian M. ; SARSTEDT, Marko: PLS-SEM: Indeed a Silver Bullet. In: *Journal of Marketing Theory and Practice* 19 (2011), No. 2, pp. 139–151

[Hardy 1982] HARDY, Andrew P.: The selection of channels when seeking information: Cost/benefit vs least-effort. In: *Information Processing & Management* 18 (1982), No. 6, pp. 289–293

[Harwell et al. 1992] HARWELL, Michael R. ; RUBINSTEIN, Elaine N. ; HAYES,
William S. ; OLDS, Corley C.: Summarizing Monte Carlo Results in Method-
ological Research: The One- and Two-Factor Fixed Effects ANOVA Cases. In:
Journal of Educational and Behavioral Statistics 17 (1992), No. 4, pp. 315–339

[Hausmann and Lage 2008] HAUSMANN, Daniel ; LAGE, Damian: Sequential
evidence accumulation in decision making: The individual desired level of confidence can explain the extent of information acquisition. In: *Judgment and
Decision Making* 3 (2008), No. 3, pp. 229–243

[van der Heijden 2004] HEIJDEN, Hans van d.: User Acceptance of Hedonic Information Systems. In: *Management Information Systems Quarterly* 28 (2004),
No. 4, pp. 695–704

[Heinrich et al. 2011] HEINRICH, Lutz J. ; HEINZL, Armin ; RIEDL, René:
Wirtschaftsinformatik: Einführung und Grundlegung. 4. Berlin, Heidelberg
: Springer, 2011

[Hemmer and Heinzl 2011] HEMMER, Erik ; HEINZL, Armin: Where is the "I" in
"IS Research"? The Quest for a Coherent Research Stream in the Context of
Human Information Behavior. In: HEINZL, Armin (Ed.) ; BUXMANN, Peter
(Ed.) ; WENDT, Oliver (Ed.) ; WEITZEL, Tim (Ed.): *Theory-Guided Model-
ing and Empiricism in Information Systems Research.* Heidelberg : Physica-
Verlag, 2011, pp. 223–246

[Hemmer and Heinzl 2012] HEMMER, Erik ; HEINZL, Armin: Determinants of
Information Channel Choice: The Impact of Task Complexity and Disposi-
tional Character Traits. In: *45th Hawaii International Conference on System
Sciences*, 2012, pp. 1717–1726

[Henelius et al. 2009] HENELIUS, Andreas ; HIRVONEN, Kati ; HOLM, Anu ; KOR-
PELA, Jussi ; MÜLLER, Kiti: Mental Workload Classification using Heart Rate
Metrics. In: *31st Annual International Conference of the IEEE Engineering in
Medicine and Biology Society*, 2009, pp. 1836–1839

[Henseler and Fassott 2010] HENSELER, Jörg ; FASSOTT, Georg: Testing Moderating Effects in PLS Path Models: An Illustration of Available Procedures. In: VINZI, Vincenzo E. (Ed.) ; CHIN, Wynne W. (Ed.) ; HENSELER, Jörg (Ed.) ; WANG, Huiwen (Ed.): *Handbook of Partial Least Squares: Concepts, Methods and Applications*. Berlin : Springer, 2010, pp. 713–735

[Henseler et al. 2009] HENSELER, Jörg ; RINGLE, Christian M. ; SINKOVICS, Rudolf R.: The Use of Partial Least Squares Path Modeling in International Marketing. In: *Advances in International Marketing* 20 (2009), pp. 277–319

[Herrnstein 1990] HERRNSTEIN, Richard J.: Rational Choice Theory: Necessary but Not Sufficient. In: *American Psychologist* 45 (1990), No. 3, pp. 356–367

[Hertel et al. 2003] HERTEL, Guido ; NIEDNER, Sven ; HERRMANN, Stefanie: Motivation of software developers in Open Source projects: an Internet-based survey of contributors to the Linux kernel. In: *Research Policy* 32 (2003), No. 7, pp. 1159–1177

[Hertzum et al. 1993] HERTZUM, M ; SOES, H ; FROKJAER, E.: Information retrieval systems for professionals: A case study of computer supported legal research. In: *European Journal of Information Systems* 2 (1993), No. 4, pp. 296–303

[Hilbig 2008] HILBIG, Benjamin E.: Individual differences in fast-and-frugal decision making: Neuroticism and the recognition heuristic. In: *Journal of Research in Personality* 42 (2008), No. 6, pp. 1641–1645

[Hirsch 2005] HIRSCH, J. E.: An index to quantify an individual's scientific research output. In: *Proceedings of the National Academy of the USA* 102 (2005), No. 46, pp. 16569?16572

[Hjortskov et al. 2004] HJORTSKOV, Nis ; RISSÉN, Dag ; BLANGSTED, Anne K. ; FALLENTIN, Nils ; LUNDBERG, Ulf ; SØGAARD, Karen: The effect of mental stress on heart rate variability and blood pressure during computer work. In: *European Journal of Applied Physiology* 92 (2004), No. 1-2, pp. 84–89

[Ho et al. 2011] HO, Shuk Y. ; BODOFF, David ; TAM, Kar Y.: Timing of Adaptive Web Personalization and Its Effects on Online Consumer Behavior. In: *Information Systems Research* 22 (2011), No. 3, pp. 660–679

[Homburg and Baumgartner 1998] HOMBURG, Christian ; BAUMGARTNER, Hans: Beurteilung von Kausalmodellen: Bestandsaufnahme und Anwendungsempfehlungen. In: HILDEBRANDT, Lutz (Ed.) ; HOMBURG, Christian (Ed.): *Die Kausalanalyse: Ein Instrument der empirischen betriebswirtschaftlichen Forschung.* Stuttgart : Schäffer-Poeschel, 1998, pp. 343–369

[Hong et al. 2004a] HONG, Weiyin ; THONG, James Y. L. ; TAM, Kar Y.: Does Animation Attract Online Users' Attention? The Effects of Flash on Information Search Performance and Perceptions. In: *Information Systems Research* 15 (2004), No. 1, pp. 60–86

[Hong et al. 2004b] HONG, Weiyin ; THONG, James Y. L. ; TAM, Kar Y.: The Effects of Information Format and Shopping Task on Consumers' Online Shopping Behavior: A Cognitive Fit Perspective. In: *Journal of Management Information Systems* 21 (2004), No. 3, pp. 149–184

[Hovorka and Larsen 2006] HOVORKA, Dirk S. ; LARSEN, Kai R.: Enabling agile adoption practices through network organizations. In: *European Journal of Information Systems* 15 (2006), No. 2, pp. 159–168

[Huber et al. 2007] HUBER, Frank ; HERRMANN, Andreas ; MEYER, Frederik ; VOGEL, Johannes ; VOLLHARDT, Kai: *Kausalmodellierung mit Partial Least Squares: Eine anwendungsorientierte Einführung.* Wiesbaden : Gabler, 2007

[Huber 1983] HUBER, G. P.: Cognitive Style as a Basis for MIS and DSS Designs: Much ado about Nothing? In: *Management Science* 29 (1983), No. 5, pp. 567–579

[Huber 1984] HUBER, George P.: Issues in the Design of Group Decision Support Systems. In: *Management Information Systems Quarterly* 8 (1984), No. 3, pp. 195–204

[Ives 1982] IVES, Blake: Graphical User Interfaces for Business Information Systems. In: *Management Information Systems Quarterly* 6 (1982, Special Issue), pp. 15–47

[Jennings et al. 1992] JENNINGS, J. R. ; KAMARCK, Thomas ; STEWART, Christopher ; EDDY, Michael ; JOHNSON, Paul: Alternate Cardiovascular Baseline

Assessment Techniques: Vanilla or Resting Baseline. In: *Psychophysiology* 29 (1992), No. 6, pp. 742–750

[Jiang et al. 2005] JIANG, Zhengrui ; MOOKERJEE, Vijay S. ; SARKAR, Sumit: Lying on the Web: Implications for Expert Systems Redesign. In: *Information Systems Research* 16 (2005), No. 2, pp. 131–148

[Johnson 2005] JOHNSON, Branden B.: Testing and Expanding a Model of Cognitive Processing of Risk Information. In: *Risk Analysis* 25 (2005), No. 3, pp. 631–650

[Jones et al. 2010] JONES, Chris ; RAMANAU, Ruslan ; CROSS, Simon ; HEALING, Graham: Net generation or Digital Natives: Is there a distinct new generation entering university? In: *Computers & Education* 54 (2010), No. 3, pp. 722–732

[Jones et al. 1993] JONES, J W. ; SAUNDERS, C ; MCLEOD, R J.: Media usage and velocity in executive information acquisition: An exploratory study. In: *European Journal of Information Systems* 2 (1993), No. 4, pp. 260

[Jones et al. 2004] JONES, Quentin ; RAVID, Gilad ; RAFAELI, Sheizaf: Information Overload and the Message Dynamics of Online Interaction Spaces: A Theoretical Model and Empirical Exploration. In: *Information Systems Research* 15 (2004), No. 2, pp. 194–210

[Junglas et al. 2008] JUNGLAS, I. A. ; JOHNSON, N. A. ; SPITZMÜLLER, C.: Personality traits and concern for privacy: an empirical study in the context of location-based services. In: *European Journal of Information Systems* 17 (2008), No. 4, pp. 387–402

[Kahneman 2003] KAHNEMAN, Daniel: A Perspective on Judgment and Choice. In: *American Psychologist* 58 (2003), No. 9, pp. 697–720

[Kahneman 2011] KAHNEMAN, Daniel: *Thinking, Fast and Slow.* Vol. 1. New York : Farrar, Straus and Giroux, 2011

[Kahneman et al. 1982] KAHNEMAN, Daniel ; SLOVIC, Paul ; TVERSKY, Amos: *Judgment under Uncertainty: Heuristics and Biases.* Vol. 1. Cambridge University Press, 1982

[Kaplan and Duchon 1988] KAPLAN, Bonnie ; DUCHON, Dennis: Combining Qualitative and Quantitative Methods in Information Systems Research: A Case Study. In: *Management Information Systems Quarterly* 12 (1988), No. 4, pp. 571–586

[Katsikopoulos and Lan 2011] KATSIKOPOULOS, Konstantinos V. ; LAN, Cherng-Horng: Herbert Simon's spell on judgment and decision making. In: *Judgment and Decision Making* 6 (2011), No. 8, pp. 722–732

[Kettinger and Li 2010] KETTINGER, William J. ; LI, Yuan: The infological equation extended: towards conceptual clarity in the relationship between data, information and knowledge. In: *European Journal of Information Systems* 19 (2010), No. 4, pp. 409–421

[Kim et al. 2009] KIM, Gimun ; SHIN, BongSik ; LEE, Ho G.: Understanding dynamics between initial trust and usage intentions of mobile banking. In: *Information Systems Journal* 19 (2009), No. 3, pp. 283–311

[Klein and Myers 1999] KLEIN, Heinz K. ; MYERS, Michael D.: A Set of Principles for Conducting and Evaluating Interpretive Field Studies in Information Systems. In: *Management Information Systems Quarterly* 23 (1999), No. 1, pp. 67–94

[Klein and Ford 2003] KLEIN, Lisa R. ; FORD, Gary T.: Consumer Search for Information in the Digital Age: An Empirical Study of Prepurchase Search for Automobiles. In: *Journal of Interactive Marketing* 17 (2003), No. 3, pp. 29–49

[Kock 2004] KOCK, Ned: The Psychbiological Model: Towards a New Theory of Computer-Mediated Communication Based on Darwinian Evolution. In: *Organization Science* 15 (2004), No. 3, pp. 327–348

[Kock 2005] KOCK, Ned: Media Richness or Media Naturalness? The Evolution of Our Biological Communication Apparatus and Its Influence on Our Behavior Toward E-Communication Tools. In: *IEEE Transactions on Professional Communication* 48 (2005), No. 2, pp. 117–130

[Kock 2009] KOCK, Ned: Information Systems Theorizing Based on Evolutionary Psychology: An Interdisciplinary Review and Theory Integration Framework. In: *Management Information Systems Quarterly* 33 (2009), No. 2, pp. 395–418

[Kogut 1990] KOGUT, Carl A.: Consumer search behavior and sunk costs. In: *Journal of Economic Behavior & Organization* 14 (1990), No. 3, pp. 381–392

[Kohli and Grover 2008] KOHLI, Rajiv ; GROVER, Varun: Business Value of IT: An Essay on Expanding Research Directions to Keep up with the Times. In: *Journal of the Association for Information Systems* 9 (2008), No. 1, pp. 23–39

[Koufaris 2002] KOUFARIS, Marios: Applying the Technology Acceptance Model and Flow Theory to Online Consumer Behavior. In: *Information Systems Research* 13 (2002), No. 2, pp. 205–223

[Kraft and Lee 1979] KRAFT, Donald H. ; LEE, T.: Stopping Rules and their Effect on Expected Search Length. In: *Information Processing & Management* 15 (1979), No. 1, pp. 47–58

[Krishnan et al. 2001] KRISHNAN, Ramayya ; LI, Xiaoping ; STEIER, David ; ZHAO, Leon: On Heterogeneous Database Retrieval: A Cognitively Guided Approach. In: *Information Systems Research* 12 (2001), No. 3, pp. 286–301

[Kruglanski and Webster 1996] KRUGLANSKI, Arie W. ; WEBSTER, Donna M.: Motivated Closing of the Mind: "Seizing" and "Freezing". In: *Psychological Review* 103 (1996), No. 2, pp. 263–283

[Kuechler and Vaishnavi 2006] KUECHLER, William L. ; VAISHNAVI, Vijay: So, Talk to Me, The Effect of Explicit Goals on the Comprehension of Business Process Narratives. In: *Management Information Systems Quarterly* 30 (2006), No. 4, pp. 961–979

[Kumar and Benbasat 2006] KUMAR, N. ; BENBASAT, I.: The Influence of Recommendations and Consumer Reviews on Evaluations of Websites. In: *Information Systems Research* 17 (2006), No. 4, pp. 425–439

[Kumar and Benbasat 2002] KUMAR, Nanda ; BENBASAT, Izak: Para-Social Presence and Communication Capabilities of a Web Site. In: *e-Service Journal* 1 (2002), No. 3, pp. 5–24

[Kumar and Benbasat 2004] KUMAR, Nanda ; BENBASAT, Izak: The Effect of Relationship Encoding, Task Type, and Complexity on Information Representation: An Empirical Evaluation of 2D and 3D Line Graphs. In: *Management Information Systems Quarterly* 28 (2004), No. 2, pp. 255–281

[Kuo et al. 2004] KUO, Feng-Yang ; CHU, Tsai-Hsin ; HSU, Meng-Hsiang ; HSIEH, Hong-Ssu: An investigation of effort-accuracy trade-off and the impact of self-efficacy on Web searching behaviors. In: *Decision Support Systems* 37 (2004), No. 3, pp. 331–342

[Kuruzovich et al. 2008] KURUZOVICH, Jason ; VISWANATHAN, Siva ; AGARWAL, Ritu ; GOSAIN, Sanjay ; WEITZMAN, Scott: Marketspace or Marketplace? Online Information Search and Channel Outcomes in Auto Retailing. In: *Information Systems Research* 19 (2008), No. 2, pp. 182–201

[Lai 2010] LAI, Linda: Maximizing without difficulty: A modified maximizing scale and its correlates. In: *Judgment and Decision Making* 5 (2010), No. 3, pp. 164–175

[Laudan 1984] LAUDAN, Larry: *Science and Values: The Aims of Science and their Role in Scientific Debate*. Berkeley : University of California Press, 1984

[Lee 1991] LEE, Allen S.: Integrating Positivist and Interpretive Approaches to Organizational Research. In: *Organization Science* 2 (1991), No. 4, pp. 342–365

[Léger et al. 2010] LÉGER, Pierre-Majorique ; DAVIS, Fred D. ; PERRET, Julien ; DUNAWAY, Mary M.: Psychophysiological Measures of Cognitive Absorption. In: *Proceedings of the Special Interest Group on Human-Computer Interaction*, 2010

[Li and Kettinger 2006] LI, Yuan ; KETTINGER, William J.: An Evolutionary Information-Processing Theory of Knowledge Creation. In: *Journal of the Association for Information Systems* 7 (2006), No. 9, pp. 593–616

[Liang and Doong 1999] LIANG, Ting-Peng ; DOONG, Her-Sen: Effect of bargaining in electronic commerce. In: *International Conference on Advance Issues of E-Commerce and Web-Based Information Systems*, 1999, pp. 174–181

[Liang et al. 2006] LIANG, Ting-Peng ; LAI, Hung-Jen ; KU, Yi-Cheng: Personalized Content Recommendation and User Satisfaction: Theoretical Synthesis and Empirical Findings. In: *Journal of Management Information Systems* 23 (2006), No. 3, pp. 45–70

[Lieberman 2000] LIEBERMAN, Matthew D.: Intuition: A Social Cognitive Neuroscience Approach. In: *Psychological Bulletin* 126 (2000), No. 1, pp. 109–137

[Lieberman 2003] LIEBERMAN, Matthew D.: Reflexive and Reflective Judgment Processes: A Social Cognitive Neuroscience Approach. In: FORGAS, Joseph P. (Ed.) ; WILLIAMS, Kipling D. (Ed.) ; HIPPEL, William von (Ed.): *Social Judgments: Implicit and Explicit Processes*. Cambridge : Cambridge University Press, 2003, pp. 44–67

[Lieberman et al. 2004] LIEBERMAN, Matthew D. ; JARCHO, Johanna M. ; SATPUTE, Ajay B.: Evidence-Based and Intuition-Based Self-Knowledge: An fMRI Study. In: *Journal of Personality and Social Psychology* 87 (2004), No. 4, pp. 421–435

[Lim et al. 2000] LIM, Kai H. ; BENBASAT, Izak ; WARD, Lawrence M.: The Role of Multimedia in Changing First Impression Bias. In: *Information Systems Research* 11 (2000), No. 2, pp. 115–136

[Lin et al. 1999] LIN, Chienting ; CHEN, Hsinchun ; NUNAMAKER, Jay F.: Verifying the Proximity and Size Hypothesis for Self-Organizing Maps. In: *Journal of Management Information Systems* 16 (1999), No. 3, pp. 57–70

[Locke and Golden-Biddle 1997] LOCKE, K. ; GOLDEN-BIDDLE, K.: Constructing Opportunities for Contribution: Structuring Intertextual Coherence and 'Problematizing' in Organizational Studies. In: *Academy of Management Journal* 40 (1997), No. 5, pp. 1023–1062

[Machlup 1983] MACHLUP, Fritz: Semantic Quirks in Studies of Information. In: MACHLUP, Fritz (Ed.) ; MANSFIELD, Una (Ed.): *The Study of Information: Interdisciplinary Messages*. New York : John Wiley & Sons, 1983

[MacInnis and Jaworski 1989] MACINNIS, Deborah J. ; JAWORSKI, Bernard J.: Information Processing from Advertisements: Toward an Integrative Framework. In: *Journal of Marketing* 53 (1989), No. 4, pp. 1–23

[Majchrzak and Jarvenpaa 2010] MAJCHRZAK, Ann ; JARVENPAA, Sirkka L.: Safe Contexts for Interorganizational Collaborations Among Homeland Security Professionals. In: *Journal of Management Information Systems* 27 (2010), No. 2, pp. 55–86

[Malik 1996] MALIK, Marek: Heart Rate Variability: Standards of Measurement, Physiological Interpretation, and Clinical Use. In: *Circulation* 93 (1996), No. 5, pp. 1043–1065

[Mani and Barua 2010] MANI, Deepa ; BARUA, Anitesh: An Empirical Analysis of the Impact of Information Capabilities Design on Business Process Outsourcing Performance. In: *Management Information Systems Quarterly* 34 (2010), No. 1, pp. 39–62

[Marewski et al. 2010] MAREWSKI, Julian N. ; GAISSMAIER, Wolfgang ; GIGERENZER, Gerd: Good judgments do not require complex cognition. In: *Cognitive processing* 11 (2010), No. 2, pp. 103–121

[Martin et al. 1993] MARTIN, Leonard L. ; WARD, David W. ; ACHEE, John W. ; WYER, Robert S. J.: Mood as Input: People Have to Interpret the Motivational Implications of Their Moods. In: *Journal of Personality and Social Psychology* 64 (1993), No. 3, pp. 317–326

[Matzler et al. 2008] MATZLER, K. ; RENZL, B. ; MÜLLER, J. ; HERTING, S. ; MOORADIAN, T. A.: Personality traits and knowledge sharing. In: *Journal of Economic Psychology* 29 (2008), No. 3, pp. 301–313

[Maynard and Hakel 1997] MAYNARD, Douglas C. ; HAKEL, Milton D.: Effects of Objective and Subjective Task Complexity on Performance. In: *Human Performance* 10 (1997), No. 4, pp. 303–330

[McComas and Trumbo 2001] MCCOMAS, Katherine A. ; TRUMBO, Craig W.: Source Credibility in Environmental Health-Risk Controversies: Application of Meyer's Credibility Index. In: *Risk Analysis* 21 (2001), No. 3, pp. 467–480

[McElroy et al. 2007] MCELROY, James C. ; HENDRICKSON, Anthony R. ; TOWNSEND, Anthony M. ; DEMARIE, Samuel M.: Dispositional Factors in Internet Use: Personality Versus Cognitive Style. In: *Management Information Systems Quarterly* 31 (2007), No. 4, pp. 809–820

[McGrath 1981] MCGRATH, Joseph E.: Dilemmatics: The Study of Research Choices and Dilemmas. In: *American Behavioral Scientist* 25 (1981), No. 2, pp. 179–210

[McKinney Jr. and Yoos II 2010] MCKINNEY JR., Earl H. ; YOOS II, Charles J.: Information About Information: A Taxonomy of Views. In: *Management Information Systems Quarterly* 34 (2010), No. 2, pp. 329–344

[Meho and Yang 2007] MEHO, Lokman I. ; YANG, Kiduk: Impact of Data Sources on Citation Counts and Rankings of LIS Faculty: Web of Science vs. Scopus and Google Scholar. In: *Journal of the American Society for Information Science and Technology* 58 (2007), No. 13, pp. 2105–2125

[Melville and Ramirez 2008] MELVILLE, Nigel ; RAMIREZ, Ronald: Information technology innovation diffusion: an information requirements paradigm. In: *Information Systems Journal* 18 (2008), No. 3, pp. 247–273

[Mendelson and Pillai 1998] MENDELSON, Haim ; PILLAI, Ravindran R.: Clockspeed and Informational Response: Evidence from the Information Technology Industry. In: *Information Systems Research* 9 (1998), No. 4, pp. 415–433

[Mennecke and Valacich 1998] MENNECKE, Brian E. ; VALACICH, Joseph S.: Information Is What You Make of It: The Influence of Group History and Computer Support on Information Sharing, Decision Quality, and Member Perceptions. In: *Journal of Management Information Systems* 15 (1998), No. 2, pp. 173–197

[Meredith et al. 1989] MEREDITH, Jack R. ; RATURI, Amitabh ; AMOAKO-GYAMPAH, Kwasi ; KAPLAN, Bonnie: Alternative Research Paradigms in Operations. In: *Journal of Operations Management* 8 (1989), No. 4, pp. 297–326

[Mesmer-Magnus and DeChurch 2009] MESMER-MAGNUS, Jessica R. ; DECHURCH, Leslie A.: Information Sharing and Team Performance: A Meta-Analysis. In: *Journal of Applied Psychology* 94 (2009), No. 2, pp. 535–546

[Metzger et al. 2010] METZGER, Miriam J. ; FLANAGIN, Andrew J. ; MEDDERS, Ryan B.: Social and Heuristic Approaches to Credibility Evaluation Online. In: *Journal of Communication* 60 (2010), No. 3, pp. 413–439

[Meyer 1982] MEYER, Robert J.: A Descriptive Model of Consumer Information Search Behavior. In: *Marketing Science* 1 (1982), No. 1, pp. 93 – 121

[Meyers-Levy and Malaviya 1999] MEYERS-LEVY, Joan ; MALAVIYA, Prashant: Consumers' Processing of Persuasive Advertisements: An Integrative Framework of Persuasion Theories. In: *Journal of Marketing* 63 (1999), No. 4, pp. 45–60

[Miller and Ireland 2005] MILLER, C. C. ; IRELAND, R. D.: Intuition in Strategic Decision Making: Friend or Foe in the Fast-Paced 21st Century? In: *The Academy of Management Executive* 19 (2005), No. 1, pp. 19–30

[Mingers 2001] MINGERS, John: Combining IS Research Methods: Towards a Pluralist Methodology. In: *Information Systems Research* 12 (2001), No. 3, pp. 240–259

[Miranda and Saunders 2003] MIRANDA, Shaila ; SAUNDERS, Carol S.: The Social Construction of Meaning: An Alternative Perspective on Information Sharing. In: *Information Systems Research* 14 (2003), No. 1, pp. 87–106

[Moore et al. 1997] MOORE, J. C. ; RAO, H. R. ; WHINSTON, A. ; NAM, K. ; RAGHU, T. S.: Information Acquisition Policies for Resource Allocation Among Multiple Agents. In: *Information Systems Research* 8 (1997), No. 2, pp. 151–170

[Morris et al. 1992] MORRIS, Andrew H. ; KASPER, George M. ; ADAMS, Dennis A.: The Effects and Limitations of Automated Text Condensing on Reading Comprehension Performance. In: *Information Systems Research* 3 (1992), No. 1, pp. 17–35

[Morris et al. 2010] MORRIS, Meredith R. ; TEEVAN, Jaime ; PANOVICH, Katrina: What Do People Ask Their Social Networks, and Why? A Survey Study of Status Message Q&A Behavior. In: *CHI 2010*. Atlanta, 2010, pp. 1739–1748

[Mudambi and Schuff 2010] MUDAMBI, Susan M. ; SCHUFF, David: What Makes a Helpful Online Review? A Study of Customer Reviews on Amazon.com. In: *Management Information Systems Quarterly* 34 (2010), No. 1, pp. 185–200

[Murata and Iwase 1998] MURATA, Atsuo ; IWASE, Hirokazu: Evaluation of Mental Workload by Fluctuation Analysis of Pupil Area. In: *Proceedings of the 20th Annual International Conference of the IEEE Engineering in Medicine and Biology Society* Vol. 20, 1998, pp. 3094–3097

[Nadkarni and Gupta 2007] NADKARNI, Sucheta ; GUPTA, Reetika: A Task-Based Model of Perceived Website Complexity. In: *Management Information Systems Quarterly* 31 (2007), No. 3, pp. 501–524

[Nelson et al. 2005] NELSON, R. R. ; TODD, Peter A. ; WIXOM, Barbara H.: Antecedents of Information and System Quality: An Empirical Examination Within the Context of Data Warehousing. In: *Journal of Management Information Systems* 21 (2005), No. 4, pp. 199–235

[Newbold et al. 2010] NEWBOLD, Paul ; CARLSON, William L. ; THORNE, Betty M.: *Statistics for Business and Economics.* 7th Edition. New Jersey : Pearson, 2010

[Newman 2001] NEWMAN, Julian: Some Observations on the Semantics of "Information". In: *Information Systems Frontiers* 3 (2001), No. 2, pp. 155–167

[Nickles et al. 1995] NICKLES, KKathryn R. ; CURLEY, Shawn P. ; BENSON, P. G.: Judgment-Based and Reasoning-Based Stopping Rules in Decision Making under Uncertainty. In: *Working Paper, Wake Forest University* (1995)

[Novak and Hoffman 2009] NOVAK, Thomas P. ; HOFFMAN, Donna L.: The Fit of Thinking Style and Situation - New Measures of Situation-Specific Experiential and Rational Cognition. In: *Journal of Consumer Research* 36 (2009), No. 1, pp. 56–72

[Orlikowski and Baroudi 1991] ORLIKOWSKI, Wanda J. ; BAROUDI, Jack J.: Studying Information Technology in Organizations: Research Approaches and Assumptions. In: *Information Systems Research* 2 (1991), No. 1, pp. 1–28

[Pacini and Epstein 1999] PACINI, Rosemary ; EPSTEIN, Seymour: The Relation of Rational and Experiential Information Processing Styles to Personality, Basic Beliefs, and the Ratio-Bias Phenomenon. In: *Journal of Personality and Social Psychology* 76 (1999), No. 6, pp. 972–987

[Payne 1982] PAYNE, John W.: Contingent Decision Behavior. In: *Psychological Bulletin* 92 (1982), No. 2, pp. 382–402

[Payne et al. 1992] PAYNE, John W. ; BETTMAN, James R. ; JOHNSON, Eric J.: Behavioral Decision Research: A Constructive Processing Perspective. In: *Annual Review of Psychology* 43 (1992), pp. 87–131

[Payne et al. 1993] PAYNE, John W. ; BETTMAN, James R. ; JOHNSON, Eric J.: *The Adaptive Decision Maker.* Cambridge : Cambridge University Press, 1993

[Petter et al. 2007] PETTER, Stacie ; STRAUB, Detmar ; RAI, Arun: Specifying Formative Constructs in Information Systems Research. In: *Management Information Systems Quarterly* 31 (2007), No. 4, pp. 623–656

[Petty et al. 2009] PETTY, Richard E. ; BRIÑOL, Pablo ; LOERSCH, Chris ; MCCASLIN, Michael J.: The Need for Cognition. In: LEARY, Mark R. (Ed.) ; HOYLE, Rick H. (Ed.): *Handbook of Individual Differences in Social Behavior.* New York : The Guilford Press, 2009, pp. 318–329

[Petty and Cacioppo 1986] PETTY, Richard E. ; CACIOPPO, John T.: The Elaboration Likelihood Model of Persuasion. In: BERKOWITZ, L. (Ed.): *Advances in Experimental Social Psychology* Vol. 19. New York : Academic Press, 1986, pp. 123–203

[Pirolli 2005] PIROLLI, Peter: Rational Analyses of Information Foraging on the Web. In: *Cognitive science* 29 (2005), No. 3, pp. 343–373

[Pitts and Browne 2004] PITTS, Mitzi G. ; BROWNE, Glenn J.: Stopping Behavior of Systems Analysts During Information Requirements Elicitation. In: *Journal of Management Information Systems* 21 (2004), No. 1, pp. 203–226

[Prabha et al. 2007] PRABHA, Chandra ; CONNAWAY, Lynn S. ; OLSZEWSKI, Lawrence ; JENKINS, Lillie R.: What is enough? Satisficing information needs. In: *Journal of Documentation* 63 (2007), No. 1, pp. 74–89

[Prensky 2001] PRENSKY, M.: Digital natives, digital immigrants. In: *On the horizon* 9 (2001), No. 5, pp. 1–6

[Qiu and Benbasat 2009] QIU, Lingyun ; BENBASAT, Izak: Evaluating Anthropo-
morphic Product Recommendation Agents - A Social Relationship Perspective
to Designing Information Systems. In: *Journal of Management Information
Systems* 25 (2009), No. 4, pp. 145–181

[Rafaeli and Ravid 2003] RAFAELI, Sheizaf ; RAVID, Gilad: Information sharing
as enabler for the virtual team: an experimental approach to assessing the role
of electronic mail in disintermediation. In: *Information Systems Journal* 13
(2003), No. 2, pp. 191–206

[Rapoport and Tversky 1970] RAPOPORT, Amnon ; TVERSKY, Amos: Choice
Behavior in an Optional Stopping Task. In: *Organizational Behavior and
Human Performance* 5 (1970), No. 2, pp. 105–120

[Reinartz et al. 2009] REINARTZ, Werner ; HAENLEIN, Michael ; HENSELER, Jörg:
An empirical comparison of the efficacy of covariance-based and variance-based
SEM. In: *International Journal of Research in Marketing* 26 (2009), No. 4,
pp. 332–344

[Reisen et al. 2008] REISEN, Nils ; HOFFRAGE, Ulrich ; MAST, Fred W.: Identifying decision strategies in a consumer choice situation. In: *Judgment and
Decision Making* 3 (2008), No. 8, pp. 641–658

[Ren et al. 2008] REN, Yuqing ; KIESLER, Sara ; FUSSELL, Susan R.: Multiple
Group Coordination in Complex and Dynamic Task Environments: Interrup-
tions, Coping Mechanisms, and Technology Recommendations. In: *Journal of
Management Information Systems* 25 (2008), No. 1, pp. 105–130

[Riedl et al. 2010a] RIEDL, René ; BANKER, Rajiv D. ; BANBASAT, Izak ; DAVIS,
Fred D. ; DENNIS, Alan R. ; DIMOKA, Angelika ; GEFEN, David ; GUPTA, Alok
; ISCHEBECK, Anja ; KENNING, Peter ; MÜLLER-PUTZ, Gernot ; PAVLOU,
Paul A. ; STRAUB, Detmar W. ; BROCKE, Jan vom ; WEBER, Bernd: On
the Foundations of NeuroIS: Reflections on the Gmunden Retreat 2009. In:
Communications of the Association for Information Systems 27 (2010), pp.
243–264

[Riedl et al. 2008] RIEDL, René ; BRANDSTÄTTER, Eduard ; ROITHMAYR, Friedrich: Identifying decision strategies: A process- and outcome-based classification method. In: *Behavior Research Methods* 40 (2008), No. 3, pp. 795–807

[Riedl et al. 2010b] RIEDL, René ; HUBERT, Marco ; KENNING, Peter: Are There Neural Gender Differences in Online Trust? An fMRI Study on the Perceived Trustworthiness of eBay Offers. In: *Management Information Systems Quarterly* 34 (2010), No. 2, pp. 397–428

[Robey and Taggart 1982] ROBEY, Daniel ; TAGGART, William: Human Information Processing in Information and Decision Support Systems. In: *Management Information Systems Quarterly* 6 (1982), No. 2, pp. 61–73

[Rudy 1996] RUDY, Ian A.: A critical review of research on electronic mail. In: *European Journal of Information Systems* 4 (1996), No. 4, pp. 198

[Saad and Russo 1996] SAAD, Gad ; RUSSO, J.Edward: Stopping Criteria in Sequential Choice. In: *Organizational Behavior and Human Decision Processes* 67 (1996), No. 3, pp. 258–270

[Scandura and Williams 2000] SCANDURA, Terri A. ; WILLIAMS, Ethlyn A.: Research Methodology in Management: Current Practices, Trends, and Implications for Future Research. In: *The Academy of Management Journal* 43 (2000), No. 6, pp. 1248–1264

[Scheepers 2006] SCHEEPERS, Rens: A conceptual framework for the implementation of enterprise information portals in large organizations. In: *European Journal of Information Systems* 15 (2006), No. 6, pp. 635

[Schmalhofer et al. 1986] SCHMALHOFER, Franz ; ALBERT, Dietrich ; ASCHENBRENNER, K. M. ; GERTZEN, Heiner: Process Traces of Binary Choices: Evidence for Selective and Adaptive Decision Heuristics. In: *The Quarterly Journal of Experimental Psychology* 38 (1986), No. 1, pp. 59–76

[Schneider and Shiffrin 1977] SCHNEIDER, Walter ; SHIFFRIN, Richard M.: Controlled and Automatic Human Information Processing: I. Detection, Search, and Attention. In: *Psychological Review* 84 (1977), No. 1, pp. 1–66

[Schoberth and Heinzl 2001] SCHOBERTH, Thomas ; HEINZL, Armin: Virtual Communities as a Communication Instrument for Infomediaries: Typologies and Properties. In: *Americas Conference on Information Systems*, 2001

[Scholl 1999] SCHOLL, Wolfgang: Restrictive Control and Information Pathologies in Organizations. In: *Journal of Social Issues* 55 (1999), No. 1, pp. 101–118

[Schultze and Orlikowski 2004] SCHULTZE, Ulrike ; ORLIKOWSKI, Wanda J.: A Practice Perspective on Technology-Mediated Network Relations: The Use of Internet-Based Self-Serve Technologies. In: *Information Systems Research* 15 (2004), No. 1, pp. 87–106

[Schunk 2009] SCHUNK, Daniel: Behavioral heterogeneity in dynamic search situations: Theory and experimental evidence. In: *Journal of Economic Dynamics & Control* 33 (2009), No. 9, pp. 1719–1738

[Schwartz et al. 2002] SCHWARTZ, Barry ; WARD, Andrew ; MONTEROSSO, John ; LYUBOMIRSKY, Sonja ; WHIE, Katherine ; LEHMAN, Darrin R.: Maximizing Versus Satisficing: Happiness Is a Matter of Choice. In: *Journal of Personality and Social Psychology* 83 (2002), No. 5, pp. 1178–1197

[Schwarz 2000] SCHWARZ, Norbert: Emotion, cognition, and decision making. In: *Cognition & Emotion* 14 (2000), No. 4, pp. 433–440

[Seale and Rapoport 1997] SEALE, Darryl ; RAPOPORT, Amnon: Sequential Decision Making with Relative Ranks: An Experimental Investigation of the "Secretary Problem". In: *Organizational Behavior and Human Decision Processes* 69 (1997), No. 3, pp. 221–236

[Shannon 1948] SHANNON, Claude E.: A Mathematical Theory of Communication. In: *The Bell System Technical Journal* 27 (1948), pp. 279–423

[Shiv and Fedorikhin 1999] SHIV, Baba ; FEDORIKHIN, Alexander: Heart and Mind in Conflict: The Interplay of Affect and Cognition in Consumer Decision Making. In: *Journal of Consumer Research* 26 (1999), No. 3, pp. 278–292

[Short et al. 1976] SHORT, John ; WILLIAMS, Ederyn ; CHRISTIE, Bruce: *The Social Psychology of Telecommunications*. London : Wiley, 1976

[Shugan 1980] SHUGAN, Steven M.:   The Cost of Thinking.   In: *Journal of Consumer Research* 7 (1980), No. 2, pp. 99–111

[Simon 1955] SIMON, Herbert A.:   A Behavioral Model of Rational Choice.   In: *The Quarterly Journal of Economics* 69 (1955), No. 1, pp. 99–118

[Simon 1982] SIMON, Herbert A.:   Designing organizations for an information-rich world. In: SIMON, H. A. (Ed.): *Models of bounded rationality* Vol. 2. Cambridge : MIT Press, 1982

[Simon 1996] SIMON, Herbert A.:   *The Sciences of the Artificial.* Cambridge : MIT Press, 1996

[Sloman 1996] SLOMAN, Steven A.:   The Empirical Case for Two Systems of Reasoning. In: *Psychological Bulletin* 119 (1996), No. 1, pp. 3–22

[Smith and DeCoster 2000] SMITH, Eliot R. ; DECOSTER, Jamie: Dual-Process Models in Social and Cognitive Psychology: Conceptual Integration and Links to Underlying Memory Systems. In: *Personality and Social Psychology Review* 4 (2000), No. 2, pp. 108–131

[Smyth and Balfe 2006] SMYTH, Barry ; BALFE, Evelyn: Anonymous personalization in collaborative web search. In: *Information Retrieval* 9 (2006), No. 2, pp. 165–190

[Sonnemans 1998] SONNEMANS, Joep: Strategies of search. In: *Journal of Economic Behavior & Organization* 35 (1998), No. 3, pp. 309–332

[Specht 1986] SPECHT, Pamela H.:   Job Characteristics as Indicants of CBIS Data Requirements. In: *Management Information Systems Quarterly* 10 (1986), No. 3, pp. 271–287

[Speier and Morris 2003] SPEIER, Cheri ; MORRIS, Michael G.:   The Influence of Query Interface Design on Decision-Making Performance. In: *Management Information Systems Quarterly* 27 (2003), No. 3, pp. 397–423

[Spetzler and Stael Von Holstein 1975] SPETZLER, Carl S. ; STAEL VON HOLSTEIN, Carl-Axel S.: Probability Encoding in Decision Analysis. In: *Management Science* 22 (1975), No. 3, pp. 340–358

[Stanovich and West 2000] STANOVICH, Keith E. ; WEST, Richard F.: Individual differences in reasoning: Implications for the rationality debate? In: *Behavioral and Brain Sciences* 23 (2000), No. 5, pp. 645–726

[Stenmark 2001] STENMARK, Dick: Leveraging Tacit Organizational Knowledge. In: *Journal of Management Information Systems* 17 (2001), No. 3, pp. 9–24

[Stigler 1961] STIGLER, George J.: The Economics of Information. In: *The Journal of Political Economy* 69 (1961), No. 3, pp. 213–225

[Storey et al. 2008] STOREY, Veda C. ; BURTON-JONES, Andrew ; SUGUMARAN, Vijayan ; PURAO, Sandeep: CONQUER: A Methodology for Context-Aware Query Processing on the World Wide Web. In: *Information Systems Research* 19 (2008), No. 1, pp. 2–25

[Strack and Deutsch 2004] STRACK, Fritz ; DEUTSCH, Roland: Reflective and Impulsive Determinants of Social Behavior. In: *Personality and Social Psychology Review* 8 (2004), No. 3, pp. 220–247

[Straub 2012] STRAUB, Detmar: Does MIS Have Native Theories? In: *Management Information Systems Quarterly* 36 (2012), No. 2, pp. iii–xii

[Straub et al. 2004] STRAUB, Detmar ; BOUDREAU, Marie-Claude ; GEFEN, David: Validation Guidelines for IS Positivist Research. In: *Communications of the Association for Information Systems* 13 (2004), No. 24, pp. 380–427

[Straub and Karahanna 1998] STRAUB, Detmar ; KARAHANNA, Elena: Knowledge Worker Communications and Recipient Availability: Toward a Task Closure Explanation of Media Choice. In: *Organization Science* 9 (1998), No. 2, pp. 160–175

[Sundar 2007] SUNDAR, S. S.: The MAIN Model: A Heuristic Approach to Understanding Technology Effects on Credibility. In: METZGER, Miriam J. (Ed.) ; FLANAGIN, Andrew J. (Ed.): *Digital Media, Youth, and Credibility.* Cambrdige : MIT Press, 2007, pp. 73–100

[Sussman and Siegal 2003] SUSSMAN, Stephanie W. ; SIEGAL, Wendy S.: Informational Influence in Organizations: An Integrated Approach to Knowledge Adoption. In: *Information Systems Research* 14 (2003), No. 1, pp. 47–65

[Sviokla 1989] SVIOKLA, John J.: Expert Systems and Their Impact on the Firm: The Effects of PlanPower Use on the Information Processing Capacity of the Financial Collaborative. In: *Journal of Management Information Systems* 6 (1989), No. 3, pp. 65–84

[Swanson 1987] SWANSON, E. B.: Information Channel Disposition and Use. In: *Decision Sciences* 18 (1987), No. 1, pp. 131–145

[Swensson and Thomas 1974] SWENSSON, Richard G. ; THOMAS, R. E.: Fixed and Optional Stopping Models for Two-Choice Discrimination Times. In: *Journal of Mathematical Psychology* 11 (1974), No. 3, pp. 213–236

[Tam and Ho 2005] TAM, Kar Y. ; HO, Shuk Y.: Web Personalization as a Persuasion Strategy: An Elaboration Likelihood Model Perspective. In: *Information Systems Research* 16 (2005), No. 3, pp. 271–291

[Tam and Ho 2006] TAM, Kar Y. ; HO, Shuk Y.: Understanding the Impact of Web Personalization on User Information Processing and Decision Outcomes. In: *Management Information Systems Quarterly* 30 (2006), No. 4, pp. 865–890

[Taraborelli 2008] TARABORELLI, Dario: How the Web Is Changing the Way We Trust. In: *Proceedings of the 2008 Conference on Current Issues in Computing and Philosophy*. Amsterdam : IOS Press Amsterdam, 2008, pp. 194–204

[Tarvainen and Niskanen 2008] TARVAINEN, Mika P. ; NISKANEN, Juha-Pekka: Kubios HRV Version 2.0 User's Guide. In: *Department of Physics, University of Kuopio, Kuopio, Finnland* (2008)

[Thompson et al. 1993] THOMPSON, Erik P. ; CHAIKEN, Shelly ; HAZLEWOOD, J. D.: Need for Cognition and Desire for Control as Moderators of Extrinsic Reward Effects: A Person X Situation Approach to the Study of Intrinsic Motivation. In: *Journal of Personality and Social Psychology* 64 (1993), No. 6, pp. 987–999

[Todd and Benbasat 1992] TODD, Peter ; BENBASAT, Izak: The Use of Information in Decision Making: An Experimental Investigation of the Impact of Computer-Based Decision Aids. In: *Management Information Systems Quarterly* 16 (1992), No. 3, pp. 373–393

[Todd and Benbasat 2000] TODD, Peter ; BENBASAT, Izak: Inducing Compensatory Information Processing through Decision Aids that Facilitate Effort Reduction: An Experimental Assessment. In: *Journal of Behavioral Decision Making* 13 (2000), No. 1, pp. 91–106

[Trochim and Donnelly 2008] TROCHIM, William M. K. ; DONNELLY, James P.: *The Research Methods Knowledge Base.* 3. Mason : Atomic Dog, 2008

[Tversky and Kahneman 1971] TVERSKY, Amos ; KAHNEMAN, Daniel: Belief in the Law of Small Numbers. In: *Psychological Bulletin* 76 (1971), No. 2, pp. 105–110

[Vakkari 1999] VAKKARI, Pertti: Task complexity, problem structure and information actions. Integrating studies on information seeking and retrieval. In: *Information Processing & Management* 35 (1999), No. 6, pp. 819–837

[Vandenbosch and Higgins 1996] VANDENBOSCH, Betty ; HIGGINS, Chris: Information Acquisition and Mental Models: An Investigation into the Relationship Between Behaviour and Learning. In: *Information Systems Research* 7 (1996), No. 2, pp. 198–214

[Vandenbosch and Huff 1997] VANDENBOSCH, Betty ; HUFF, Sid L.: Searching and Scanning: How Executives Obtain Information from Executive Information Systems. In: *Management Information Systems Quarterly* 21 (1997), No. 1, pp. 81–107

[Venkatesh and Johnson 2002] VENKATESH, Viswanath ; JOHNSON, Philip: Telecommuting Technology Implementations: A Within- and Between-Subjects Longitudinal Field Study. In: *Personel Psychology* 55 (2002), No. 3, pp. 661–687

[Vessey and Galletta 1991] VESSEY, Iris ; GALLETTA, Dennis: Cognitive Fit: An Empirical Study of Information Acquisition. In: *Information Systems Research* 2 (1991), No. 1, pp. 63–84

[Vodanovich et al. 2010] VODANOVICH, Shahper ; SUNDARAM, David ; MYERS, Michael: Digital Natives and Ubiquitous Information Systems. In: *Information Systems Research* 21 (2010), No. 4, pp. 711–723

[Vreeken 2002] VREEKEN, Arjan: Notions of Information: A Review of Literature. In: *Sprouts: Working Papers on Information Systems* 2 (2002), No. 7

[Walther 1992] WALTHER, Joseph B.: Interpersonal Effects in Computer-Mediated Interaction: A Relational Perspective. In: *Communication Research* 19 (1992), No. 1, pp. 52–90

[Wang and Benbasat 2005] WANG, Weiquan ; BENBASAT, Izak: Trust in and Adoption of Online Recommendation Agents. In: *Journal of the Association for Information Systems* 6 (2005), No. 3, pp. 72–101

[Wang and Benbasat 2009] WANG, Weiquan ; BENBASAT, Izak: Interactive Decision Aids for Consumer Decision Making in E-Commerce: The Influence of Perceived Strategy Restrictiveness. In: *Management Information Systems Quarterly* 33 (2009), No. 2, pp. 293–320

[Watson and Clark 1997] WATSON, David ; CLARK, Lee A.: Extraversion and its positive emotional core. In: HOGAN, Robert (Ed.): *Handbook of Personality Psychology.* San Diego : Academic Press, 1997

[Watson 1990] WATSON, Richard T.: Influences on the IS Manager's Perceptions of Key Issues: Information Scanning and the Relationship With the CEO. In: *Management Information Systems Quarterly* 14 (1990), No. 2, pp. 217–231

[Watson-Manheim and Bélanger 2007] WATSON-MANHEIM, Mary B. ; BÉLANGER, France: Communication Media Repertoires: Dealing with the Multiplicity of Media Choices. In: *Management Information Systems Quarterly* 31 (2007), No. 2, pp. 267–293

[Weber 2004] WEBER, Ron: Editor's Comments: The Rhetoric of Positivism versus Interpretivism: A Personal View. In: *Management Information Systems Quarterly* 28 (2004), No. 1, pp. iii–xii

[Weber 2012] WEBER, Ron: Evaluating and Developing Theories in the Information Systems Discipline. In: *Journal of the Association for Information Systems* 13 (2012), No. 1, pp. 1–30

[Webster and Kruglanski 1994] WEBSTER, Donna M. ; KRUGLANSKI, Arie W.:
Individual Differences in Need for Cognitive Closure. In: *Journal of Personality
and Social Psychology* 67 (1994), No. 6, pp. 1049–1062

[Wetherbe 1991] WETHERBE, James C.: Executive Information Requirements:
Getting It Right. In: *Management Information Systems Quarterly* 15 (1991),
No. 1, pp. 51–65

[Whetten 1989] WHETTEN, David A.: What Constitutes a Theoretical Contribution? In: *Academy of Management Review* 14 (1989), No. 4, pp. 490–495

[Wilensky 1967] WILENSKY, Harold L.: *Organizational Intelligence: Knowledge
and Policy in Government and Industry*. Basic Books, 1967

[Wilson 1981] WILSON, Thomas D.: On user studies and information needs. In:
Journal of Documentation 37 (1981), No. 1, pp. 3–15

[Wilson 1999] WILSON, Thomas D.: Models in Information Behaviour Research.
In: *Journal of Documentation* 55 (1999), No. 3, pp. 249–270

[Wilson 2000] WILSON, Thomas D.: Human Information Behavior. In: *Informing
Science* 3 (2000), No. 2, pp. 49–55

[Wirth et al. 2007] WIRTH, Werner ; BÖCKING, Tabea ; KARNOWSKI, Veronika ;
PAPE, Thilo von: Heuristic and Systematic Use of Search Engines. In: *Journal
of Computer-Mediated Communication* 12 (2007), No. 3, pp. 778–800

[Wittmann 1959] WITTMANN, Waldemar: *Unternehmung und unvollkommene
Information*. Köln und Opladen : Westdeutscher Verlag, 1959

[Wold 1982] WOLD, Herman O.: Soft Modeling: The Basic Design and Some
Extensions. In: JÖRESKOG, K. G. (Ed.) ; WOLD, Herman O. (Ed.): *Sys-
tems Under Indirect Observation: Causality, Structure, and Prediction, Part
II*. Amsterdam : North Holland, 1982, pp. 1–54

[Wood 1986] WOOD, Robert E.: Task Complexity: Definition of the Construct.
In: *Organizational Behavior and Human Performance* 37 (1986), No. 1, pp.
60–82

[Wynn and Williams 2012] WYNN, Donald J. ; WILLIAMS, Clay K.: Principles for Conducting Critical Realist Case Study Research in Information Systems. In: *Management Information Systems Quarterly* 36 (2012), No. 3, pp. 787–810

[Yin 2009] YIN, Robert K.: *Case Study Research: Design and Methods.* 4. Thousand Oaks : SAGE Publications, 2009

[Yoo and Alavi 2001] YOO, Youngjin ; ALAVI, Maryam: Media and Group Cohesion: Relative Influences on Social Presence, Task Participation, and Group Consensus. In: *Management Information Systems Quarterly* 25 (2001), No. 3, pp. 371–390

[Yu et al. 2011] YU, Tian ; BENBASAT, Izak ; CENFETELLI, Ronald: Toward Deep Understanding of Persuasive Product Recommendation Agents. In: *Proceedings of the International Conference on Information Systems*, 2011

[Zach 2005] ZACH, Lisl: When Is "Enough" Enough? Modeling the Information-Seeking and Stopping Behavior of Senior Arts Administrators. In: *Journal of the American Society for Information Science and Technology* 56 (2005), No. 1, pp. 23–35

[Zhang et al. 2009] ZHANG, Ping ; LI, Na ; SCIALDONE, Michael J. ; CAREY, Jane: The Intellectual Advancement of Human-Computer Interaction Research: A Critical Assessment of the MIS Literature (1990-2008). In: *Transactions on Human-Computer Interaction* 1 (2009), No. 3, pp. 55–107

[Zhang et al. 2011] ZHANG, Tongxiao ; AGARWAL, Ritu ; LUCAS, Henry C. J.: The Value of IT-Enabled Retailer Learning: Personalized Product Recommendations and Customer Store Loyalty in Electronic Markets. In: *Management Information Systems Quarterly* 35 (2011), No. 4, pp. 859–881

[Zhang and Watts 2008] ZHANG, Wei ; WATTS, Stephanie A.: Capitalizing on Content: Information Adoption in Two Online communities. In: *Journal of the Association for Information Systems* 9 (2008), No. 2, pp. 72–93

[van Zuuren and Wolfs 1991] ZUUREN, Florence J. ; WOLFS, Heleen M.: Styles of Information Seeking under Threat: Personal and Situational Aspects of Monitoring and Blunting. In: *Personality and Individual Differences* 12 (1991), No. 2, pp. 141–149

[Zwick et al. 2003] ZWICK, Rami ; RAPOPORT, Amnon ; LO, Alison King C. ;
MUTHUKRISHNAN, A. V.: Consumer Sequential Search: Not Enough or Too
Much? In: *Marketing Science* 22 (2003), No. 4, pp. 503–519

ENTSCHEIDUNGSUNTERSTÜTZUNG FÜR ÖKONOMISCHE PROBLEME

Herausgegeben von Christian Becker, Wolfgang Gaul, Armin Heinzl,
Alexander Mädche und Martin Schader

Band 1 Ingo Böckenholt: Mehrdimensionale Skalierung qualitativer Daten. Ein Instrument zur Unterstützung von Marketingentscheidungen. 1989.

Band 2 Jürgen Joseph: Arbeitswissenschaftliche Aspekte der betrieblichen Einführung neuer Technologien am Beispiel von Computer Aided Design (CAD). Felduntersuchung zur Ermittlung arbeitswissenschaftlicher Empfehlungen für die Einführung neuer Technologien. 1990.

Band 3 Eva Schönfelder: Entwicklung eines Verfahrens zur Bewertung von Schichtsystemen nach arbeitswissenschaftlichen Kriterien. 1992.

Band 4 Michael Bargl: Akzeptanz und Effizienz computergestützter Dispositionssysteme in der Transportwirtschaft. Empirische Studien zur Implementierungsforschung von Entscheidungsunterstützungssystemen am Beispiel computergestützter Tourenplanungssysteme. 1994.

Band 5 Reinhold Decker: Analyse und Simulation des Kaufverhaltens auf Konsumgütermärkten. Konzeption eines modell- und wissensorientierten Systems zur Auswertung von Paneldaten. 1994.

Band 6 Wolfgang Gaul / Martin Schader (Hrsg.): Wissensbasierte Marketing-Datenanalyse. Das WIMDAS-Projekt. 1994.

Band 7 Daniel Baier: Konzipierung und Realisierung einer Unterstützung des kombinierten Einsatzes von Methoden bei der Positionierungsanalyse. 1994.

Band 8 Ulrich Lutz: Preispolitik im internationalen Marketing und westeuropäische Integration. 1994.

Band 9 Kirsten Petersen: Design eines Courseware-Entwicklungssystems für den computerunterstützten universitären Unterricht. CULLIS-Teilprojekt I. 1996.

Band 10 Stefan Neumann: Einsatz von Interactive Video im computerunterstützten universitären Unterricht. CULLIS Teilprojekt II. 1996.

Band 11 Eberhard Aust: Simultane Conjointanalyse, Benefitsegmentierung, Produktlinien- und Preisgestaltung. 1996.

Band 12 Peter Heydebreck: Technologische Verflechtung. Ein Instrument zum Erreichen von Produkt- und Prozeßinnovationserfolg. 1996.

Band 13 Michael Pesch: Effiziente Verkaufsplanung im Investitionsgütermarketing. 1997.

Band 14 Frank Wartenberg: Entscheidungsunterstützung im persönlichen Verkauf. 1997.

Band 15 Thomas Lechler: Erfolgsfaktoren des Projektmanagements. 1997.

Band 16 Alexandre Saad: Anbahnung und Erfolg von europäischen kooperativen F&E-Projekten. Eine empirische Analyse anhand von ESPRIT-Projekten. 1998.

Band 17 Michael Löffler: Integrierte Preisoptimierung. 1999.

Band 18 Frank Säuberlich: KDD und Data Mining als Hilfsmittel zur Entscheidungsunterstützung. 2000.

Band 38   Jessica Katharina Winkler: International Entry Mode Choices of Software Firms. An Analysis of Product-Specific Determinants. 2009.

Band 39   Martin J. Lafleur: *Loyalty Profiling*. Erfolgsdimensionen und Modellansätze eines effizienten und effektiven Customer Relationship Management. 2010.

Band 40   Ingo Ott: Effizientes Prozessmanagement im öffentlichen Dienst. 2010.

Band 41   Stefan Seedorf: Ontologie-gestützte Entwicklung komponentenbasierter Anwendungssysteme. Ein wissensbasiertes Informationssystem zur Unterstützung der Entwicklung und Wartung von Geschäftskomponenten (KompIS). 2010.

Band 42   Dominic Gastes: Erhebungsprozesse und Konsistenzanforderungen im Analytic Hierarchy Process (AHP). 2011.

Band 43   *erscheint in Kürze*

Band 44   Olaf Thiele: Informationsvisualisierungen auf mobilen Endgeräten zur Unterstützung des betrieblichen Datenmanagements. 2011.

Band 45   Krisztian Antal Buza: Fusion Methods for Time-Series Classification. 2011.

Band 46   Thomas Kude: The Coordination of Inter-Organizational Networks in the Enterprise Software Industry. The Perspective of Complementors. 2012.

Band 47   Alexandra Rebecca Klages: Clusteranalyse für Netzwerke. 2012.

Band 48   Christian Thum: Enabling Lightweight Real-time Collaboration. 2012.

Band 49   Miroslav Lazic: The Impact of Information Technology Governance on Business Performance. 2013.

Band 50   Verena Elisabeth Majuntke: Application Coordination in Pervasive Systems. 2013.

Band 51   Lars Klimpke: Konzeption und Realisierung eines integrierten Mikroblog-basierten Kommunikationsansatzes für die verteilte Softwareentwicklung. 2013.

Band 52   Erik Hemmer: Information Seeking Stopping Behavior in Online Scenarios. The Impact of Task, Technology and Individual Characteristics. 2013.

www.peterlang.de